CLOUD ORCHESTRATION UNLEASHED

COMPREHENSIVE JOURNEY FROM NOVICE TO GURU

4 BOOKS IN 1

BOOK 1
CLOUD ORCHESTRATION DEMYSTIFIED: A BEGINNER'S GUIDE

BOOK 2
MASTERING CLOUD ORCHESTRATION: INTERMEDIATE TECHNIQUES AND BEST PRACTICES

BOOK 3
CLOUD ORCHESTRATION FOR ENTERPRISE: ADVANCED STRATEGIES AND CASE STUDIES

BOOK 4
CLOUD ORCHESTRATION MASTERY: EXPERT-LEVEL AUTOMATION AND SCALABILITY

ROB BOTWRIGHT

Published by Rob Botwright
Library of Congress Cataloging-in-Publication Data
ISBN 978-1-83938-519-3
Cover design by Rizzo

Disclaimer

The contents of this book are based on extensive research and the best available historical sources. However, the author and publisher make no claims, promises, or guarantees about the accuracy, completeness, or adequacy of the information contained herein. The information in this book is provided on an "as is" basis, and the author and publisher disclaim any and all liability for any errors, omissions, or inaccuracies in the information or for any actions taken in reliance on such information.

The opinions and views expressed in this book are those of the author and do not necessarily reflect the official policy or position of any organization or individual mentioned in this book. Any reference to specific people, places, or events is intended only to provide historical context and is not intended to defame or malign any group, individual, or entity.

The information in this book is intended for educational and entertainment purposes only. It is not intended to be a substitute for professional advice or judgment. Readers are encouraged to conduct their own research and to seek professional advice where appropriate.

Every effort has been made to obtain necessary permissions and acknowledgments for all images and other copyrighted material used in this book. Any errors or omissions in this regard are unintentional, and the author and publisher will correct them in future editions.

TABLE OF CONTENTS – BOOK 1 - CLOUD ORCHESTRATION DEMYSTIFIED: A BEGINNER'S GUIDE

TABLE OF CONTENTS – BOOK 2 - MASTERING CLOUD ORCHESTRATION: INTERMEDIATE TECHNIQUES AND BEST PRACTICES

TABLE OF CONTENTS – BOOK 3 - CLOUD ORCHESTRATION FOR ENTERPRISE: ADVANCED STRATEGIES AND CASE STUDIES

TABLE OF CONTENTS – BOOK 4 - CLOUD ORCHESTRATION MASTERY: EXPERT-LEVEL AUTOMATION AND SCALABILITY

Introduction

Welcome to "Cloud Orchestration Unleashed: Comprehensive Journey from Novice to Guru," an extraordinary book bundle that will take you on an enlightening voyage through the dynamic and ever-evolving realm of cloud orchestration. In this four-book collection, we embark on an exhilarating journey designed to transform you from a curious novice into a confident orchestration guru. Together, we will explore the intricate landscape of cloud orchestration, scaling the heights of knowledge and expertise.

Book 1: Cloud Orchestration Demystified: A Beginner's Guide
In this first installment, we begin our journey by demystifying the fundamental concepts and principles of cloud orchestration. We unravel complex terminologies, explore foundational technologies, and provide you with a strong foundation on which to build your orchestration expertise. Whether you're new to cloud technology or looking to expand your horizons, this beginner's guide will equip you with the essential knowledge needed to navigate the world of orchestration.

Book 2: Mastering Cloud Orchestration: Intermediate Techniques and Best Practices
As our journey progresses, we delve deeper into the orchestration landscape. In Book 2, we explore intermediate techniques and best practices that will elevate your orchestration skills to the next level. From orchestrating containerized workloads to harnessing the power of automation and resource optimization, you'll gain practical insights and real-world experience to orchestrate cloud environments effectively.

Book 3: Cloud Orchestration for Enterprise: Advanced Strategies and Case Studies
Enterprise orchestration introduces unique challenges and opportunities, and Book 3 is your guide to conquering them. We delve into advanced strategies and present real-life case studies that shed light on orchestrating complex workflows, ensuring compliance, and optimizing performance in enterprise settings. By the end of this book, you'll be well-prepared to tackle intricate orchestration challenges within your organization.

Book 4: Cloud Orchestration Mastery: Expert-Level Automation and Scalability

In our final installment, we ascend to the pinnacle of expertise in cloud orchestration. Book 4 is dedicated to expert-level automation and scalability techniques that will empower you to manage large-scale deployments with finesse. You'll explore innovations in orchestration architecture, resource scaling, and performance optimization, making you a true master of cloud orchestration.

"Cloud Orchestration Unleashed" is not just a book bundle; it's a comprehensive journey that equips you with the knowledge, skills, and confidence to navigate the intricate world of cloud orchestration. Whether you're orchestrating workloads for personal projects, leading orchestration initiatives within your organization, or architecting complex multicloud environments, this bundle is your passport to orchestration success.

Are you ready to embark on this transformative journey? As we turn the pages of "Cloud Orchestration Unleashed," we invite you to unlock the doors to a world of possibilities in the cloud. It's a world where automation, scalability, efficiency, and innovation converge to shape the future of IT. Whether you're a novice, an intermediate practitioner, or an expert, this bundle has been meticulously crafted to empower you to orchestrate the cloud with confidence and mastery.

Join us on this exhilarating adventure through the clouds, and together, we'll unleash the power of cloud orchestration like never before.

BOOK 1
CLOUD ORCHESTRATION DEMYSTIFIED
A BEGINNER'S GUIDE

ROB BOTWRIGHT

Chapter 1: Introduction to Cloud Orchestration

Cloud Orchestration: What Is It? Cloud orchestration is a concept that forms the backbone of modern cloud computing. It's all about efficiently managing and automating the provisioning, configuration, and coordination of cloud resources. When we talk about cloud resources, we're referring to things like virtual machines, storage, databases, and networking components that are hosted in the cloud. Now, let me explain why this concept is so crucial in today's technology landscape.

In recent years, cloud computing has become the go-to solution for many businesses and organizations looking to scale their operations, reduce costs, and improve flexibility. With cloud services offered by providers like Amazon Web Services (AWS), Microsoft Azure, and Google Cloud, companies can access computing resources without the need to invest in and maintain physical infrastructure. However, managing these cloud resources efficiently can be a complex task, especially as organizations grow and their needs evolve.

This is where cloud orchestration comes into play. It provides a systematic way to manage and automate various cloud-related tasks, ensuring that resources are allocated, configured, and scaled as needed. Think of it as a conductor leading an orchestra of cloud services to play in harmony. With orchestration, you can streamline your operations, reduce manual errors, and optimize resource utilization, all while maintaining a high level of control and visibility over your cloud infrastructure.

But how does cloud orchestration work, you might wonder? Well, it relies on a combination of tools, scripts, and workflows to define and manage cloud resources. These tools can range from simple scripting languages to sophisticated orchestration platforms.

Now, let's dive a bit deeper into the components of cloud orchestration. At its core, orchestration involves defining a series of steps or tasks that need to be executed to achieve a particular outcome. These tasks can include provisioning virtual machines, configuring network settings, deploying applications, and more.

One of the key benefits of cloud orchestration is automation. Automation is what allows you to eliminate repetitive manual tasks. For example, instead of manually creating and configuring virtual machines every time you need them, you can define an orchestration workflow that automates this process. This not only saves time but also reduces the risk of human error.

Additionally, orchestration provides a level of abstraction. It abstracts the complexity of underlying cloud infrastructure and services, allowing you to work with a higher-level representation of your resources. This makes it easier to manage and scale your applications without having to delve into the nitty-gritty details of cloud services.

Now, let's talk about some practical scenarios where cloud orchestration shines. Imagine you're running a web application that experiences fluctuating traffic. During peak times, you need to scale up your infrastructure to handle increased user demand, and during off-peak times, you want to scale down to save costs. With orchestration, you can define rules and triggers that automatically adjust your resource allocation based on real-time traffic data. This dynamic scaling ensures your application performs optimally without manual intervention.

Furthermore, cloud orchestration can help with disaster recovery and high availability. You can set up orchestration workflows that replicate your data and applications across multiple data centers or regions. If one data center experiences an outage, your orchestration system can seamlessly redirect traffic to a backup location, minimizing downtime and ensuring business continuity.

Security and compliance are also critical aspects of cloud orchestration. You can define security policies and compliance checks as part of your orchestration workflows. This ensures that resources are provisioned and configured according to your organization's security standards, reducing the risk of vulnerabilities and ensuring regulatory compliance.

In essence, cloud orchestration is a powerful tool for managing the complexities of the cloud environment. It empowers organizations to harness the full potential of cloud computing while maintaining control, efficiency, and scalability. Whether you're a startup looking to streamline your operations or a large enterprise managing a vast cloud infrastructure, understanding and implementing cloud orchestration can significantly benefit your organization. In summary, cloud orchestration is the conductor of the cloud computing orchestra. It brings order and efficiency to the cloud, enabling businesses to harness the full potential of cloud resources while maintaining control, security, and scalability. As technology continues to evolve, mastering the art of cloud orchestration will be essential for organizations seeking to thrive in the digital age.

The importance of orchestration in modern computing cannot be overstated. It plays a pivotal role in the management and optimization of complex computing environments. To grasp its significance, one must first understand the evolving landscape of technology.

In today's fast-paced digital world, businesses and organizations rely on technology more than ever. Computing resources have become the lifeblood of operations, powering everything from web applications to data analytics. However, the sheer scale and complexity of modern IT infrastructure pose significant challenges.

This is where orchestration steps in. At its core, orchestration is the art of coordinating and automating tasks, ensuring that they work together seamlessly. In the realm of computing, this means managing a diverse set of resources, including servers, storage, networking components, and software applications.

Think of a symphony orchestra. Each instrument plays a unique role, and their harmonious collaboration creates beautiful music. Similarly, in computing, various components must work together in harmony to deliver a reliable and efficient system. This is where orchestration takes center stage.

Orchestration provides a structured approach to managing these intricate systems. It simplifies complex workflows, reduces manual intervention, and enhances resource utilization. With orchestration, organizations can achieve several critical objectives.

Efficiency is a fundamental goal. In an era where time is money, orchestrating routine tasks eliminates repetitive manual work. For example, provisioning and configuring virtual machines can be automated, reducing the risk of human error and freeing up valuable human resources for more strategic tasks.

Scalability is another key benefit. In today's dynamic business environment, the ability to scale resources up or down rapidly is essential. Orchestration enables organizations to respond to changes in demand, ensuring that resources are allocated efficiently to meet workload requirements. Furthermore, orchestration enhances agility. In a world where innovation and adaptation are paramount, businesses must respond swiftly to evolving market demands. Orchestration enables rapid deployment and adaptation of applications and services, helping organizations stay ahead in competitive markets.

But orchestration is not just about efficiency, scalability, and agility; it's also about control and visibility. In a complex computing environment, maintaining oversight is challenging. Orchestration provides a unified view of the entire system, allowing administrators to monitor and manage resources effectively.

Moreover, orchestration fosters consistency. It ensures that tasks are executed according to predefined standards and best practices. This consistency is critical for compliance with industry regulations and security policies.

Security, indeed, is a paramount concern. With the growing sophistication of cyber threats, safeguarding data and systems is non-negotiable. Orchestration allows organizations to enforce security measures consistently, from access controls to encryption, across their entire infrastructure.

In summary, orchestration is the conductor of the digital symphony. It brings order, efficiency, and harmony to the complex world of modern computing. By automating tasks, enhancing scalability, and ensuring consistency and security, orchestration empowers organizations to harness the full potential of their technology infrastructure.

However, orchestration is not a one-size-fits-all solution. The specific needs and challenges vary from one organization to another. Therefore, it's crucial to choose the right orchestration tools and strategies that align with your unique requirements.

There are various orchestration approaches to consider. One common approach is infrastructure orchestration, which focuses on managing and automating the provisioning of computing resources, such as servers, storage, and networking.

Another approach is application orchestration, which is geared toward automating the deployment and management of software applications. This is particularly relevant in a world where containerization and microservices architecture are gaining popularity.

Workflow orchestration, on the other hand, concentrates on automating complex sequences of tasks and processes. It is often used in scenarios where multiple steps need to be executed in a specific order, such as in data processing pipelines or business workflows.

Cloud orchestration is a specialized form that is tailored for managing resources in cloud computing environments. With the rise of cloud services, organizations must adapt their orchestration strategies to leverage the flexibility and scalability that the cloud offers.

Container orchestration, exemplified by tools like Kubernetes, is designed to manage the deployment, scaling, and orchestration of containerized applications. Containers have become a favored method for packaging and deploying applications due to their portability and efficiency.

These orchestration approaches can often be combined to meet the intricate needs of modern IT ecosystems. The choice of which to use—or whether to use a combination—depends on factors such as the organization's size, industry, technology stack, and specific goals.

To implement orchestration successfully, organizations must also consider the human factor. Skilled professionals who understand both the technology and the business processes are essential. Training and education are vital to ensure that the orchestration team can effectively design, implement, and maintain orchestration workflows.

Additionally, collaboration across teams is crucial. Orchestration touches various aspects of an organization, from IT operations to development and security. Effective communication and cooperation among these teams are necessary to create and manage orchestration workflows that align with business objectives.

In summary, the importance of orchestration in modern computing cannot be overstated. It empowers organizations to streamline operations, enhance scalability, and ensure security and compliance. Whether orchestrating infrastructure, applications, workflows, or cloud resources, the right orchestration approach can transform how businesses operate in the digital age. It's not just about automating tasks; it's about orchestrating success in a rapidly evolving technological landscape.

Chapter 2: Understanding Cloud Computing Fundamentals

When we talk about cloud computing, one of the fundamental concepts that you'll encounter is the cloud service model, and it's worth understanding the nuances of Infrastructure as a Service (IaaS), Platform as a Service (PaaS), and Software as a Service (SaaS). These three service models represent different layers of abstraction and management when it comes to cloud resources and applications.

Let's begin with Infrastructure as a Service or IaaS. This service model provides you with the foundational building blocks of cloud computing. Essentially, it offers virtualized computing resources over the internet. Think of it as renting virtual machines, storage, and networking components from a cloud provider. With IaaS, you have the flexibility to deploy and manage your operating systems, applications, and data on these virtualized resources.

IaaS is particularly valuable when you need full control over the infrastructure, whether it's for running custom software, hosting web applications, or managing databases. It's like having an empty data center at your disposal, but without the headache of hardware procurement and maintenance. You can scale your resources up or down as needed, pay only for what you use, and avoid the capital expenses associated with owning physical hardware.

Platform as a Service or PaaS takes things a step further. With PaaS, you're provided with not just the infrastructure but also the entire development and runtime environment for your applications. In essence, it abstracts away many of the underlying complexities, allowing you to focus solely on your code and the functionality of your applications.

Think of it as a fully equipped kitchen in a restaurant. You have the tools, ingredients, and appliances you need to cook, but you don't need to worry about maintaining the kitchen itself. PaaS offerings often include development frameworks, databases, middleware, and other tools to streamline application development, deployment, and scaling.

This service model is ideal for developers and development teams who want to accelerate the development and delivery of applications. It promotes collaboration, allows for continuous integration and continuous delivery (CI/CD), and reduces the time and effort required to manage infrastructure. Whether you're building web applications, mobile apps, or data analytics solutions, PaaS simplifies the process.

Now, let's talk about Software as a Service or SaaS. SaaS is the most user-friendly of the three service models. It's all about delivering software applications over the internet on a subscription basis. Instead of purchasing and installing software on your local devices or servers, you access and use it through a web browser.

Think of SaaS as a service you subscribe to, like streaming movies or music. You don't need to worry about installation, maintenance, or updates; the service provider takes care of all that. Popular examples of SaaS applications include email services like Gmail, productivity suites like Microsoft 365, and customer relationship management (CRM) software like Salesforce.

SaaS is highly convenient for businesses and individuals alike. It offers cost savings by eliminating the need for in-house infrastructure and IT support for software maintenance. It also ensures that users always have access to the latest features and security updates.

In summary, these three cloud service models, IaaS, PaaS, and SaaS, represent different levels of abstraction and management when it comes to cloud computing. IaaS provides you with virtualized infrastructure, PaaS gives you a development and runtime environment, and SaaS offers fully hosted and managed software applications. Each model has its unique strengths and use cases, and the choice among them depends on your specific needs and objectives.

When considering which service model to use, it's important to assess your organization's requirements, technical expertise, and budget constraints. You may find that a combination of these service models, known as a hybrid approach, is the most suitable for your business. Ultimately, the cloud service model you choose should align with your goals and enable you to leverage the benefits of cloud computing effectively.

When it comes to deploying cloud services, you'll encounter several deployment models, each with its own characteristics and considerations, and understanding these models—public, private, hybrid, and multi-cloud—is essential for making informed decisions about your cloud strategy.

Let's start with the public cloud deployment model. In a public cloud, cloud resources and services are owned and operated by a third-party cloud service provider and made available to the general public or a broad audience. Essentially, it's like renting space on a shared infrastructure, and some well-known public cloud providers include Amazon Web Services (AWS), Microsoft Azure, and Google Cloud.

Public clouds offer several advantages, including scalability, cost-efficiency, and the ability to access a vast array of services and resources. They are particularly appealing to startups and small businesses because they eliminate the need for significant upfront capital investments in physical hardware.

However, it's important to note that public clouds are, by their nature, shared environments, which means your data and applications coexist with those of other customers on the same infrastructure. Security and compliance considerations are critical, and organizations must carefully manage access controls and data protection measures.

Next, let's explore the private cloud deployment model. A private cloud, as the name suggests, is a cloud infrastructure dedicated solely to a single organization. It can be hosted on-premises, in a data center, or by a third-party provider. Private clouds offer enhanced control, security, and customization compared to public clouds. They are often favored by enterprises that require strict regulatory compliance or have specific data privacy and security requirements. With a private cloud, you have more control over the physical infrastructure and can tailor it to meet your organization's specific needs.

The hybrid cloud deployment model combines elements of both public and private clouds. In a hybrid cloud, you have the flexibility to move workloads and data between the public and private environments as needed. This allows you to leverage the scalability and cost-effectiveness of the public cloud while retaining control and security in the private cloud.

Hybrid clouds are particularly valuable for organizations with fluctuating workloads. During periods of high demand, you can burst into the public cloud to scale resources quickly, and during times when data sensitivity or compliance requirements come to the fore, you can run workloads in the private cloud. Lastly, let's delve into the multi-cloud deployment model. Multi-cloud refers to the practice of using more than one cloud provider to meet different business needs. It can involve a combination of public clouds, private clouds, or hybrid clouds from various providers.

The appeal of a multi-cloud approach lies in its ability to mitigate vendor lock-in and enhance redundancy and disaster recovery capabilities. By distributing workloads across multiple cloud providers, organizations reduce the risk of being dependent on a single vendor's ecosystem and gain the flexibility to choose the best-fit services from each provider.

However, managing a multi-cloud environment can be complex. It requires careful orchestration and coordination to ensure that data and applications are effectively distributed and that security, compliance, and governance standards are consistently maintained across all cloud platforms.

In summary, these cloud deployment models—public, private, hybrid, and multi-cloud—offer a spectrum of options to meet diverse business requirements. Public clouds provide scalability and cost-efficiency, private clouds offer control and security, hybrid clouds combine the best of both worlds, and multi-clouds enhance flexibility and redundancy.

The choice of which deployment model to adopt depends on factors such as an organization's data sensitivity, compliance needs, scalability requirements, and overall cloud strategy. As organizations continue to embrace cloud computing, understanding these deployment models is crucial for making informed decisions and optimizing the use of cloud resources.

Chapter 3: The Role of Orchestration in Cloud Management

When we delve into the realm of cloud orchestration, we quickly encounter a fundamental principle: orchestrating resources for efficiency. Efficiency is at the heart of why organizations turn to orchestration in the first place. It's all about optimizing the use of resources, streamlining processes, and achieving more with less.

Think of orchestrating resources as conducting a symphony. Each instrument in an orchestra has a role to play, and the conductor ensures that they all work together harmoniously. Similarly, in the world of cloud computing, a multitude of resources - virtual machines, storage, databases, networking, and more - must come together seamlessly to deliver a reliable and efficient system.

Orchestration provides the conductor's baton in this scenario. It coordinates and automates various tasks and processes, ensuring that they work in perfect harmony. The goal is to minimize manual intervention, eliminate inefficiencies, and optimize resource allocation.

Let's consider a practical example. Imagine a web application hosted in the cloud that experiences variable traffic throughout the day. During peak hours, it needs more computing power and resources to handle increased user demand. During off-peak times, it can scale down to save costs. Manually adjusting resources according to this fluctuating demand would be cumbersome and prone to errors.

Orchestration, however, enables organizations to define rules and triggers that automatically adjust resource allocation based on real-time data. This dynamic scaling ensures that the application performs optimally without the need for constant human intervention. It's like having an orchestra that adjusts its tempo and volume in response to the audience's energy.

Efficiency in resource allocation extends beyond scaling. It also encompasses load balancing. In a cloud environment, applications may run on multiple servers or instances to distribute the workload and ensure high availability. Load balancers, orchestrated by cloud management systems, evenly distribute incoming network traffic across these instances, preventing any single server from becoming overwhelmed. This not only improves performance but also enhances fault tolerance.

Furthermore, orchestration contributes to the efficient use of cloud storage. It can automate data backup and archiving processes, ensuring that critical data is protected and that storage resources are utilized optimally. This is particularly important in industries with stringent data retention requirements, such as healthcare and finance.

Automation is the driving force behind this efficiency. Orchestrating repetitive and time-consuming tasks saves organizations valuable time and resources. It minimizes the risk of human error, enhances consistency, and allows IT teams to focus on more strategic and value-added activities.

In essence, orchestration simplifies the orchestration of complex workflows, reduces operational costs, and enhances resource utilization. It empowers organizations to respond rapidly to changing demands, all while maintaining a high level of control and visibility over their cloud infrastructure.

But orchestration doesn't stop at efficiency. It also plays a vital role in the optimization of resource costs. Cloud providers often charge based on resource usage, and without proper orchestration, organizations may find themselves overpaying for underutilized resources.

Orchestration tools and platforms can analyze resource usage patterns and recommend optimizations. For example, they can identify idle or underutilized virtual machines and suggest their termination to reduce costs. This proactive approach to resource management ensures that organizations get the most value from their cloud investments.

Moreover, orchestration can assist in rightsizing resources. It's common for organizations to allocate more resources than necessary to ensure performance and availability. However, this can lead to unnecessary expenses. Orchestration can continuously monitor resource usage and adjust allocations accordingly, striking the right balance between performance and cost.

Security is another crucial aspect of orchestrating resources. As organizations scale their operations in the cloud, ensuring the security of resources and data becomes paramount. Orchestrating security measures and compliance checks as part of resource provisioning workflows is essential.

Orchestration tools can enforce security policies, such as access controls and encryption, consistently across all resources. They can also automate security audits and compliance checks, helping organizations adhere to industry regulations and internal security standards. This proactive approach minimizes the risk of security breaches and data leaks.

In summary, orchestrating resources for efficiency is a core principle in cloud computing. It's about conducting the various components of a cloud environment like a symphony, ensuring that they work together harmoniously to deliver optimal performance, cost-effectiveness, and security.

Orchestration achieves this by automating resource allocation, load balancing, and storage management. It proactively identifies opportunities for cost optimization, such as rightsizing resources and eliminating idle instances. Moreover, orchestration plays a pivotal role in enforcing security measures and compliance checks, safeguarding data and applications in the cloud.

As organizations continue to embrace the cloud and expand their digital presence, the role of orchestration in resource management will only become more critical. It's the conductor that keeps the cloud orchestra in tune, ensuring that every resource plays its part in delivering an efficient, secure, and cost-effective performance.

When it comes to harnessing the full power of cloud computing, orchestrating for scalability and automation takes center stage. It's a dynamic duo that empowers organizations to meet the ever-changing demands of the digital landscape with agility and efficiency.

Let's start by unraveling the concept of scalability. Scalability is about the ability to adapt and grow as your needs evolve. In the realm of cloud computing, this translates to the capacity to increase or decrease computing resources on demand. Think of it as the ability to seamlessly expand or shrink your digital infrastructure as traffic surges or subsides. Scalability is essential because it allows organizations to handle varying workloads effectively. In today's digital world, applications must be prepared to face unpredictable spikes in user activity. Consider an online retailer during a holiday shopping season or a streaming platform during a popular live event. Scalability ensures that these services continue to perform optimally, delivering a seamless user experience.

The cloud, with its vast pool of resources, is ideally suited for scalability. However, achieving scalability requires more than just having resources available. It requires intelligent orchestration to allocate these resources dynamically as needed.

Orchestration for scalability involves creating predefined rules and triggers that automatically adjust resource allocation based on real-time data. For instance, if a web application experiences a sudden surge in traffic, orchestration can spin up additional virtual servers to handle the load. When traffic subsides, it can reduce resources to save costs.

This dynamic allocation of resources, driven by orchestration, ensures that you pay only for what you use, avoid over-provisioning, and maintain a responsive and cost-effective infrastructure.

But scalability isn't limited to just scaling up. It also involves scaling down when demand decreases. Orchestration plays a crucial role here by automatically decommissioning resources that are no longer needed. This prevents wastage of computing power and helps control expenses.

Now, let's shift our focus to automation. Automation is the secret sauce that makes scalability possible. It's about minimizing manual intervention in routine tasks and processes. In the context of cloud computing, automation encompasses everything from provisioning virtual machines to deploying applications and managing data.

Consider a scenario where you need to replicate your web application across multiple regions to ensure high availability. Doing this manually would be time-consuming and error-prone. Automation, facilitated by orchestration, enables you to define templates and scripts that can be executed to replicate and configure resources consistently across different locations.

Automation doesn't stop at deployment; it extends to ongoing management. For example, if one of your virtual machines experiences a hardware failure, automation can detect the issue and automatically migrate your workload to a healthy server without any human intervention. This reduces downtime and ensures continuous service availability.

Moreover, automation enhances consistency. In a complex cloud environment with numerous resources, ensuring that configurations remain consistent across all instances is challenging. Automation scripts and templates enforce uniformity, reducing the risk of configuration drift and vulnerabilities.

The benefits of automation go beyond scalability and consistency; it also boosts efficiency. Tasks that once required hours or days of manual work can now be executed in minutes or seconds. This frees up IT teams to focus on strategic initiatives rather than mundane, repetitive tasks.

For instance, patch management is critical for security. With automation, you can schedule and automate the installation of security patches across your entire infrastructure. This ensures that your systems are always up-to-date with the latest security fixes, reducing the risk of vulnerabilities.

In essence, orchestration for scalability and automation is a powerhouse combination that empowers organizations to thrive in the digital age. It's the engine that drives the modern cloud infrastructure, enabling organizations to handle dynamic workloads, improve resource utilization, enhance security, and boost operational efficiency.

But it's important to note that achieving effective orchestration for scalability and automation requires careful planning and strategy. Organizations must define clear objectives, identify key performance indicators, and establish governance and security policies.

Additionally, selecting the right orchestration tools and platforms is crucial. There's a wide range of options available, each with its strengths and limitations. The choice depends on factors such as the complexity of your environment, the skills of your team, and your specific use cases.

Furthermore, organizations must invest in the necessary training and skill development. Orchestrating for scalability and automation requires expertise in scripting, coding, and the intricacies of cloud services. Skilled professionals who understand both the technical aspects and the business requirements are essential for success.

In summary, orchestrating for scalability and automation is the linchpin of modern cloud computing. It's the enabler that allows organizations to scale their infrastructure dynamically, respond to changing demands, and improve operational efficiency. As digital ecosystems continue to evolve, mastering the art of orchestration for scalability and automation will be paramount for organizations seeking to thrive in a rapidly changing technological landscape.

Chapter 4: Getting Started with Cloud Service Providers

When it comes to choosing a cloud service provider, my aim is to provide you with a friendly and informative overview of the major players in the cloud computing arena, helping you make an informed decision that aligns with your organization's needs.

First on our list is Amazon Web Services (AWS), often considered the pioneer and leader in the cloud industry. AWS boasts a vast global network of data centers, enabling it to offer a comprehensive range of services that cater to organizations of all sizes and industries. From computing power with Amazon EC2 to scalable storage with Amazon S3, AWS provides a robust and feature-rich platform.

Microsoft Azure, a formidable contender, is next on our exploration. With a strong focus on enterprise solutions and an extensive suite of services, Azure has gained popularity among businesses seeking seamless integration with Microsoft products like Windows Server and Office 365. Azure's global presence ensures reliability, and its services span computing, networking, databases, AI, and more.

Google Cloud Platform (GCP), powered by the technology giant Google, has made significant strides in cloud computing. Known for its expertise in data analytics and machine learning, GCP offers a robust infrastructure along with powerful AI and data processing capabilities. If data-driven insights are at the heart of your business, GCP may be a compelling choice.

IBM Cloud, backed by the legacy of IBM's technology innovation, is another notable player. It provides a wide range of cloud services, including AI, blockchain, and IoT solutions. IBM Cloud is particularly appealing to enterprises seeking hybrid cloud solutions that integrate seamlessly with their existing on-premises infrastructure.

Alibaba Cloud, often referred to as Aliyun, is a dominant force in the Asian cloud market and is gaining global recognition. It's known for its affordability and strong presence in China. Alibaba Cloud offers a wide array of services, including computing, storage, networking, and AI, making it a viable option for organizations with international ambitions.

Oracle Cloud, fueled by the tech giant Oracle, focuses on database and enterprise applications. If your organization relies heavily on Oracle's software stack, Oracle Cloud provides a tailored environment for running Oracle databases and applications, along with a range of cloud services.

Salesforce, renowned for its customer relationship management (CRM) software, has ventured into the cloud space with Salesforce Cloud. While it may not offer the extensive infrastructure services of other providers, it excels in providing a platform for developing and deploying customer-centric applications and services.

Now, let's talk about some key factors to consider when comparing these cloud service providers. One of the primary considerations is the range and depth of services offered. AWS, Azure, and GCP are known for their extensive service catalogs, making them versatile choices for various use cases. On the other hand, if your organization has specialized requirements, such as specific AI or database needs, you may find value in providers like IBM Cloud or Alibaba Cloud.

Global reach and data center locations are essential aspects, especially if your organization operates on a global scale. AWS has a wide-reaching network of data centers, followed closely by Azure and GCP. Consider which provider has the geographic presence that aligns with your business's operational footprint.

Pricing models and cost management tools are critical factors in your decision-making process. Each provider has its pricing structure and cost management tools, so it's vital to understand how their pricing aligns with your budget and consumption patterns. AWS, for instance, offers a pay-as-you-go model, while Azure provides various pricing options, including reserved instances for cost optimization.

Security and compliance are non-negotiable when it comes to cloud services. You'll want to evaluate each provider's security measures, certifications, and compliance offerings. AWS, Azure, and GCP have robust security practices and numerous compliance certifications, making them appealing choices for organizations with strict security and regulatory requirements.

Ease of use and management is another factor that can significantly impact your experience with a cloud provider. Consider the user interfaces, management tools, and APIs offered by each provider. AWS and Azure have comprehensive management consoles, while GCP is known for its developer-friendly environment.

Community and support resources play a crucial role in your cloud journey. A strong user community, documentation, and customer support can make a significant difference in troubleshooting issues and optimizing your cloud environment. AWS, Azure, and GCP have vibrant communities and extensive documentation.

Ultimately, the choice of a cloud service provider should align with your organization's specific needs, objectives, and constraints. It's essential to evaluate each provider's offerings, pricing, and capabilities in the context of your unique requirements.

Keep in mind that the cloud landscape is continually evolving, with providers regularly introducing new features and services. Therefore, staying informed and periodically reassessing your choice is a good practice to ensure that your cloud provider aligns with your evolving business needs.

In this ever-evolving landscape, your choice of a cloud service provider is a critical decision that can significantly impact your organization's success. By carefully evaluating factors such as service offerings, global reach, pricing models, security, ease of use, and community support, you can make an informed choice that empowers your business to thrive in the digital age.

As we embark on the journey of setting up your first cloud account, let's start by demystifying the process and understanding why it's a crucial step in today's digital landscape. When you decide to take the plunge into cloud computing, whether for personal projects, business ventures, or educational pursuits, creating your first cloud account is akin to acquiring a passport to the digital world.

Your cloud account will serve as your gateway to a vast ecosystem of computing resources, services, and technologies. It's your key to accessing the flexibility, scalability, and innovation that the cloud offers. Before we dive into the practical steps of setting up your account, let's explore some essential concepts and considerations.

First and foremost, it's important to choose the right cloud service provider for your needs. We've previously discussed major cloud providers like Amazon Web Services (AWS), Microsoft Azure, Google Cloud Platform (GCP), and others. Each has its strengths and specialties. Your choice will depend on factors such as your specific requirements, budget, and familiarity with the provider's services.

Once you've made your choice, the next step is to navigate to the provider's website and initiate the sign-up process. This typically involves providing your email address, creating a password, and agreeing to the terms of service. Keep in mind that cloud providers take security seriously, so you'll often encounter robust password requirements to protect your account.

Authentication and identity verification are crucial steps in ensuring the security of your cloud account. Many providers offer multi-factor authentication (MFA) as an additional layer of security. It's highly recommended to enable MFA, as it adds an extra level of protection by requiring a second form of verification, such as a text message code or a mobile app.

Now, let's talk about billing. Most cloud providers offer a free tier with limited resources for new users. This allows you to explore and experiment without incurring charges initially. However, as you begin to use more resources or specific premium services, you'll want to set up billing information. This typically involves providing a credit card or other payment method.

Understanding the provider's billing model is essential. Some providers offer pay-as-you-go pricing, where you pay only for the resources you consume. Others may offer reserved instances or subscription plans, which can provide cost savings for predictable workloads. Be sure to explore the billing options that align with your usage patterns and budget.

With your account created and billing set up, you're now ready to explore the cloud console. The cloud console is the web-based interface that allows you to manage your cloud resources. It's your control center, where you can create virtual machines, set up databases, configure networking, and more. Spend some time familiarizing yourself with the console, as it will be your primary tool for managing your cloud environment.

Organizations often use a hierarchical structure to manage cloud resources efficiently. This structure typically involves grouping resources into projects or resource groups. Each project can have its permissions and access controls. This hierarchy allows for better organization, security, and resource allocation.

When setting up your first cloud account, consider the naming conventions and tagging strategies you'll use to keep your resources organized. Naming conventions help you quickly identify and manage resources, while tags provide metadata that can be used for cost allocation, tracking, and management purposes.

Security is a top priority in cloud computing, and securing your cloud account is essential. Cloud providers offer a range of security features, such as identity and access management (IAM), firewalls, encryption, and monitoring tools. Take the time to configure these security measures to protect your account and data.

It's also important to establish clear access controls and permissions. Define who can access your cloud resources and what actions they can perform. Role-based access control (RBAC) is a common approach that allows you to assign roles and permissions to users or groups.

Backup and disaster recovery planning should not be overlooked. Cloud providers offer backup and snapshot capabilities that enable you to protect your data and applications. Regularly schedule backups and test your disaster recovery procedures to ensure business continuity.

Finally, as you embark on your cloud journey, embrace the learning curve. Cloud computing offers a world of possibilities, but it also comes with complexity and new concepts. Don't be afraid to explore, experiment, and seek out resources like documentation, tutorials, and community forums to expand your knowledge.

Setting up your first cloud account is not just a technical process; it's a gateway to innovation, scalability, and the digital future. It empowers you to harness the power of the cloud to build, deploy, and scale applications and services with unprecedented flexibility and efficiency.

So, as you embark on this exciting journey, remember that your cloud account is more than just a collection of resources; it's a canvas for your digital aspirations, a realm of endless possibilities, and a testament to the transformative potential of cloud computing.

Chapter 5: Tools and Platforms for Cloud Orchestration

Welcome to the exciting world of orchestration tools, where we'll embark on a journey to explore the technology that enables the automation and coordination of complex tasks in today's digital landscape. Imagine having a team of tireless assistants who follow your instructions with precision, ensuring that your workflows run seamlessly, efficiently, and error-free. Orchestration tools are your virtual assistants in the realm of IT and beyond.

At its core, orchestration is all about making things happen in a structured and efficient manner. It involves coordinating a series of tasks, often across multiple systems or platforms, to achieve a specific objective. Orchestration is the conductor of the digital symphony, ensuring that every component and process plays its part harmoniously.

Now, you might be wondering why orchestration is so important. Well, in today's fast-paced and highly connected world, businesses and organizations rely on an intricate web of processes and systems to function. Whether it's provisioning resources in a cloud environment, automating repetitive tasks, managing complex workflows, or responding to dynamic conditions, orchestration is the key to efficiency, agility, and reliability.

To illustrate the significance of orchestration, let's consider a scenario. Imagine you run an e-commerce website, and you're launching a limited-time promotion that involves updating product prices, inventory levels, and advertising across multiple channels. Without orchestration, you'd need to manually update each product, monitor inventory changes, and coordinate advertising campaigns—a time-consuming and error-prone endeavor.

Orchestration tools, however, can streamline this process. You can create a workflow that automatically adjusts product prices, updates inventory levels, and triggers advertising campaigns based on predefined rules and conditions. The result? A seamless and efficient promotion that delights your customers and boosts your sales.

Now that we've established the importance of orchestration, let's dive into the world of orchestration tools. These tools are software solutions designed to facilitate the automation, coordination, and management of complex workflows. They come in various shapes and sizes, each tailored to specific use cases and industries.

One of the key characteristics of orchestration tools is their ability to work across heterogeneous environments. This means they can orchestrate tasks and processes involving a mix of technologies, systems, and applications. Whether you're dealing with on-premises servers, cloud services, databases, or IoT devices, orchestration tools provide a unified platform to manage them all.

So, what are some common use cases for orchestration tools? Well, the possibilities are vast. Let's explore a few scenarios to give you a taste of their versatility:

Cloud Resource Provisioning: Orchestration tools are often used to automate the provisioning of cloud resources. Whether you're spinning up virtual machines, configuring storage, or deploying containers in the cloud, orchestration tools can streamline the process and ensure consistency.

DevOps and Continuous Integration/Continuous Deployment (CI/CD): In the world of DevOps, orchestration tools play a pivotal role. They automate the building, testing, and deployment of software, enabling faster and more reliable software releases.

IT Service Management (ITSM): Orchestration tools are valuable for managing IT service requests and incident resolution. They can automate ticket routing, escalate issues, and trigger notifications to keep IT operations running smoothly.

Data ETL (Extract, Transform, Load): Data integration and transformation are critical in today's data-driven world. Orchestration tools can automate the ETL process, ensuring that data flows seamlessly from source to destination, undergoes necessary transformations, and gets loaded into data warehouses or analytics platforms.

Security Incident Response: Orchestration tools can enhance cybersecurity by automating threat detection and response. They can isolate compromised systems, block malicious activity, and generate alerts for further investigation.

Business Process Automation: In the realm of business operations, orchestration tools can streamline workflows across departments. This includes tasks like employee onboarding, procurement, and financial approvals.

Now, let's talk about the features and capabilities of orchestration tools. At their core, these tools offer workflow design and automation capabilities. They provide a visual interface or scripting language that allows users to define workflows, specify conditions, and automate tasks. Think of it as a digital canvas where you paint the steps of your process.

Orchestration tools also excel in handling dependencies. They understand the sequence of tasks and ensure that each task completes successfully before moving on to the next. This prevents errors and ensures that complex workflows progress smoothly.

Exception handling is another essential feature. Orchestration tools allow you to define how the system should respond when things don't go as planned. For example, you can specify actions to take when a task fails, such as sending a notification or triggering a manual intervention.

Many orchestration tools offer integrations with a wide range of systems and applications. This means you can connect your orchestration workflows with databases, cloud services, APIs, and more, enabling seamless data exchange and interaction.

Monitoring and reporting capabilities are crucial for visibility and accountability. Orchestration tools provide dashboards and logs that allow you to track the progress of workflows, monitor resource usage, and generate reports for analysis and compliance.

Finally, security features are paramount. Orchestration tools often include role-based access control (RBAC) and encryption to protect sensitive data and restrict access to authorized users.

As you explore orchestration tools, you'll encounter a diverse landscape. Some popular names in the orchestration tool arena include Apache NiFi, Ansible, Kubernetes (for container orchestration), Apache Airflow, and ServiceNow, to name a few. Each of these tools caters to specific use cases and has its unique strengths.

In summary, orchestration tools are your digital assistants in the world of complex workflows and processes. They empower organizations to automate tasks, coordinate activities, and respond to dynamic conditions efficiently. Whether you're managing cloud resources, streamlining DevOps pipelines, or automating business processes, orchestration tools are the key to unlocking efficiency and agility in today's digital age.

So, as you embark on your journey into the realm of orchestration tools, remember that you're stepping into a world of endless possibilities, where automation and coordination are the keys to success. With the right orchestration tools at your disposal, you have the power to orchestrate your digital symphony and achieve remarkable feats of efficiency and reliability.

Welcome to the exciting world of cloud orchestration platforms, where we'll embark on a journey to discover the tools and platforms that enable organizations to automate and streamline their cloud operations with ease. Imagine having a robust set of instruments at your disposal, each designed to help you manage and optimize your cloud resources efficiently. Cloud orchestration platforms are your toolkit for orchestrating complex workflows, automating repetitive tasks, and achieving operational excellence in the cloud.

To begin our exploration, let's understand the significance of cloud orchestration platforms in today's digital landscape. The cloud has transformed the way organizations operate, providing unprecedented scalability, flexibility, and agility. However, with these benefits come complexities in managing diverse cloud resources, services, and deployments. This is where cloud orchestration platforms step in.

At its core, cloud orchestration is about ensuring that various cloud components work together harmoniously to deliver a seamless and efficient cloud environment. It's the art of coordinating the provisioning, configuration, and management of cloud resources to meet business objectives. Cloud orchestration platforms are the enablers of this art, offering a wide array of tools and features to simplify and automate complex tasks.

One of the primary roles of cloud orchestration platforms is to automate resource provisioning. Whether you need to deploy virtual machines, create storage volumes, or configure networking, these platforms allow you to define templates and workflows that automate these processes. This automation not only saves time but also reduces the risk of human error.

Scalability is another key focus area. Cloud orchestration platforms enable organizations to dynamically scale their resources based on demand. Imagine a scenario where your e-commerce website experiences a sudden surge in traffic during a holiday sale. With cloud orchestration, you can set up rules to automatically add more virtual servers to handle the increased load and scale back down when traffic subsides, ensuring a smooth customer experience.

Automation is at the heart of cloud orchestration platforms. They provide the ability to automate routine tasks and workflows, such as software deployment, configuration management, and patching. Automation not only improves efficiency but also enhances consistency across your cloud environment.

Centralized management is a significant advantage offered by these platforms. They provide a single interface or dashboard to manage all your cloud resources, regardless of the cloud provider or service. This centralized view simplifies administration and reduces the complexity of managing a multi-cloud environment.

When it comes to choosing a cloud orchestration platform, you'll encounter a variety of options, each with its strengths and capabilities. Let's explore some of the popular cloud orchestration platforms:

AWS CloudFormation: If you're operating in the Amazon Web Services (AWS) ecosystem, CloudFormation is a natural choice. It allows you to define infrastructure as code (IaC) using JSON or YAML templates, making it easy to provision and manage AWS resources.

Azure Resource Manager (ARM): Microsoft Azure users rely on ARM to orchestrate and manage Azure resources. ARM templates enable the definition of resource groups and their dependencies, providing a consistent approach to Azure resource management.

Google Cloud Deployment Manager: For those in the Google Cloud Platform (GCP) realm, Deployment Manager offers a solution. It uses templates written in YAML to describe GCP resources and their configurations, allowing for efficient resource provisioning and management.

HashiCorp Terraform: Terraform is a popular choice for multi-cloud environments. It provides a domain-specific language (HCL) to define infrastructure as code and supports various cloud providers, making it versatile for managing resources across clouds.

Apache CloudStack: CloudStack is an open-source platform that offers cloud orchestration capabilities. It's designed for building and managing public, private, or hybrid clouds and supports various hypervisors.

OpenStack Heat: OpenStack users often turn to Heat for orchestration needs. Heat templates allow users to define resources and their dependencies in an OpenStack environment, simplifying resource provisioning.

Ansible: While not exclusively an orchestration platform, Ansible is a popular automation tool widely used for cloud orchestration. It uses YAML-based playbooks to automate tasks and configurations across cloud providers.

Kubernetes: When it comes to container orchestration, Kubernetes stands out. It manages containerized applications and their resources efficiently, making it an excellent choice for microservices architectures and container-based workloads.

ServiceNow: ServiceNow is a comprehensive platform that offers IT service management (ITSM) and cloud orchestration capabilities. It's often used for managing IT services and automating workflows.

These platforms cater to a range of use cases, from infrastructure provisioning to application deployment and configuration management. Your choice will depend on factors like your cloud provider, the complexity of your environment, and your specific automation needs.

Beyond resource provisioning and automation, cloud orchestration platforms often provide features like monitoring, scaling policies, and reporting. They give you the tools to optimize resource utilization, track costs, and ensure compliance with organizational policies and industry regulations.

Security is a paramount concern in the cloud, and orchestration platforms address it through features like access control, encryption, and auditing. They enable organizations to implement robust security measures and maintain the integrity of their cloud environments.

In summary, cloud orchestration platforms are the indispensable tools that empower organizations to harness the full potential of the cloud. They automate, coordinate, and streamline cloud operations, enabling efficiency, scalability, and agility in a digital world. Whether you're managing resources in a single cloud or navigating a multi-cloud landscape, these platforms are your trusted companions on your cloud journey.

As you explore the realm of cloud orchestration platforms, remember that you're embarking on a journey of empowerment, where you have the tools to automate and optimize your cloud operations with precision. With the right platform at your fingertips, you're well-equipped to orchestrate your cloud resources and achieve operational excellence in the cloud.

Chapter 6: Creating Your First Orchestration Workflow

Designing a simple orchestration flow is like composing a beautiful piece of music, where each note and instrument plays a specific role in creating a harmonious melody, and in the world of IT and cloud orchestration, the melody is the smooth and efficient execution of tasks.

The first step in this creative process is to define your objective clearly; think of it as the melody you want to play. What do you want to achieve with your orchestration flow? Is it provisioning cloud resources, automating software deployment, or something entirely different? Having a clear objective is the foundation of a successful orchestration flow.

Once you have your objective in mind, it's time to break it down into smaller, manageable tasks. These tasks are like the individual notes in your melody. They can be simple or complex, but they should all contribute to the overall goal. Take some time to identify the tasks involved in achieving your objective, and consider their sequence.

Now, let's talk about the tools and instruments you'll use to create your orchestration flow. In the world of orchestration, these are the automation and orchestration platforms, scripting languages, or tools specific to your environment. Just as a musician selects the right instruments for a piece of music, you'll choose the tools that best suit your orchestration needs.

For many orchestration tasks, scripting languages like Python, PowerShell, or Bash are valuable instruments. They allow you to write scripts that automate specific actions, such as configuring server settings or deploying software. Alternatively, you might opt for dedicated orchestration platforms like Ansible, Terraform, or Kubernetes if you need to manage complex workflows or multiple systems.

Now, let's create our simple orchestration flow together. Imagine you have a scenario where you need to automate the process of setting up a web server and deploying a website on it. Your objective is to achieve this efficiently and consistently.

We'll start with the first task in our orchestration flow: provisioning a virtual machine in a cloud environment. To do this, you might choose a cloud orchestration platform like AWS CloudFormation or Azure Resource Manager. These platforms allow you to define the infrastructure as code, specifying the virtual machine's size, storage, and networking requirements in a template.

With your virtual machine provisioned, the next task in your flow is to configure the operating system and install the necessary software. Here, scripting languages like PowerShell or Bash come into play. You can write scripts that automatically configure the server, install web server software like Apache or Nginx, and prepare it for hosting your website.

As you compose this part of your orchestration flow, think about error handling. What should happen if the script encounters an error during configuration or software installation? You can include logic to handle errors gracefully, such as sending notifications or rolling back changes.

Now, let's move on to the final task in our simple orchestration flow: deploying the website. Depending on your specific requirements, you might use a tool like Ansible to automate the deployment process. Ansible playbooks can define the steps needed to copy website files, configure the web server to serve them, and start the web server.

In your orchestration flow, consider the order of tasks. You want to ensure that each task completes successfully before moving on to the next. For instance, you wouldn't want to deploy the website before the virtual machine is fully provisioned and configured.

As you design your orchestration flow, also think about input parameters. These are like the variables in your musical composition. They allow you to customize the flow for different scenarios. For example, you might want to specify the size of the virtual machine or the URL of the website as input parameters to your orchestration.

Testing is a crucial step in the orchestration flow design process. Just as a musician rehearses before performing, you should test your orchestration flow in a controlled environment to ensure that it achieves the desired outcome. Be prepared to make adjustments and refinements based on your testing results.

Error handling is another important aspect to consider. What should happen if a task fails at any point in the flow? You can design your orchestration to detect failures and take appropriate actions, whether that's notifying an administrator or triggering a rollback to a known good state.

Documentation plays a role in your orchestration flow's success. Just as musical scores guide musicians, documentation provides guidance to those who will use or maintain your orchestration flow in the future. Include clear instructions, comments, and explanations to make your flow understandable and maintainable.

When your orchestration flow is complete and thoroughly tested, it's time to put it into action. You'll execute the flow in your production environment, enjoying the fruits of your orchestration labor as it automates the provisioning and deployment process with precision and efficiency.

Remember that simplicity is often a virtue in orchestration flow design. Start with a clear objective, break it down into manageable tasks, choose the right tools, and test thoroughly. Simplicity not only makes your flow easier to understand and maintain but also reduces the potential for errors.

In the world of orchestration, your creativity is the limit. Whether you're automating cloud resource provisioning, configuring servers, or deploying applications, designing a simple orchestration flow is your opportunity to compose a symphony of efficiency and reliability. So, let your creativity flow, and may your orchestration efforts be as harmonious as a well-orchestrated piece of music.

Welcome to the fascinating world of implementing orchestration templates, where we'll delve into the practical steps of turning your orchestration flow design into a reality. Think of this process as taking your musical composition and transforming it into a live performance, where each instrument and note plays its part seamlessly, creating a beautiful symphony of automation.

To kick off our journey into implementation, let's revisit the orchestration flow we designed earlier, where we automated the setup of a web server and the deployment of a website. Now, it's time to turn that design into actionable templates that the orchestration platform can understand and execute.

In orchestration, templates serve as the sheet music for your automation orchestra. They contain the instructions and parameters needed to perform your orchestration flow. In our scenario, we'll need templates for provisioning a virtual machine, configuring the server, and deploying the website.

Let's start with the first task: provisioning a virtual machine. In the world of cloud orchestration, templates often come in the form of Infrastructure as Code (IaC). These templates use a declarative language like JSON or YAML to describe the desired state of your infrastructure.

For instance, if you're using AWS CloudFormation, you'd create a CloudFormation template. In this template, you specify the virtual machine's characteristics, such as its instance type, storage, and networking configuration. You define the resources, like the virtual machine itself, security groups, and key pairs, all in code.

Once you've created your virtual machine provisioning template, it's time to move on to the second task: configuring the server. This is where scripting languages like PowerShell or Bash come into play. You'll create scripts that automate the server setup, including tasks like installing software, configuring settings, and securing the server.

Here, you can integrate your scripts into your template by using a tool like Ansible or Terraform. These tools allow you to embed script execution as part of your infrastructure provisioning process. This ensures that server configuration happens automatically after the virtual machine is provisioned.

Now, let's talk about the final task: deploying the website. Just as we used scripting languages for server configuration, we can use them here as well. You'll create scripts that automate the deployment process, copying website files to the server, configuring the web server software, and starting it.

In your template, you can define the sequence of tasks to ensure that the deployment script runs after the server configuration is complete. This sequencing ensures that your website deployment is coordinated and orderly.

As you work on your templates, consider the flexibility they offer. You can parameterize your templates, allowing you to customize the orchestration for different scenarios. For example, you might define parameters for the virtual machine size, web server configuration, or website URL. These parameters make your templates adaptable to various needs.

Testing is a critical step in the implementation process. Just as musicians rehearse before performing, you should thoroughly test your templates to ensure they work as expected. Create testing environments that mimic your production environment, and execute your templates in these controlled settings.

Pay close attention to error handling during testing. What happens if a task fails? Ensure that your templates include error-handling logic, such as retry mechanisms or notifications, to address potential issues gracefully.

Documentation remains essential as you implement your templates. Just as musical scores guide musicians, your documentation should guide users and administrators who will work with your templates. Include clear instructions, parameter descriptions, and any prerequisites or dependencies.

Security is a paramount concern in the implementation process. Consider how your templates handle sensitive information like passwords or access keys. Ensure that your templates adhere to security best practices and that any secrets are managed securely.

With your templates thoroughly tested and documented, it's time to put them into action in your production environment. You'll execute your templates using the orchestration platform, watching as your automation symphony unfolds with precision and efficiency.

Continuous improvement is a valuable mindset during the implementation process. Just as musicians refine their performances over time, you can refine your templates based on feedback and real-world usage. As your environment evolves, your templates can evolve with it to meet changing requirements.

Monitoring is a crucial aspect of orchestration template implementation. Keep an eye on your automated processes, tracking their progress, resource usage, and any errors or exceptions. Monitoring helps you maintain the health and reliability of your automation.

Scalability is another consideration. As your organization grows, your templates should scale with it. Ensure that your templates can handle increased workloads and resource demands by designing them with scalability in mind.

Resource optimization is an ongoing effort. Periodically review your templates to identify opportunities for efficiency and cost savings. Are there resources that can be right-sized or decommissioned? Are there optimizations you can apply to your orchestration processes?

In summary, implementing orchestration templates is the journey from design to execution, where your automation vision becomes a reality. Just as musicians transform musical notes into a live performance, you're transforming your orchestration flow into orchestrated actions that drive efficiency and reliability in your IT operations.

As you embark on this implementation journey, remember that you're wielding the power of automation to streamline tasks, reduce errors, and accelerate processes. Your templates are the blueprints for orchestrating your digital symphony, where each task and action plays its part in creating a harmonious and efficient environment.

So, embrace this creative process, refine your templates over time, and may your orchestration efforts continue to produce melodies of automation that resonate throughout your organization.

Chapter 7: Automating Resource Provisioning

Welcome to the realm of automating virtual machine deployment, a fascinating journey where we'll explore the art of orchestrating the creation and configuration of virtual machines with precision and efficiency. Imagine having the power to provision virtual machines effortlessly, whether it's for development, testing, or production purposes, and to do so consistently and reliably. This is the promise of automation in virtual machine deployment.

In our automation adventure, the first step is to understand the why. Why automate virtual machine deployment? Well, in today's dynamic and fast-paced IT landscape, the ability to rapidly provision and configure virtual machines is a game-changer. It reduces manual errors, accelerates resource allocation, and empowers IT teams to respond swiftly to changing business needs.

Now, let's dive into the how. How do we automate virtual machine deployment? The key lies in leveraging automation tools and scripts that can perform the tasks traditionally done manually. Picture these tools and scripts as your digital assistants, tirelessly executing your instructions to create and configure virtual machines exactly as you desire.

One of the fundamental tools for automating virtual machine deployment is a cloud orchestration platform like AWS CloudFormation, Azure Resource Manager, or Google Cloud Deployment Manager. These platforms enable you to define your virtual machine's characteristics, such as its size, storage, and networking, using Infrastructure as Code (IaC) templates.

Imagine you're using AWS CloudFormation. You'd create a CloudFormation template, written in JSON or YAML, that describes your virtual machine's configuration. This template acts as the blueprint for your virtual machine deployment.

In this template, you specify details like the virtual machine's instance type, storage volumes, security groups, and any additional software you want pre-installed. It's like providing the construction plan for your virtual machine.

Once you've crafted your CloudFormation template, it's time to orchestrate the deployment. You simply submit the template to AWS, and CloudFormation takes care of the rest. It provisions the virtual machine based on your template's specifications, configuring it according to your predefined instructions.

But our orchestration journey doesn't stop here. After provisioning the virtual machine, there's often a need for further configuration. This is where scripting languages like PowerShell, Bash, or Python come into play.

Consider this: you've automated the creation of a virtual machine, but it's a blank canvas waiting to be customized. Scripts are your brushes, and they allow you to paint the server with your desired configurations.

Let's say you want your virtual machine to serve as a web server. You can write a script that installs the necessary web server software, sets up your website files, and configures the server to respond to HTTP requests. These scripts are your instruments of customization.

Now, here's the beauty of automation: you can seamlessly integrate these scripts into your virtual machine deployment process. With orchestration tools like Ansible, Terraform, or even simple cloud-init scripts, you can execute these customization scripts automatically after the virtual machine is provisioned.

Imagine orchestrating a symphony where the deployment template serves as the conductor, directing the initial setup, and the scripts act as the talented musicians, adding the finishing touches to the performance.

As you work on automating virtual machine deployment, error handling becomes an important consideration. Just as a conductor guides the orchestra through unexpected turns, your orchestration should be prepared to handle errors gracefully.

Scripts and orchestration tools often allow you to define error-handling mechanisms. For example, you can include logic that retries a failed task a certain number of times before reporting an error or rolling back to a known good state.

Testing is another pivotal part of the automation process. Before you showcase your virtual machine deployment symphony in a live performance, you must rehearse in a controlled environment. Create testing environments that mimic your production setup, and execute your automation scripts and templates there.

Thoroughly validate that your virtual machines are provisioned and configured correctly. Test different scenarios, including those where errors may occur, to ensure your automation can handle various situations.

Documentation remains a guiding star in your automation journey. Just as musical scores provide instructions to musicians, your documentation should offer clear guidance to those who will interact with your automation. Include detailed instructions, parameter explanations, and any prerequisites or dependencies.

Security is of paramount importance in virtual machine deployment automation. Just as a conductor ensures the orchestra plays in harmony, you must safeguard your virtual machines. Take measures to protect sensitive information like passwords and access keys. Implement security best practices in your scripts and templates to fortify your automation symphony.

Finally, when you're ready to showcase your automated virtual machine deployment, do so in your production environment. Witness how your orchestration and scripts seamlessly provision and configure virtual machines, saving time and reducing the potential for human error.

Remember that automation is an ongoing journey of improvement. Just as musicians refine their performance over time, you can refine your automation scripts and templates based on real-world usage and feedback. As your needs evolve, your automation can evolve with them.

In summary, automating virtual machine deployment is your chance to conduct a symphony of efficiency and reliability. Whether you're provisioning virtual machines for development, testing, or production, automation streamlines the process, reduces errors, and empowers you to respond rapidly to changing demands.

So, embrace the automation orchestra, compose your templates and scripts, and let your virtual machines sing in harmony. May your automation efforts create a symphony of efficiency that resonates throughout your IT operations.

Welcome to the realm of scaling resources on demand, a fascinating journey where we'll explore the art of dynamically adjusting your computing resources to meet the ever-changing needs of your organization. Imagine having the ability to seamlessly expand or contract your infrastructure, ensuring that you always have the right amount of resources available, whether it's to handle increased customer traffic during a product launch or to optimize costs during periods of low demand.

Scaling resources on demand is like having a magical elastic band that stretches or shrinks to fit your needs, providing you with agility and cost-efficiency in your IT operations.

To begin our exploration, let's understand why scaling on demand is essential in today's fast-paced digital landscape. In the world of IT, change is constant. Customer demands fluctuate, seasonal trends come and go, and unexpected traffic spikes can occur at any moment. The ability to scale your resources to meet these dynamic requirements is not just a convenience; it's a strategic advantage.

Now, let's delve into the "how" of scaling on demand. The key lies in leveraging cloud computing and virtualization technologies. Imagine these technologies as the tools in your toolkit, allowing you to adjust your infrastructure with precision and ease.

In the cloud, you have the power to provision and de-provision virtual machines, storage, and networking resources in minutes. Think of these resources as building blocks that you can assemble or disassemble as needed. When your organization experiences a surge in demand, you can quickly add more resources to handle the load. Conversely, during periods of reduced demand, you can release unneeded resources, optimizing cost-efficiency.

The orchestration of scaling resources on demand often involves the use of automation and monitoring tools. Automation is like your trusted assistant, ready to execute predefined actions when specific conditions are met. Monitoring tools are your watchful eyes, constantly observing resource utilization and performance.

Imagine a scenario where your e-commerce website experiences a sudden influx of visitors due to a flash sale. Your monitoring tools detect the increased traffic and alert your automation system. In response, the automation system triggers the provisioning of additional web server instances to ensure a smooth shopping experience for your customers.

The beauty of automation is that it can be tailored to your organization's unique needs. You define the rules and conditions for scaling. You decide when and how resources should be added or removed. This level of control allows you to align resource scaling with your business goals and objectives.

Testing plays a pivotal role in the scaling process. Just as a performer rehearses before a live show, you must validate that your scaling mechanisms work as intended. Create testing environments that simulate real-world scenarios, including scenarios with varying levels of demand. Test your automated scaling processes rigorously to ensure they respond appropriately.

Remember that scaling isn't limited to handling traffic spikes. It's also about optimizing resource allocation. Imagine you operate a cloud-based data analytics platform. During weekdays, when your data scientists are actively working, you scale up your computing resources to handle intensive data processing tasks. However, on weekends, when activity slows down, you scale down your resources to save costs. This intelligent allocation of resources is a hallmark of efficient scaling on demand.

Security is a critical consideration in the world of scaling. Just as a vigilant guard protects a castle, you must ensure that your scaled resources are secure. Implement access controls, encryption, and security best practices to safeguard your infrastructure, even as it dynamically adjusts to meet demand.

Documentation remains a valuable companion in your scaling journey. Just as a map guides a traveler, your documentation guides your team in understanding and operating your scaling mechanisms. Include clear instructions, procedures, and insights gained from testing to facilitate efficient scaling.

Cost optimization is another benefit of scaling on demand. The ability to release unneeded resources during periods of low demand helps control operational costs. Imagine the cost savings achieved by automatically shutting down idle virtual machines during non-business hours. This optimization can have a significant impact on your organization's bottom line.

In summary, scaling resources on demand is your ticket to agility, efficiency, and cost optimization in the world of IT. Whether you're managing web applications, data processing workloads, or any other IT resources, the ability to flexibly adjust your infrastructure to meet the needs of the moment is a powerful advantage.

As you navigate the journey of scaling on demand, remember that you're not just managing resources; you're orchestrating a symphony of efficiency. You have the tools, automation, and monitoring at your disposal to ensure that your infrastructure always strikes the right chord, whether you're facing a sudden crescendo of activity or enjoying the harmony of optimized costs during quieter moments.

So, embrace the magic of scaling resources on demand, fine-tune your automation, and orchestrate a performance that keeps your organization in tune with the dynamic rhythms of the digital world. May your scaling efforts bring agility, efficiency, and harmony to your IT operations.

Chapter 8: Monitoring and Optimization in Cloud Orchestration

Welcome to the exciting world of implementing real-time monitoring, where we'll explore the art of keeping a vigilant eye on your systems, applications, and infrastructure as they operate in real-time. Imagine having the ability to detect issues the moment they arise, swiftly respond to anomalies, and ensure the optimal performance of your digital landscape. This is the power of real-time monitoring, a valuable practice in today's fast-paced IT environment.

To embark on this journey of real-time monitoring, it's important to understand why it matters. In the digital age, your systems are the lifeblood of your organization. They support critical business functions, serve customers, and handle data vital to your operations. Real-time monitoring is like having a radar system that constantly scans the horizon for potential storms, allowing you to navigate smoothly and proactively address any challenges.

Now, let's delve into the "how" of implementing real-time monitoring. Think of it as setting up an intricate web of sensors and alerts that keep you informed and ready to take action. This web is created through a combination of tools, sensors, and configurations that allow you to collect, analyze, and respond to data in real-time.

Imagine you have a web application that serves thousands of users. Real-time monitoring for this application involves installing monitoring agents on your servers. These agents act as your eyes and ears, continuously collecting data on server performance, application health, and user interactions.

This collected data is like the pieces of a puzzle. Real-time monitoring tools are your puzzle solvers. They aggregate, correlate, and analyze this data to provide you with a clear picture of what's happening in your environment.

Picture this scenario: your monitoring tools detect a sudden spike in CPU usage on one of your servers. This is akin to your radar system detecting an unexpected turbulence in the sky. Real-time alerts, configured in your monitoring setup, immediately notify your team of the issue.

Automation plays a significant role in real-time monitoring. Think of it as your trusty assistant that can take predefined actions in response to specific events. For example, in the case of the CPU spike, your automation scripts could be set up to automatically scale your server resources to handle the increased load, ensuring uninterrupted service for your users.

Testing is a crucial part of the implementation process. Just as a pilot undergoes rigorous training, your real-time monitoring setup must be tested to ensure it responds accurately to various scenarios. Create testing scenarios that mimic real-world situations, such as simulated traffic spikes or server failures, and verify that your monitoring tools and alerts function as expected.

Documentation is your compass in the world of real-time monitoring. Just as a map guides an explorer, your documentation guides your team in understanding and operating your monitoring setup. Include clear instructions on setting up alerts, configuring thresholds, and interpreting monitoring data.

Security remains a top priority when implementing real-time monitoring. Just as a vigilant guard watches over a fortress, you must ensure that your monitoring setup is secure. Implement access controls, encryption, and best practices to protect the sensitive data collected by your monitoring tools.

Scalability is a consideration for organizations that experience growth. As your environment expands, your real-time monitoring setup should scale with it. Ensure that your monitoring tools and agents can handle increased data volume and complexity.

Resource optimization is another benefit of real-time monitoring. Just as a well-tuned engine delivers optimal performance, monitoring helps you identify resource bottlenecks and inefficiencies. You can make data-driven decisions to optimize resource allocation and cost-effectiveness.

Real-time monitoring isn't limited to reactive measures. It's also about proactive insights. Imagine your monitoring tools providing predictive analytics, warning you of potential issues before they occur. This proactive approach allows you to address problems before they impact your users or business.

In summary, implementing real-time monitoring is your key to staying ahead of the curve in the world of IT operations. Whether you're managing applications, servers, or network infrastructure, the ability to detect, analyze, and respond to events in real-time is a strategic advantage.

As you embark on this journey of real-time monitoring, remember that you're not just setting up tools; you're building a watchful guardian that keeps your digital landscape safe and efficient. With the right tools, configurations, and automation, you can navigate the complexities of modern IT with confidence.

So, embrace the power of real-time monitoring, fine-tune your setup, and let your monitoring tools be your eyes and ears in the ever-changing world of IT. May your real-time insights guide you to smooth operations and optimal performance.

Welcome to the fascinating world of identifying optimization opportunities, where we'll embark on a journey of discovery to uncover ways to enhance the efficiency, performance, and cost-effectiveness of your IT operations. Imagine having the ability to fine-tune your systems and processes, making them run smoother and smarter. This is the essence of optimization, a practice that holds immense value in the ever-evolving landscape of technology.

To begin our exploration, let's understand why identifying optimization opportunities is crucial. In the world of IT, change is constant. New technologies emerge, user demands evolve, and business goals shift. What works efficiently today may not be as effective tomorrow. Optimization is like a compass that guides you in navigating these changes, ensuring that your IT ecosystem remains aligned with your organization's objectives.

Now, let's delve into the "how" of identifying optimization opportunities. Think of it as wearing a detective's hat, ready to investigate your systems, processes, and workflows for clues that point to areas in need of improvement. This investigative work involves a combination of data analysis, performance monitoring, and strategic thinking.

Imagine you're responsible for managing a cloud-based web application. Optimization opportunities in this scenario could be hiding in various places. For example, you might notice that your application's response time has increased over time, impacting user experience. This observation is a valuable clue, signaling a potential optimization opportunity.

Performance monitoring tools act as your magnifying glass in this detective work. They provide detailed insights into your application's behavior, helping you identify bottlenecks, resource constraints, or inefficient code. It's like having a microscope to examine the smallest details of your IT environment.

Data analysis is another critical aspect of the process. Imagine your monitoring tools generate a wealth of data, including metrics on server utilization, network traffic, and application performance. Analyzing this data can reveal patterns and anomalies that point to areas where optimization can yield significant benefits.

As a detective, you might notice that during certain hours of the day, your application experiences a surge in user activity, causing response times to slow down. This pattern suggests an optimization opportunity: scaling your resources to accommodate peak usage hours.

Automation is a valuable ally in the quest for optimization. Think of it as your trusted assistant, ready to execute predefined actions when optimization opportunities are identified. For example, if your detective work reveals that server utilization consistently exceeds a certain threshold during peak hours, automation scripts can be set up to automatically provision additional resources to handle the increased load.

Testing is a crucial step in the optimization process. Just as a scientist conducts experiments to validate hypotheses, you should create testing environments that mimic your production setup. Test various optimization strategies to ensure they deliver the expected results without introducing new issues.

Documentation is your reference guide as you navigate the optimization journey. Think of it as the detective's notebook, where you record your findings, strategies, and outcomes. Documenting optimization opportunities and their resolutions helps ensure that knowledge is shared and retained within your organization.

Security remains a top priority throughout the optimization process. Imagine you're optimizing your application by implementing caching mechanisms to improve response times. While optimization is the goal, you must ensure that security measures are not compromised. Implement access controls, encryption, and other security best practices to safeguard your system.

Resource optimization is a significant benefit of identifying optimization opportunities. Think of it as decluttering and organizing your IT environment, ensuring that resources are used efficiently. For example, you might discover that certain virtual machines are consistently underutilized. By right-sizing these resources or decommissioning them, you can optimize costs.

Cost optimization is another compelling reason to identify optimization opportunities. Imagine you're managing a cloud infrastructure, and your monthly costs are consistently higher than expected. Through analysis and detective work, you identify instances of resource over-provisioning. By adjusting resource allocations, you can reduce costs without sacrificing performance.

In summary, identifying optimization opportunities is your key to maintaining a competitive edge in the world of IT. Whether you're managing applications, infrastructure, or workflows, the ability to pinpoint areas in need of improvement is a strategic advantage.

As you embark on this journey of optimization, remember that you're not just optimizing systems; you're optimizing outcomes. With the right tools, analysis, and automation, you can uncover hidden potential within your IT ecosystem, making it more efficient, cost-effective, and aligned with your organization's goals.

So, embrace the role of a detective, follow the clues in your data, and let optimization be your guide to a smarter and more efficient IT environment. May your detective work lead you to uncover opportunities that enhance the performance and value of your technology investments.

Chapter 9: Security and Compliance Considerations

Welcome to the realm of securing orchestration workflows, where we embark on a journey to safeguard the heartbeats of your automated processes, ensuring that they operate securely and without compromise. Imagine orchestrating complex workflows that power your organization, from provisioning resources to automating tasks, all while keeping security as a top priority. This is the essence of securing orchestration, a critical aspect of modern IT operations.

To begin our exploration, let's understand why securing orchestration workflows is paramount. In today's digital landscape, where cyber threats are ever-present, your automated workflows can be tempting targets. They control access to sensitive data, execute critical operations, and manage your infrastructure. Security breaches can have devastating consequences. Securing orchestration is like placing a fortress around your automation, defending it from potential threats.

Now, let's delve into the "how" of securing orchestration workflows. Think of it as constructing layers of protection around your automation processes, ensuring that only authorized actions are executed and that sensitive information remains confidential. This multifaceted approach involves a combination of access controls, encryption, authentication, and monitoring.

Imagine you have an orchestration workflow responsible for provisioning virtual machines in your cloud environment. Securing this workflow begins with defining who has access to it. Access controls act as your gatekeepers, allowing only authorized users or systems to interact with the workflow.

Authentication is another crucial element. Think of it as your virtual bouncer, verifying the identity of those seeking access to your orchestration. Implement strong authentication mechanisms, such as multi-factor authentication (MFA), to ensure that only trusted individuals can initiate workflows.

Encryption adds an extra layer of protection to your orchestration. Just as you would encrypt sensitive documents, encrypt data transmitted between components of your automation. Secure communication channels using protocols like HTTPS or SSH to prevent eavesdropping.

Access logs play a pivotal role in securing orchestration workflows. Imagine these logs as your digital surveillance cameras, recording every interaction with your automation. Monitoring and auditing access logs help you detect suspicious activities and ensure compliance with security policies.

Automation doesn't mean relinquishing control. Instead, it offers the opportunity to enforce strict security policies consistently. For example, you can create automation scripts that ensure virtual machines are launched with up-to-date security patches and configurations that adhere to your organization's security standards.

Testing is an essential part of securing orchestration workflows. Just as a security system undergoes rigorous testing, your orchestration security measures should be evaluated for vulnerabilities. Conduct penetration testing and vulnerability assessments to identify weaknesses that attackers might exploit.

Documentation remains your guiding light in the realm of orchestration security. Just as a map assists a traveler, your documentation guides your team in understanding and adhering to security practices. Include clear instructions on configuring security settings, managing access controls, and responding to security incidents.

Security incident response is a crucial aspect of securing orchestration workflows. Imagine you detect an unauthorized attempt to execute a critical workflow. Having a well-defined incident response plan in place allows you to take immediate action, investigate the incident, and mitigate any potential damage.

Regular security audits are like health checkups for your orchestration. Periodically review and assess your security measures to ensure they remain effective and up-to-date. Technology and threats evolve, and your security practices should evolve with them.

Integration with existing security tools is a smart move. Just as you'd connect surveillance cameras to a central monitoring system, integrate your orchestration security with your organization's overall security infrastructure. This allows you to leverage existing threat intelligence and incident response capabilities.

Resource isolation is a strategy to consider. Just as you'd keep valuable assets in a secure vault, isolate critical orchestration components from less secure parts of your network. Implement network segmentation and micro-segmentation to limit the exposure of your orchestration workflows to potential threats.

Remember that security is an ongoing process. Just as you'd continuously monitor a fortress, regularly review and update your orchestration security measures. Stay informed about emerging threats and security best practices, and adapt your security strategy accordingly.

In summary, securing orchestration workflows is your shield against potential threats and vulnerabilities. Whether you're managing resource provisioning, automating tasks, or orchestrating complex processes, security should be an integral part of your automation strategy.

As you navigate the world of securing orchestration workflows, remember that you're not just protecting automation; you're safeguarding the integrity, confidentiality, and availability of your organization's operations. With the right security measures in place, you can orchestrate with confidence, knowing that your automated workflows are resilient in the face of potential threats.

So, embrace the role of a guardian, fortify your orchestration security, and let your automation processes thrive in a secure and protected environment. May your security efforts shield your organization from harm and enable the seamless operation of your automated workflows.

Welcome to the world of compliance with industry regulations, where we'll embark on a journey to ensure that your organization operates within the legal and regulatory boundaries of your specific industry. Imagine navigating through a complex web of rules and standards, all designed to protect consumers, maintain fair competition, and uphold the integrity of your sector. This journey is not just about following the rules; it's about building trust, reducing risks, and ensuring the sustainability of your business.

To begin our exploration, let's understand why complying with industry regulations is crucial. In today's interconnected global economy, businesses must adhere to a multitude of regulations that vary by industry, location, and function. Failure to comply can result in legal consequences, reputational damage, and financial penalties. Compliance is like the compass that guides your organization through the regulatory landscape, helping you avoid pitfalls and navigate safely.

Now, let's delve into the "how" of complying with industry regulations. Think of it as a structured approach to understanding, implementing, and monitoring the rules that apply to your industry. This approach involves a combination of research, policy development, risk assessment, and ongoing monitoring.

Imagine you're operating a financial services firm. Compliance with industry regulations in this context involves understanding the laws and regulations that govern financial markets, customer protection, and anti-money laundering measures. This understanding is your foundation for building a compliant organization.

Policy development is your next step. Think of it as creating a set of rules and procedures that align with industry regulations. These policies should cover everything from customer data protection to financial reporting. They act as your organization's guidebook for ensuring compliance.

Risk assessment is a critical aspect of the compliance process. Imagine it as a safety inspection of your operations, identifying areas where you might fall short of regulatory requirements. Conduct thorough risk assessments to pinpoint potential compliance vulnerabilities and prioritize corrective actions.

Compliance is not a one-time effort; it's an ongoing commitment. Regular monitoring and auditing are your tools for ensuring continued compliance. Just as you'd perform regular maintenance on a vehicle, monitor your operations to detect any deviations from regulatory standards.

Documentation is your record-keeping companion throughout the compliance journey. Think of it as your organization's diary, where you document compliance efforts, policies, procedures, and audit results. Detailed records demonstrate your commitment to compliance and provide a valuable resource for regulators.

Training and education are essential components of compliance. Just as a driver's education course prepares you for the road, train your employees on industry regulations and your organization's compliance policies. Ensure that everyone understands their role in maintaining compliance.

Compliance with industry regulations often involves reporting to regulatory authorities. Imagine it as filing your taxes; timely and accurate reporting is essential. Establish procedures for submitting required reports and ensure that deadlines are met.

Technology can be a valuable ally in compliance efforts. Implement compliance management software and tools that help you track, document, and report on your compliance activities. These tools can streamline your compliance processes and reduce the risk of oversight.

Risk management is a crucial consideration in the compliance journey. Just as you'd take precautions to prevent accidents, proactively manage risks associated with non-compliance. Identify potential compliance risks, develop mitigation strategies, and establish contingency plans.

Integration with industry associations and peer groups can provide valuable insights into compliance best practices. Collaborate with others in your industry to stay informed about regulatory changes, emerging trends, and successful compliance strategies.

In summary, complying with industry regulations is a fundamental responsibility for organizations across various sectors. Whether you're in finance, healthcare, manufacturing, or any other industry, adherence to regulations is a non-negotiable aspect of doing business.

As you navigate the world of compliance, remember that you're not just following rules; you're building a foundation of trust and credibility. Compliance enhances your organization's reputation, reduces risks, and positions you as a responsible and ethical player in your industry.

So, embrace the journey of compliance, invest in the necessary resources, and let it be a testament to your commitment to doing business the right way. May your compliance efforts not only keep you within the boundaries of industry regulations but also propel your organization toward sustainable success.

Chapter 10: Scaling Your Cloud Orchestration Environment

Welcome to the world of horizontal and vertical scaling strategies, where we explore two fundamental approaches to expanding the capacity and performance of your IT infrastructure. Imagine your organization growing, and with that growth comes the need to ensure your systems can handle increased demands. This journey is all about finding the right balance between adding more resources and optimizing existing ones to meet your evolving needs.

To begin our exploration, let's understand what horizontal scaling and vertical scaling mean. Horizontal scaling is like adding more lanes to a highway, where you increase capacity by adding more servers or instances to your infrastructure. Vertical scaling, on the other hand, is like upgrading your car to a faster and more powerful model, where you enhance performance by adding more resources (such as CPU, RAM, or storage) to a single server or instance.

Horizontal scaling offers the advantage of elasticity. Picture this: your e-commerce website experiences a surge in traffic during holiday sales. With horizontal scaling, you can effortlessly add more web servers to distribute the load and handle the increased user requests. When the shopping frenzy subsides, you can reduce the number of servers to save costs.

Vertical scaling, on the other hand, provides improved performance within a single server. Consider a database server that stores critical customer data. As your database grows, you can vertically scale by adding more CPU cores, RAM, or storage capacity to handle larger datasets and more complex queries. This approach ensures that your database maintains optimal performance as your business expands.

The choice between horizontal and vertical scaling depends on your specific needs and circumstances. Imagine you're operating a content delivery network (CDN). Horizontal scaling is a natural choice here because it allows you to distribute content across multiple servers geographically, reducing latency and improving response times for users worldwide.

In contrast, think of a scientific research project that requires massive computational power for simulations. Vertical scaling would be the preferred strategy in this case, as you can equip a single server with high-performance CPUs and ample RAM to handle the computational demands efficiently.

Automation plays a significant role in scaling strategies. Imagine you've implemented an auto-scaling system that automatically adds or removes virtual machines based on predefined triggers, such as CPU utilization or incoming traffic. This automation ensures that your infrastructure adapts to changing workloads without manual intervention.

Testing is a crucial step in both horizontal and vertical scaling. Picture this scenario: you've added additional web servers to handle increased traffic during a product launch. Testing ensures that the newly added servers work seamlessly with the existing ones and that the load balancer evenly distributes requests. Similarly, when vertically scaling a database server, rigorous testing ensures that the upgraded configuration performs as expected without data corruption or downtime.

Documentation is your guiding compass in scaling endeavors. Imagine you've documented the procedures for adding more resources to a virtual machine or configuring load balancing rules. These documents provide your team with clear instructions, reducing the risk of errors during scaling operations.

Resource monitoring is essential for both horizontal and vertical scaling strategies. Picture this: your application's memory usage gradually increases over time. Monitoring tools can alert you when the memory utilization reaches a predefined threshold, prompting you to take action, such as adding more RAM or optimizing your application's memory usage.

Security considerations are crucial in scaling. Imagine you're scaling your web application horizontally by adding more servers. Each new server should be configured with the same security policies and access controls as existing ones to maintain a consistent security posture.

Cost optimization is a significant benefit of scaling strategies. Think of it as ensuring that you pay only for the resources you need. With horizontal scaling, you can scale up or down based on demand, optimizing costs during both peak and off-peak periods. Vertical scaling allows you to allocate resources precisely where they are needed, avoiding overprovisioning.

In summary, horizontal and vertical scaling strategies are essential tools in managing the growth and performance of your IT infrastructure. Whether you're expanding your web services, databases, or other resources, these strategies provide flexibility, performance improvements, and cost control.

As you navigate the world of scaling, remember that you're not just adding or upgrading resources; you're ensuring that your infrastructure aligns with your organization's goals and adapts to changing demands. With the right scaling strategy in place, you can confidently accommodate growth, maintain optimal performance, and keep costs in check.

So, embrace the power of scaling, choose the strategy that fits your needs, and let it be a driving force that propels your organization toward success in an ever-evolving digital landscape. May your scaling efforts enable you to meet the challenges of tomorrow with confidence and efficiency.

Welcome to the exciting world of load balancing and auto-scaling configurations, where we'll explore two essential techniques that ensure your applications and services remain highly available, performant, and responsive to fluctuating user demands. Imagine a scenario where your website experiences a sudden surge in traffic due to a viral social media post or a flash sale event. Load balancing and auto-scaling are like the dynamic duo that steps in to handle such spikes in usage, ensuring a seamless user experience.

Let's start our journey by understanding the concept of load balancing. Think of it as the conductor of an orchestra, ensuring that each instrument plays in harmony to create beautiful music. In the realm of IT, load balancing distributes incoming network traffic across multiple servers, preventing any single server from becoming overwhelmed and maintaining optimal performance.

Imagine you have a web application that receives user requests. Without load balancing, all those requests would hit a single server, potentially causing it to slow down or even crash during traffic spikes. Load balancing acts as a traffic cop, directing requests to multiple servers in a balanced way, ensuring that each server's load remains manageable.

Load balancers come in various forms, such as hardware appliances or software solutions. They use algorithms to determine how to distribute traffic among servers. Some algorithms prioritize evenly distributing requests, while others consider server health and performance metrics to make intelligent routing decisions.

Auto-scaling, on the other hand, is like having a magical workforce that expands or shrinks in response to demand. Imagine you run an e-commerce website, and during the holiday season, you expect a significant increase in traffic. Auto-scaling allows you to automatically add more servers or resources when demand surges and remove them when it subsides, all without manual intervention.

The key to successful load balancing and auto-scaling configurations is automation. Automation ensures that these processes respond quickly to changing conditions. For example, when your website experiences a sudden influx of visitors, your auto-scaling system can detect the increased load and automatically spin up additional web servers to handle the traffic.

Testing is a crucial step in configuring load balancing and auto-scaling. Imagine you're setting up a load balancer for your web application. Thoroughly test its configuration to ensure that traffic is evenly distributed, and failover mechanisms work seamlessly. Similarly, when configuring auto-scaling, test how well it responds to varying levels of demand.

Documentation plays a pivotal role in ensuring the effectiveness of load balancing and auto-scaling configurations. Imagine you're part of a team responsible for managing these configurations. Clear and detailed documentation guides your team in understanding how load balancing and auto-scaling are set up, making it easier to troubleshoot issues and make improvements.

Resource monitoring is your watchful guardian in load balancing and auto-scaling. Just as a lifeguard keeps a close eye on swimmers in the pool, monitoring tools track the health and performance of your servers and resources. They provide real-time insights into traffic patterns, server utilization, and response times, allowing you to make informed decisions.

Security considerations are paramount when configuring load balancing and auto-scaling. Imagine you have a load balancer in front of a cluster of web servers. Ensure that the load balancer is protected from unauthorized access, and implement secure communication channels between the load balancer and servers. Security measures should be integrated into the configuration from the beginning.

Cost optimization is a significant benefit of auto-scaling configurations. Think of it as a smart thermostat that adjusts heating and cooling based on occupancy. With auto-scaling, you can allocate resources precisely when needed, minimizing costs during periods of low demand and maximizing performance during peaks.

Scaling strategies depend on the specific needs of your application or service. Imagine you're running a video streaming platform. Auto-scaling is essential here because it allows you to dynamically add more video servers to handle increased streaming demand during popular events like live sports broadcasts.

In contrast, consider a financial institution with a critical database server. Load balancing might not be the primary concern in this case, but vertical scaling, where you add more resources to a single server, can ensure that the database remains responsive and available during heavy transaction periods.

In summary, load balancing and auto-scaling configurations are fundamental tools for ensuring the reliability and performance of your applications and services. Whether you're running a website, a cloud-based application, or a complex network, these configurations provide the flexibility and responsiveness needed to adapt to changing conditions.

As you navigate the world of load balancing and auto-scaling, remember that you're not just optimizing resource usage; you're ensuring that your users have a smooth and uninterrupted experience. With the right configurations in place, you can confidently handle traffic spikes, deliver consistent performance, and keep your services running smoothly, even in the face of unexpected demand.

So, embrace the power of load balancing and auto-scaling, tailor your configurations to your specific requirements, and let them be your allies in delivering reliable and high-performance services to your users. May your load balancing and auto-scaling configurations keep your digital infrastructure in perfect harmony, even in the face of the most challenging conditions.

BOOK 2
MASTERING CLOUD ORCHESTRATION
INTERMEDIATE TECHNIQUES AND BEST PRACTICES

ROB BOTWRIGHT

Chapter 1: Reviewing Cloud Orchestration Fundamentals

Welcome to the world of cloud orchestration, where we'll explore key concepts that form the foundation of this essential practice in modern IT. Imagine orchestrating a symphony of cloud resources, from virtual machines to containers, all working together harmoniously to meet your organization's goals. Cloud orchestration is like the conductor who directs this complex ensemble, ensuring that resources are provisioned, configured, and managed efficiently.

Let's begin our journey by understanding what cloud orchestration means. Think of it as the art of automating and coordinating tasks in the cloud, where you define a sequence of actions to achieve a specific outcome. Imagine you want to deploy a web application with multiple components, including databases, web servers, and load balancers. Cloud orchestration allows you to automate the provisioning of these resources, configure them correctly, and ensure they work together seamlessly.

Templates play a pivotal role in cloud orchestration. Imagine you're an architect designing a building. You create blueprints that detail the structure's layout and specifications. Similarly, in cloud orchestration, you use templates to define the infrastructure and application configurations. These templates serve as the instructions that automation tools follow to create and manage resources.

Automation is the heart of cloud orchestration. Picture this: you have a repetitive task, like launching virtual machines whenever new employees join your organization. Automation allows you to define rules and workflows that execute these tasks automatically. This not only saves time but also reduces the risk of human error.

Orchestration tools are your trusted companions in this journey. Think of them as your orchestra members, each playing a unique role. These tools help you define, manage, and execute the orchestrated workflows. They can range from open-source solutions like Ansible and Terraform to cloud provider-specific tools like AWS CloudFormation or Azure Resource Manager.

Resource abstraction is a crucial concept in cloud orchestration. Imagine you're driving a car. You don't need to understand every mechanical detail to operate it. Similarly, cloud orchestration abstracts the complexity of underlying cloud resources. You define what you need (e.g., a virtual machine with specific configurations), and the orchestration tool handles the technical details.

Parameterization is a key feature of orchestration templates. Picture this: you're baking cookies, and you have a recipe with ingredients that can vary, like the type of chocolate chips. Parameterization allows you to customize your orchestration templates by specifying values for different parameters, making them adaptable to various scenarios.

Dependencies are a fundamental consideration in cloud orchestration. Imagine building a house. You can't install the roof before erecting the walls. Similarly, orchestration templates often involve resources with dependencies. You define the order in which resources are created and specify any interdependencies to ensure a smooth workflow.

Conditional logic adds flexibility to cloud orchestration. Think of it as decision-making in your daily life. For example, if it's raining, you might take an umbrella. In orchestration, you can include conditional statements in templates. These statements allow you to create workflows that adapt to different conditions, such as deploying additional resources if traffic spikes occur.

Orchestration in the cloud is not limited to infrastructure alone. Imagine you're cooking a multi-course meal. You coordinate not only the main dishes but also the side dishes, beverages, and desserts. Similarly, cloud orchestration can encompass both infrastructure provisioning and application deployment, ensuring that all components work together seamlessly.

Scalability is a core concept in cloud orchestration. Picture this: your online store experiences a sudden surge in traffic during a holiday sale. Scalability allows you to dynamically allocate additional resources to handle the increased load and then release them when traffic subsides, ensuring that your application remains responsive and cost-effective.

Version control is essential for managing orchestration templates. Think of it as keeping track of changes in a document. Version control systems allow you to maintain a history of your templates, track modifications, and collaborate with team members effectively. This ensures that your orchestration configurations are consistent and well-managed.

Error handling is a critical aspect of cloud orchestration. Imagine you're flying a plane, and an unexpected issue arises. Error handling mechanisms in orchestration allow you to define how to respond to errors or failures gracefully. You can specify actions like rollback, notification, or retry to ensure the reliability of your workflows.

In summary, cloud orchestration is the art of automating and coordinating tasks in the cloud, using templates, automation tools, and orchestrated workflows. It abstracts the complexity of cloud resources, allowing you to define, manage, and execute tasks efficiently.

As you navigate the world of cloud orchestration, remember that it's not just about automation; it's about achieving desired outcomes with precision and efficiency. With the right orchestration tools and templates in place, you can confidently manage your cloud resources, deploy applications, and adapt to changing requirements in a dynamic and agile manner.

So, embrace the conductor's role, master the orchestration techniques, and let cloud orchestration be your guiding baton in orchestrating a symphony of cloud resources to create harmony in your IT operations. May your orchestration efforts bring efficiency, reliability, and scalability to your cloud endeavors.

Welcome to the world of workflow automation, where we'll explore the concept, significance, and practical applications of this transformative technology. Imagine streamlining your daily tasks, eliminating repetitive actions, and optimizing processes to boost productivity. Workflow automation is like having a virtual assistant that tirelessly handles routine work, allowing you to focus on more strategic and creative endeavors.

Let's begin our journey by understanding what workflow automation means. Think of it as the magic wand that simplifies complex processes. In essence, workflow automation involves using technology to design, execute, and manage a sequence of tasks or steps in a predefined order. These tasks could be anything from data entry and document approval to customer onboarding and inventory management.

Automation tools are the engines behind workflow automation. Imagine having a toolbox filled with versatile gadgets that can perform various tasks. These tools enable you to define workflows, set rules, and trigger actions based on specific conditions. Some popular automation tools include Zapier, Microsoft Power Automate, and WorkflowMax.

Efficiency is a key driver of workflow automation. Picture this: you're running a small e-commerce business, and each day, you receive a flood of customer inquiries and order notifications. With workflow automation, you can create rules that automatically route inquiries to the right department, send order confirmations to customers, and update inventory levels in real-time. This not only saves time but also reduces errors and ensures a seamless customer experience.

Streamlining repetitive tasks is a fundamental application of workflow automation. Imagine you work in human resources, and you regularly receive job applications. Automation allows you to set up a workflow that automatically sorts, filters, and responds to incoming applications, making the hiring process more efficient and consistent.

Data integration is another powerful aspect of workflow automation. Think of it as connecting different parts of a puzzle. Automation tools can fetch data from various sources, like databases, spreadsheets, or online forms, and consolidate it into a single, unified view. This streamlines data analysis and decision-making processes.

Notification and alerting mechanisms are essential components of workflow automation. Imagine you're a project manager, and you want to stay updated on critical project milestones. Automation tools can be set up to send you notifications when specific conditions are met, such as when a task is completed or a deadline is approaching.

Customization is a hallmark of effective workflow automation. Picture this: you run a marketing campaign, and you need to send personalized follow-up emails to customers who've shown interest in your product.

Automation tools allow you to create custom workflows that tailor messages based on individual customer interactions, enhancing engagement and conversion rates.

Error reduction is a significant benefit of workflow automation. Think of it as having a proofreader for your documents. Automation tools can validate data, perform consistency checks, and alert you when anomalies or errors are detected. This ensures that processes run smoothly and accurately.

Scalability is a key consideration in workflow automation. Imagine your business is growing rapidly, and you need to expand your customer support team. With automation, you can easily scale your workflows to accommodate increased workloads. Whether you're handling ten or ten thousand inquiries, automation adapts to your needs.

Collaboration and communication are enhanced through workflow automation. Picture this: you work in a remote team, and you need to coordinate tasks with colleagues in different time zones. Automation tools can facilitate collaboration by automatically assigning tasks, sending reminders, and updating team members on progress, ensuring everyone stays in sync. Auditing and compliance are critical in many industries. Think of it as following a recipe to ensure food safety. Automation tools can record every step of a workflow, providing a detailed audit trail. This helps organizations maintain compliance with regulations and standards and facilitates transparency in processes.

Mobile accessibility is a feature that modern automation tools offer. Imagine you're on the go, and you need to approve an important document. Mobile-friendly automation apps allow you to access and manage workflows from your smartphone or tablet, providing flexibility and convenience.

Integration with existing software is a seamless process in workflow automation. Picture this: your organization uses a combination of tools, from customer relationship management (CRM) systems to accounting software. Automation tools can integrate with these existing systems, enabling data flow and process automation across your software ecosystem.

Testing and optimization are ongoing activities in workflow automation. Think of it as fine-tuning a musical instrument for the best performance. After setting up automation workflows, it's essential to monitor their effectiveness, gather feedback, and make improvements. Regular testing ensures that workflows remain efficient and aligned with business goals.

In summary, workflow automation is a transformative technology that simplifies processes, enhances efficiency, reduces errors, and improves collaboration. Whether you're managing business operations, customer interactions, or project workflows, automation tools empower you to create customized, adaptable solutions that align with your specific needs.

As you navigate the world of workflow automation, remember that it's not about replacing human efforts; it's about enhancing them. Automation allows you to focus on strategic tasks, creativity, and innovation, while routine and repetitive work is handled efficiently by the technology.

So, embrace the power of workflow automation, tailor it to your unique requirements, and let it be your reliable ally in streamlining processes, enhancing productivity, and achieving your business objectives. May your automation endeavors bring newfound efficiency and effectiveness to your professional journey.

Chapter 2: Advanced Tools and Frameworks

Welcome to the advanced realm of orchestration tools, where we dive deeper into sophisticated solutions that enable you to orchestrate complex workflows with precision and efficiency. Imagine orchestrating a grand symphony with an array of instruments, each playing a unique role in creating a harmonious masterpiece. Advanced orchestration tools are like seasoned conductors, offering a refined and nuanced approach to automating intricate processes.

Let's embark on our journey by understanding the significance of advanced orchestration tools. Think of them as the Swiss Army knives of automation, equipped with a wide range of features and capabilities. These tools go beyond basic orchestration by offering advanced functionalities that cater to the most complex and demanding workflows.

Complexity handling is a defining feature of advanced orchestration tools. Picture this: you manage a multinational supply chain with multiple suppliers, warehouses, and distribution channels. Advanced tools can handle the intricacies of orchestrating resources, data, and actions across geographically dispersed operations, ensuring seamless coordination.

Extensibility is a key advantage of advanced orchestration tools. Imagine you have a unique business requirement that standard solutions can't address. Advanced tools offer extensibility through custom scripting, plugins, and integrations, allowing you to tailor the orchestration process to your specific needs.

Service orchestration is a vital capability in advanced tools. Think of it as managing a high-stakes theatrical production with various performers, costumes, and props. Advanced orchestration tools excel in coordinating complex service workflows, such as provisioning cloud resources, configuring network services, and deploying applications across hybrid environments.

Parallel processing is a noteworthy feature in advanced orchestration. Picture this: you need to process a massive dataset with millions of records. Advanced tools can parallelize tasks, distributing the workload across multiple processors or servers to accelerate execution and optimize resource utilization.

Orchestration of microservices and containers is a specialized domain within advanced tools. Think of it as directing a troupe of actors in a play, each playing a specific role. Advanced orchestration tools like Kubernetes and Docker Swarm excel in managing microservices and containerized applications, ensuring scalability, fault tolerance, and efficient resource utilization.

Role-based access control is a crucial security aspect of advanced orchestration tools. Imagine you have a team of administrators with varying levels of access and responsibilities. These tools provide granular control over user permissions, allowing you to define who can perform specific actions within the orchestration process.

Integration with external systems is seamless with advanced orchestration tools. Think of it as connecting various pieces of a puzzle to complete a picture. These tools offer robust APIs, connectors, and adapters to integrate with external systems, databases, and cloud services, ensuring data consistency and workflow continuity.

Complex workflow modeling is a strength of advanced tools. Picture this: you have a multi-step workflow with conditional branching and dynamic decision-making. Advanced orchestration tools provide graphical or code-based interfaces for creating intricate workflow models, facilitating the automation of even the most complex processes.

Real-time monitoring and analytics are indispensable features in advanced orchestration tools. Think of them as the conductor's baton that keeps tempo in a symphony. These tools offer comprehensive dashboards, alerts, and reporting capabilities to monitor the progress and performance of orchestration workflows in real-time, allowing you to make data-driven decisions and optimize processes.

Fault tolerance and disaster recovery are top priorities for advanced orchestration tools. Imagine a scenario where a critical component in your workflow fails. Advanced tools implement fault tolerance mechanisms like automated failover, backup and recovery, and load balancing to ensure continuity and minimize downtime.

Version control and auditing are essential in advanced orchestration tools. Think of it as keeping a detailed logbook of every performance in a theater production. These tools maintain version history of orchestration workflows, enabling you to track changes, roll back to previous configurations, and meet compliance and auditing requirements.

Security and compliance features are robust in advanced orchestration tools. Picture this: you're orchestrating workflows that involve sensitive data or regulatory requirements. These tools offer encryption, access controls, and compliance templates to ensure that your orchestration processes meet industry-specific security and compliance standards.

Multi-cloud and hybrid cloud support is a hallmark of advanced orchestration tools. Think of it as conducting a symphony that includes musicians from different orchestras. These tools excel in orchestrating resources across diverse cloud providers and on-premises environments, ensuring seamless interoperability and resource management.

In summary, advanced orchestration tools are versatile and powerful solutions designed to meet the demands of complex and diverse automation scenarios. Whether you're orchestrating intricate service workflows, managing microservices, or ensuring compliance in regulated industries, these tools offer a wide array of capabilities to streamline processes, enhance security, and optimize resource utilization.

As you venture into the world of advanced orchestration tools, keep in mind that they are your allies in orchestrating complex processes with precision and agility. With their sophisticated features and extensibility, you can confidently tackle the most intricate automation challenges, ensuring that your organization operates at its highest level of efficiency and effectiveness.

So, embrace the conductor's baton of advanced orchestration tools, explore their capabilities, and let them guide you in orchestrating complex workflows with finesse and expertise. May your orchestration endeavors lead to seamless coordination, enhanced productivity, and the successful realization of your automation goals.

Welcome to the world of leveraging frameworks for complex workflows, where we'll explore the use of structured frameworks to orchestrate intricate processes with efficiency and reliability. Imagine you have a toolkit filled with specialized instruments, each designed for a specific task. Frameworks are like these specialized tools, providing a structured approach to automating complex workflows in a way that simplifies design, execution, and management.

Let's embark on our journey by understanding what frameworks are and why they are essential in handling complex workflows. Think of a framework as a blueprint for building a complex structure, like a skyscraper. It provides a predefined structure and set of rules that guide the construction process. Similarly, in the context of workflow orchestration, frameworks offer a structured foundation for designing, executing, and managing complex workflows.

Complexity management is a key benefit of using frameworks. Picture this: you are orchestrating a healthcare process that involves patient data management, appointment scheduling, and insurance claims processing. A framework provides a structured approach to manage the intricacies of such a complex workflow, ensuring that all components work together seamlessly.

Reusability is a defining feature of frameworks. Imagine you've designed an efficient workflow for a specific task. With a framework, you can reuse the same design and structure for similar tasks, reducing the time and effort required to create new workflows. This not only saves resources but also promotes consistency across processes.

Standardization is crucial in complex workflows. Think of it as following a set of best practices in a manufacturing process to ensure quality and consistency. Frameworks enforce standardization by providing predefined templates, guidelines, and best practices, helping organizations maintain consistency and compliance in their processes.

Modularity is a strength of frameworks in managing complexity. Picture this: you have a complex software application with multiple modules. A framework allows you to break down the application into modular components, each with its own well-defined function. This modularity simplifies development, testing, and maintenance of the workflow.

Interoperability is a vital consideration in complex workflows. Imagine you're integrating various software systems, each with its own protocols and data formats.

Frameworks often come with built-in support for integrating diverse technologies and systems, ensuring seamless interoperability within the workflow.

Scalability is a critical aspect of complex workflows. Think of it as being able to expand a manufacturing process to meet increased demand. Frameworks are designed to handle scalability challenges by providing mechanisms to add or remove components as needed, ensuring that the workflow can adapt to changing requirements.

Error handling and recovery mechanisms are robust in frameworks. Picture this: during the execution of a complex workflow, unexpected errors or failures can occur. Frameworks offer built-in error handling and recovery mechanisms, allowing workflows to gracefully handle exceptions and continue processing.

Dependency management is a key consideration in complex workflows. Think of it as ensuring that all parts of a machine work together smoothly. Frameworks provide tools for defining and managing dependencies between workflow components, ensuring that tasks are executed in the correct order and that interdependencies are well-managed.

Parallelism and concurrency support are essential in complex workflows. Imagine you have a workflow that needs to process multiple tasks simultaneously. Frameworks offer features for parallel execution, enabling tasks to run concurrently, improving performance and efficiency.

Monitoring and analytics capabilities are integral to frameworks. Think of them as instruments that allow you to measure the performance and health of your workflow. Frameworks often include built-in monitoring and analytics tools, providing insights into the execution of the workflow and enabling data-driven decision-making.

Security and access control are paramount in complex workflows. Picture this: you're orchestrating a financial transaction process that involves sensitive data. Frameworks offer security features such as encryption, authentication, and role-based access control, ensuring that data remains secure and compliant with regulations.

Adaptability to changing requirements is a strength of frameworks. Think of it as being able to modify the design of a building as new requirements emerge. Frameworks are flexible and allow you to adapt workflows to changing business needs, ensuring that your processes remain relevant and effective over time.

Version control and auditability are crucial in complex workflows. Imagine you need to track changes and maintain a history of workflow modifications. Frameworks provide version control mechanisms, allowing you to document changes, track revisions, and meet compliance and auditing requirements.

Integration with external systems is seamless with frameworks. Think of it as connecting different components of a complex machine. Frameworks offer APIs, connectors, and adapters that facilitate integration with external systems, databases, and services, ensuring data flow and process continuity.

In summary, leveraging frameworks for complex workflows is like having a structured guide to orchestrate intricate processes with efficiency, reliability, and scalability. Whether you're managing complex healthcare workflows, financial transactions, or manufacturing processes, frameworks offer a structured approach to handling complexity and ensuring that all components work together seamlessly.

As you explore the world of frameworks for complex workflows, remember that they are your trusted companions in designing, executing, and managing intricate processes. With their structured approach, best practices, and scalability, frameworks empower you to navigate the challenges of complexity with confidence, enabling your organization to operate efficiently and adapt to changing demands.

So, embrace the structured foundation that frameworks provide, tailor them to your unique requirements, and let them guide you in orchestrating complex workflows with precision and expertise. May your journey with frameworks lead to streamlined processes, enhanced productivity, and successful automation of even the most intricate tasks.

Chapter 3: Orchestration Patterns and Workflows

Welcome to the world of designing efficient orchestration workflows, where we'll delve into the art and science of creating workflows that not only automate tasks but do so with precision, speed, and resource optimization. Imagine orchestrating a complex dance performance where every move is perfectly choreographed, and the result is a seamless and captivating spectacle. Efficient orchestration workflows are like the choreographers of automation, ensuring that tasks flow smoothly and harmoniously.

Let's embark on our journey by understanding the essence of designing efficient orchestration workflows. Think of it as creating a well-organized recipe that guides you through the steps of preparing a delicious meal. In the world of automation, workflows serve as those recipes, outlining a sequence of actions, decisions, and conditions that need to be executed to achieve a specific outcome.

Efficiency is a central theme in designing workflows. Picture this: you're managing a customer onboarding process for an e-commerce platform. An efficient workflow ensures that customer data is verified, accounts are created, and welcome emails are sent in the shortest time possible, providing an exceptional customer experience.

Process mapping is an essential step in designing efficient workflows. Think of it as drawing a detailed map before embarking on a journey. Mapping involves visualizing the entire workflow, identifying the steps, decision points, and dependencies, and understanding the flow of data and resources.

Automation suitability assessment is a crucial consideration. Imagine you have a manual process that involves frequent human judgment and creativity. Not all processes are equally suitable for automation, and it's important to assess whether automation would bring efficiency or hinder the process.

Resource allocation and optimization are key goals in workflow design. Picture this: you're managing a data analysis workflow that requires substantial computing resources. Efficient workflows allocate resources dynamically, ensuring that tasks have access to the right amount of computing power, storage, and network bandwidth.

Conditional logic is a powerful element in designing workflows. Think of it as creating a "choose your own adventure" story, where the path depends on the choices made. Conditional logic allows workflows to adapt based on specific conditions, making them versatile and capable of handling diverse scenarios.

Parallel processing is a significant efficiency booster in workflow design. Imagine you have a task that can be divided into multiple sub-tasks, all of which can be executed simultaneously. Efficient workflows leverage parallel processing to reduce processing time and increase throughput.

Error handling and recovery mechanisms are crucial in efficient workflows. Picture this: during the execution of a complex workflow, unexpected errors or exceptions can occur. Efficient workflows are designed with built-in error handling mechanisms that can identify issues, trigger appropriate actions, and continue processing.

Resource scaling and de-scaling strategies are vital for efficient workflows. Think of it as having a thermostat that adjusts the temperature in your home based on your comfort level. Efficient workflows can scale up resources during peak demand and de-scale during periods of low activity, optimizing resource utilization and costs.

Monitoring and analytics capabilities are integral to efficient workflow design. Imagine you're driving a car, and you have a dashboard that provides real-time information about the vehicle's performance. Efficient workflows offer comprehensive monitoring and analytics tools that allow you to track the progress, performance, and bottlenecks within the workflow.

User interaction and decision points are important considerations. Picture this: you're orchestrating an order processing workflow, and there are cases where human intervention is required for decision-making. Efficient workflows incorporate user interaction points, ensuring that tasks are routed to the right individuals for timely decisions.

Workflow versioning and change management are essential for maintaining efficiency. Think of it as updating software to fix bugs and add new features. Efficient workflows have version control mechanisms that allow you to make changes, track revisions, and ensure that the workflow remains aligned with evolving business needs.

Documentation and knowledge sharing are key aspects of efficient workflow design. Imagine you're passing on a family recipe to the next generation. Efficient workflows are well-documented, making it easy for team members to understand and maintain them. Documentation also aids in onboarding new team members and ensuring knowledge continuity.

Security and compliance considerations are paramount in workflow design. Picture this: you're handling sensitive financial transactions. Efficient workflows incorporate security features like encryption, access controls, and audit trails to safeguard data and ensure compliance with industry regulations.

Integration with external systems and services is seamless in efficient workflows. Think of it as connecting different pieces of a puzzle to complete a picture. Efficient workflows offer robust integration capabilities, allowing you to connect with external databases, APIs, cloud services, and third-party applications.

Adaptability and flexibility are qualities of efficient workflows. Imagine your business evolves, and new requirements emerge. Efficient workflows are designed to be adaptable, allowing you to modify, expand, or reconfigure them to meet changing business needs without significant disruption.

In summary, designing efficient orchestration workflows is an art that requires careful consideration of process mapping, resource optimization, conditional logic, error handling, and many other elements. Whether you're automating customer onboarding, data analysis, or order processing, efficient workflows ensure that tasks are executed with precision, speed, and resource efficiency.

As you embark on the journey of designing efficient workflows, remember that they are your partners in orchestrating processes that drive efficiency and productivity. With thoughtful design and optimization, you can create workflows that not only save time and resources but also enhance the overall effectiveness of your organization.

So, embrace the role of the choreographer in designing efficient workflows, craft them with precision and creativity, and let them lead your organization in a dance of automation that captivates with its efficiency and grace. May your journey in workflow design be filled with harmonious processes and seamless automation.

Welcome to the fascinating world of common orchestration

patterns in practice, where we'll explore tried-and-true approaches to orchestrating processes effectively. Think of orchestration patterns as the building blocks of automation, each with a unique design and purpose, allowing you to create efficient and reliable workflows for a wide range of tasks.

Let's embark on our journey by understanding what orchestration patterns are and why they are essential in the world of automation. Imagine you're a chef in a bustling kitchen, and you have a set of recipes that guide you in preparing different dishes. Orchestration patterns are like those recipes, providing structured instructions on how to coordinate and execute various tasks to achieve a specific goal.

Sequential execution is one of the most fundamental orchestration patterns. Picture this: you're assembling a piece of furniture, and the instructions guide you step by step, from assembling the frame to attaching the components. Sequential execution involves executing tasks in a linear order, ensuring that each task completes before the next one begins.

Parallel execution is another essential orchestration pattern. Think of it as juggling multiple tasks simultaneously, each performed independently. Parallel execution allows you to execute multiple tasks concurrently, which can significantly reduce processing time and improve efficiency.

Conditional branching is a powerful orchestration pattern that introduces decision-making into workflows. Imagine you're automating an order processing system, and you need to determine the appropriate shipping method based on the customer's location. Conditional branching allows you to evaluate conditions and execute different tasks based on the outcomes.

Looping, or iteration, is a versatile orchestration pattern that involves repeating a set of tasks until a specified condition is met. Think of it as brewing the perfect cup of tea, where you steep the tea bag until it reaches the desired strength. Looping patterns are valuable when you need to perform a task multiple times or until a specific criterion is satisfied.

Error handling is an essential aspect of orchestration patterns. Picture this: during the execution of a workflow, unexpected errors or exceptions can occur, such as a server outage or a data validation failure. Error handling patterns enable you to gracefully handle these exceptions, trigger appropriate actions, and ensure the workflow's robustness.

State management is crucial in many orchestration patterns. Think of it as remembering where you left off in a complex task. State management patterns allow you to keep track of the workflow's progress, store intermediate results, and resume execution from a specific point, even after interruptions.

Resource allocation and optimization patterns are essential in orchestrating tasks that require computing resources, such as data processing or rendering. Imagine you're rendering a high-definition video, and you want to distribute the rendering tasks across multiple servers to speed up the process. Resource allocation patterns help you optimize resource usage and scalability.

Fan-out and fan-in patterns are valuable when you need to distribute tasks to multiple workers or processes and then aggregate their results. Think of it as organizing a team of specialists to work on different aspects of a project and then bringing their contributions together. Fan-out distributes tasks, and fan-in collects and combines the results.

Workflow chaining, or composition, is a pattern that involves connecting multiple workflows together to achieve a more extensive automation process. Imagine you have separate workflows for user registration and email verification. Workflow chaining patterns allow you to connect these workflows seamlessly, creating an end-to-end process.

Event-driven orchestration patterns are suited for scenarios where tasks should be triggered in response to specific events or signals. Picture this: you have an e-commerce platform, and you want to send order confirmation emails immediately after a successful purchase. Event-driven patterns allow you to respond to events in real-time and initiate the corresponding tasks.

Coordinated orchestration patterns come into play when multiple tasks need to be synchronized or coordinated to achieve a common goal. Think of it as orchestrating a grand performance with multiple actors who need to enter the stage at the right moment. Coordinated patterns ensure that tasks are synchronized to work harmoniously together.

Data flow and transformation patterns are essential in scenarios involving data manipulation, conversion, and transformation. Imagine you're processing and aggregating data from various sources to generate reports. Data flow patterns help you design workflows that efficiently move, transform, and analyze data.

Human interaction patterns are valuable when tasks involve user input or approval. Picture this: you're automating a travel expense approval process, and managers need to review and approve expenses. Human interaction patterns introduce tasks that require human intervention, such as reviewing documents or making decisions.

Integration patterns enable you to connect and interact with external systems, services, and APIs seamlessly. Think of it as building bridges between different islands of data and functionality. Integration patterns provide standardized approaches to integrate with third-party systems, ensuring data exchange and interoperability.

Versioning and change management patterns are crucial for maintaining and evolving orchestration workflows over time. Imagine your business processes evolve, and you need to update your workflows to accommodate new requirements. Versioning and change management patterns help you manage and document workflow changes effectively.

Logging and auditing patterns ensure that you have a record of workflow executions for monitoring, compliance, and debugging. Think of it as keeping a detailed journal of each performance in a theater production. Logging and auditing patterns help you track workflow execution, errors, and outcomes, ensuring transparency and accountability.

In summary, common orchestration patterns are like a rich toolbox that empowers you to design and automate a wide range of tasks and processes efficiently. Whether you're orchestrating sequential tasks, making decisions, handling errors, or coordinating complex workflows, these patterns provide proven approaches to achieving automation goals.

As you explore the world of orchestration patterns, remember that they are your allies in orchestrating processes with precision, flexibility, and reliability. With the right pattern at your disposal, you can confidently tackle automation challenges and create workflows that streamline operations and enhance productivity.

So, embrace the versatility of orchestration patterns, apply them creatively to your automation endeavors, and let them guide you in orchestrating processes that captivate with their efficiency and effectiveness. May your journey in automation be filled with harmonious workflows and successful automation projects.

Chapter 4: Optimizing Resource Allocation

Welcome to the world of resource optimization strategies, where we'll explore techniques and approaches to make the most of your resources, whether they are computing power, storage, or human talent. Think of resource optimization as a way to maximize efficiency and minimize waste, much like a skilled chef who uses every part of an ingredient to create a delicious meal.

Let's dive into the fascinating realm of resource optimization and uncover the strategies that can help you achieve efficiency and cost-effectiveness. Picture this: you're managing a cloud infrastructure, and you want to ensure that you're not overprovisioning resources, which can lead to unnecessary expenses. Resource optimization strategies come to the rescue by helping you strike the right balance between resource allocation and utilization.

Rightsizing is a fundamental concept in resource optimization. Think of it as ensuring that you have the right-sized shoes for your feet. In the context of computing resources, rightsizing means allocating just the right amount of CPU, memory, and storage to a workload. This prevents overprovisioning, where resources sit idle, and underprovisioning, which can lead to poor performance.

Load balancing is a crucial strategy in resource optimization. Imagine you're hosting a website that experiences varying levels of traffic throughout the day. Load balancing ensures that incoming requests are distributed evenly across multiple servers, preventing any single server from becoming a bottleneck and optimizing response times.

Dynamic scaling is a resource optimization technique that allows you to adjust resources in response to changing workloads. Think of it as having a thermostat in your home that automatically adjusts the temperature based on your preferences. Dynamic scaling can automatically add or remove resources as needed to handle spikes in demand, ensuring optimal performance and cost control.

Resource pooling is a strategy commonly used in virtualization and cloud environments. Picture this: you have a pool of virtual machines or storage that can be dynamically allocated to different workloads. Resource pooling optimizes resource utilization by allowing resources to be shared and allocated on-demand, reducing waste and improving efficiency.

Automated provisioning is a powerful resource optimization technique. Imagine you're setting up a development environment for your software team. Automated provisioning allows you to automate the process of creating and configuring resources, such as virtual machines, databases, and networks, saving time and reducing the risk of manual errors.

Resource consolidation is a strategy that focuses on combining multiple resources into a single, more efficient resource. Think of it as decluttering your workspace by merging similar tools into one. Resource consolidation can involve consolidating physical servers into virtual machines or combining storage volumes to reduce complexity and improve resource utilization.

Efficient data storage and management are essential aspects of resource optimization. Picture this: you're managing a vast amount of data, and you want to ensure that it's stored efficiently to minimize storage costs. Efficient data storage techniques, such as data deduplication and compression, help reduce storage requirements while maintaining data integrity.

Idle resource identification is a resource optimization practice that involves identifying and reclaiming idle or underutilized resources. Imagine you have virtual machines that are rarely used but consume resources. Identifying and reclaiming these idle resources can free up capacity for more critical workloads, improving efficiency and cost-effectiveness.

Resource tagging and labeling provide visibility and control over resources in complex environments. Think of it as labeling items in your pantry to easily find what you need. Resource tagging allows you to categorize and label resources, making it easier to track usage, allocate costs, and enforce policies.

Resource optimization policies are guidelines that help you make informed decisions about resource allocation and utilization. Picture this: you want to ensure that resources are allocated according to business priorities and compliance requirements. Resource optimization policies provide a framework for making resource allocation decisions based on predefined criteria.

Resource monitoring and analytics are integral to resource optimization. Imagine you're driving a car, and you have a dashboard that displays real-time information about fuel consumption and engine performance. Resource monitoring and analytics provide insights into resource utilization, helping you identify areas where optimization is needed and making data-driven decisions.

Human expertise and collaboration play a vital role in resource optimization. Think of it as a team of skilled chefs working together to create a gourmet meal. Human expertise allows you to analyze complex resource optimization challenges, make strategic decisions, and implement optimization strategies effectively.

Resource optimization tools and software are valuable assets in the quest for efficiency. Picture this: you have a toolbox filled with specialized tools for different tasks. Resource optimization tools provide automation, visibility, and control over resources, simplifying the process of identifying and implementing optimization opportunities.

Sustainable practices are becoming increasingly important in resource optimization. Imagine you're managing a data center, and you want to reduce energy consumption and environmental impact. Sustainable resource optimization involves implementing energy-efficient technologies, such as cooling systems and renewable energy sources, to reduce resource waste and promote sustainability.

Resource optimization is an ongoing process that requires continuous monitoring and adaptation. Think of it as tending to a garden, where you regularly prune and nurture to achieve a bountiful harvest. By continuously evaluating resource utilization, identifying optimization opportunities, and adapting to changing demands, you can maintain efficiency and cost-effectiveness over time.

In summary, resource optimization strategies are your trusted companions in the quest for efficiency and cost-effectiveness. Whether you're managing computing resources, storage, or any other valuable assets, these strategies provide a roadmap to make the most of what you have.

As you explore the world of resource optimization, remember that it's not just about saving costs but also about improving performance, sustainability, and the overall effectiveness of your operations. With the right strategies and a proactive approach, you can navigate the challenges of resource management with confidence, ensuring that your organization operates at its best.

So, embrace resource optimization as a journey of continuous improvement, apply these strategies creatively to your unique challenges, and let them guide you in maximizing efficiency, reducing waste, and achieving sustainable success. May your path in resource optimization be marked by smart decisions, resourceful solutions, and a thriving, optimized environment.

Welcome to the world of dynamic resource allocation techniques, where we'll explore the art and science of adjusting computing resources on the fly to meet the changing needs of your applications and workloads. Think of dynamic resource allocation as having a magical toolbox that allows you to instantly conjure more computing power when your applications demand it and return resources to the pool when they're no longer needed.

Dynamic resource allocation is all about flexibility and responsiveness. Imagine you're hosting a popular e-commerce website, and during a flash sale, the website experiences a sudden surge in traffic. Dynamic resource allocation ensures that your website can seamlessly scale up to handle the increased load without a hiccup.

Scaling up, also known as vertical scaling, is a technique where you add more resources to a single instance of an application to boost its performance. Picture this: you're playing a video game, and you want to improve the graphics and frame rate. Scaling up involves upgrading the CPU, memory, or other resources of your gaming computer to achieve a better gaming experience.

Scaling out, or horizontal scaling, is the counterpart of scaling up. Think of it as having multiple identical copies of your application running in parallel to distribute the workload. Scaling out is like assembling a team of superheroes to tackle a challenging task together. It involves adding more instances of your application to handle increased traffic or workload.

Auto-scaling is a dynamic resource allocation technique that automates the process of scaling based on predefined criteria. Imagine you're managing a cloud-based application, and you want it to automatically add or remove instances in response to changes in traffic. Auto-scaling uses triggers, such as CPU usage or network traffic, to determine when to scale.

Elasticity is a concept closely related to auto-scaling. Picture this: you have a rubber band that stretches and contracts based on the force applied to it. Elasticity in computing refers to the ability of a system to automatically adapt to changing workloads by adding or removing resources as needed. It's about maintaining optimal performance while controlling costs.

Load balancing is a key component of dynamic resource allocation. Think of it as distributing the weight evenly among a group of people carrying a heavy object. Load balancing ensures that incoming requests or tasks are distributed across multiple resources or servers, preventing overloading and optimizing response times.

Resource pools are a valuable technique in dynamic allocation. Imagine you have a shared swimming pool where people can jump in and use it as needed. Resource pools allocate resources from a common pool and return them when they're no longer in use. It's an efficient way to manage resources in a shared environment.

Resource reservations are a practice in dynamic allocation where you reserve a portion of resources for specific workloads or applications. Picture this: you're hosting a conference, and you want to ensure that a reserved section is available for VIP guests. Resource reservations guarantee that a certain amount of resources is dedicated to critical tasks.

Resource priorities are a technique that allows you to assign different priorities to tasks or workloads. Think of it as a priority boarding system at an airport. Resource priorities ensure that high-priority tasks get access to resources first, while lower-priority tasks wait in line, optimizing resource allocation based on importance.

Resource capping is a strategy in dynamic allocation where you set a maximum limit on resource usage for specific tasks or applications. Imagine you're at an all-you-can-eat buffet, but you decide to cap your plate with a specific portion to avoid overindulgence. Resource capping prevents resource-intensive tasks from consuming excessive resources, maintaining fairness and stability.

Resource affinity and anti-affinity are techniques that control the placement of tasks or workloads on specific resources. Picture this: you have a puzzle, and some pieces fit together perfectly, while others don't. Resource affinity ensures that related tasks run on the same resources, optimizing communication and performance, while anti-affinity ensures that conflicting tasks are kept apart to avoid interference.

Dynamic resource allocation is particularly valuable in cloud computing environments. Think of it as having access to a vast pool of resources in the cloud that you can allocate and de-allocate as needed. Cloud providers offer services that enable you to dynamically scale your applications based on actual usage, helping you avoid overprovisioning and reducing costs.

Resource orchestration is a practice that combines various dynamic allocation techniques to optimize resource usage. Imagine you're conducting an orchestra, and each musician plays their part at the right time and in harmony with others. Resource orchestration involves coordinating the allocation, scaling, and management of resources across multiple components of an application or system.

Resource allocation algorithms are the brains behind dynamic allocation. Picture this: you have a smart thermostat that adjusts the temperature based on your preferences and energy efficiency. Resource allocation algorithms use data and criteria to make intelligent decisions about when and how to allocate resources, optimizing efficiency and performance.

Monitoring and analytics are critical aspects of dynamic resource allocation. Think of it as having a control panel that displays real-time information about resource usage and performance. Monitoring and analytics tools provide insights into resource utilization, allowing you to make informed decisions and adjustments.

Resource allocation policies are guidelines that help you define how resources should be allocated and managed. Imagine you have a set of rules that dictate who gets access to specific resources and under what conditions. Resource allocation policies ensure that resource allocation aligns with business objectives, compliance requirements, and best practices.

Resource allocation is not just about computing resources; it extends to other types of resources, such as storage, network bandwidth, and even human resources. Picture this: you're managing a project, and you need to allocate team members with specific skills to different tasks. Resource allocation techniques can optimize human resource allocation, ensuring that the right people are assigned to the right tasks.

In summary, dynamic resource allocation techniques are your allies in the quest for efficiency and performance optimization. Whether you're scaling up, scaling out, or automating resource allocation, these techniques empower you to adapt to changing demands and make the most of your resources.

As you explore the world of dynamic resource allocation, remember that it's about finding the right balance between resource availability and utilization. With the right techniques and tools at your disposal, you can confidently navigate the dynamic landscape of resource allocation, ensuring that your applications and workloads run smoothly and efficiently.

Chapter 5: Advanced Monitoring and Troubleshooting

Welcome to the world of proactive monitoring for orchestration, a journey into the realm of staying ahead of potential issues and ensuring the smooth operation of your orchestrated workflows. Think of proactive monitoring as having a vigilant guardian that watches over your orchestration environment, identifying and addressing concerns before they escalate.

Proactive monitoring is all about staying one step ahead. Imagine you're driving a car, and you have sensors that warn you about low tire pressure before a flat tire occurs. Proactive monitoring in orchestration serves a similar purpose, providing insights into the health and performance of your orchestrated processes.

Real-time visibility is a fundamental aspect of proactive monitoring. Picture this: you're piloting a ship through treacherous waters, and you need a clear view of your surroundings to navigate safely. Real-time visibility in orchestration provides continuous insights into the status of your workflows, resources, and components.

Alerting and notification mechanisms are essential in proactive monitoring. Think of them as your orchestra's conductor, alerting musicians when it's time to play their instruments. Alerting and notification systems in orchestration send alerts when predefined conditions or thresholds are met, ensuring that you're informed about potential issues promptly.

Performance metrics and key performance indicators (KPIs) are your guiding stars in proactive monitoring. Imagine you're an athlete training for a marathon, and you track your running speed and heart rate to monitor your progress.

Performance metrics and KPIs in orchestration provide quantitative data about the efficiency and effectiveness of your workflows.

Predictive analytics is a powerful tool in proactive monitoring. Picture this: you're a weather forecaster using historical data and patterns to predict upcoming weather conditions. Predictive analytics in orchestration uses historical data and machine learning algorithms to anticipate potential issues or bottlenecks, allowing you to take preventive actions.

Resource utilization analysis is crucial in proactive monitoring. Think of it as managing the balance of your financial investments to ensure optimal returns. Resource utilization analysis in orchestration assesses how efficiently your computing resources, such as CPU, memory, and storage, are used, helping you identify areas for optimization.

Anomaly detection is like having a security system that flags unusual behavior in your home. In orchestration, anomaly detection algorithms monitor workflows and components for deviations from expected behavior, signaling potential issues or security threats.

Capacity planning is a proactive strategy that involves forecasting resource needs based on historical data and expected growth. Imagine you're an event planner, and you need to estimate the number of guests and seating arrangements for a party. Capacity planning in orchestration ensures that you have the right amount of resources to support current and future workloads.

Health checks and self-healing mechanisms are like having a personal trainer and a first-aid kit in one. In orchestration, health checks continuously assess the well-being of components and workflows, and self-healing mechanisms automatically take corrective actions when issues are detected, ensuring system resilience.

Incident response and escalation procedures are part of proactive monitoring's playbook. Think of them as your orchestra's emergency plan in case something goes wrong during a performance. Incident response procedures in orchestration define how to address and resolve issues, while escalation procedures ensure that critical problems are elevated to the appropriate teams or individuals.

Compliance monitoring is essential in industries with regulatory requirements. Picture this: you're a quality control inspector ensuring that products meet safety standards. Compliance monitoring in orchestration verifies that your workflows adhere to industry-specific regulations and policies, reducing the risk of non-compliance.

Log management and auditing are your record-keeping companions in proactive monitoring. Log management collects and stores data about workflow execution, errors, and events, while auditing tracks changes and access to sensitive information, providing a trail of actions for security and compliance purposes.

Automated remediation is the superhero of proactive monitoring. Imagine you have a guardian angel who can swiftly intervene and fix issues without your direct involvement. Automated remediation in orchestration uses predefined scripts or actions to resolve common problems, reducing manual intervention and downtime.

Continuous improvement is the philosophy that underpins proactive monitoring. Think of it as a commitment to always fine-tune and optimize your orchestra's performance. Continuous improvement in orchestration involves regularly reviewing monitoring data, analyzing trends, and making adjustments to enhance efficiency and effectiveness.

Collaboration and communication are integral to proactive monitoring. Picture this: you're conducting an orchestra, and you need seamless communication with each musician to maintain harmony. Collaboration tools and communication channels in orchestration enable teams to coordinate responses to issues and share insights, ensuring a collective and proactive approach.

Proactive monitoring extends to multi-cloud and hybrid environments. Think of it as having multiple stages for a grand performance, each with its unique set of instruments and musicians. Proactive monitoring solutions for multi-cloud and hybrid environments provide visibility and control across diverse platforms, ensuring consistent monitoring and response.

Machine learning and artificial intelligence (AI) are the future of proactive monitoring. Imagine having an assistant that learns from past experiences and predicts potential challenges. Machine learning and AI in orchestration can analyze vast amounts of data, identify patterns, and make intelligent recommendations for optimization and issue prevention.

Proactive monitoring is not a one-size-fits-all approach. It requires tailoring to your specific orchestration environment, goals, and challenges. Think of it as customizing your orchestra's repertoire to match the occasion and the audience. By adapting proactive monitoring strategies to your unique context, you can maximize its benefits and effectively safeguard your orchestration environment.

In summary, proactive monitoring is your ally in the world of orchestration, ensuring that you anticipate, detect, and address issues before they impact your workflows and operations. It's about staying ahead of the curve, leveraging data-driven insights, and fostering a culture of continuous improvement.

As you embark on your journey of proactive monitoring, remember that it's not just a set of tools and techniques but a mindset and a commitment to proactive action. By embracing proactive monitoring, you can navigate the complexities of orchestration with confidence, maintain peak performance, and deliver exceptional results to your audience, whether they're customers, stakeholders, or colleagues.

Welcome to the intricate world of troubleshooting complex orchestration scenarios, where we dive into the art of unraveling intricate issues in your orchestrated workflows. Picture this journey as an expedition through a dense jungle, where every twist and turn may hold the key to uncovering and resolving the most perplexing orchestration challenges.

Troubleshooting in orchestration begins with a detective's mindset. Imagine you're a detective examining clues to solve a mystery, piecing together evidence to uncover the truth. In the world of orchestration, troubleshooting involves collecting and analyzing data to diagnose and resolve issues.

Logs are your primary source of information when troubleshooting. Think of them as the breadcrumbs left behind by a traveler in the woods, offering hints about their journey. Logs in orchestration record events, errors, and activities, providing a trail to follow when investigating problems.

Understanding the workflow's context is essential for effective troubleshooting. Picture this scenario: you receive a cryptic message, and deciphering it depends on knowing the context of the conversation. In orchestration, comprehending the workflow's context means knowing the sequence of tasks, dependencies, and inputs that define its behavior.

Dependency mapping is like creating a map of interconnected cities, indicating routes and distances. In orchestration, dependency mapping involves identifying relationships between tasks, services, and resources within your workflow. This mapping helps you pinpoint where issues may be causing disruptions.

Monitoring tools act as your eyes and ears when troubleshooting. Think of them as a pair of binoculars that allow you to observe distant landscapes. Monitoring tools in orchestration provide real-time insights into the health and performance of your workflows, enabling you to detect anomalies and issues as they arise.

Error handling is your safety net in orchestration troubleshooting. Imagine you're a trapeze artist, and when you miss a catch, there's a safety net to prevent a fall. Error handling mechanisms in orchestration define how your workflow responds to unexpected situations, such as errors or exceptions, ensuring that it continues to function or gracefully exits.

Isolating issues involves narrowing down the scope of the problem. Picture this: you're troubleshooting a malfunctioning gadget, and you start by checking individual components to identify the faulty one. In orchestration, isolating issues means identifying whether the problem lies within a specific task, service, or resource, or if it's a systemic issue affecting the entire workflow. Testing hypotheses is part of the troubleshooting process. Think of it as conducting experiments to verify or refute possible explanations for a problem. In orchestration, you may formulate hypotheses about what's causing an issue and then test them by making controlled changes to your workflow or configuration. Documentation is your guidebook in troubleshooting complex scenarios. Imagine you're exploring an intricate maze, and you have a detailed map to help you navigate. In orchestration, documentation includes records of your workflow's design, configuration settings, and past troubleshooting efforts, providing valuable context for resolving issues.

Collaboration and knowledge sharing are invaluable in orchestration troubleshooting. Picture this: you're solving a puzzle with friends, and each person brings their unique insights and expertise. Collaborative troubleshooting involves working with colleagues, teams, or online communities to tap into collective knowledge and problem-solving skills.

Error codes and messages are like a foreign language dictionary when troubleshooting. In orchestration, error codes and messages provide clues about what went wrong and where. Understanding these codes can help you pinpoint the root cause of an issue and take appropriate corrective actions.

Pattern recognition is a skill that seasoned troubleshooters develop. Think of it as recognizing recurring shapes or motifs in a tapestry. In orchestration, pattern recognition involves spotting common issues or symptoms that may indicate a specific problem. Recognizing these patterns can expedite troubleshooting by leading you to known solutions.

Escalation procedures are your emergency plan when troubleshooting reaches an impasse. Imagine you're on a ship facing a storm, and you have a protocol to call for assistance if needed. In orchestration, escalation procedures define when and how to involve higher-level support or specialists to address particularly challenging issues.

Regression testing is a safeguard against unintended consequences when troubleshooting. Picture this: you've repaired a leaky roof, and now you want to ensure that the fix didn't create new problems. In orchestration, regression testing involves retesting your workflow after making changes or fixes to confirm that the issue is resolved without introducing new issues.

Documentation is worth emphasizing again, as it's your trusty companion throughout the troubleshooting journey. Think of it as a traveler's journal that captures your experiences, lessons learned, and successful troubleshooting strategies. Proper documentation ensures that you can revisit and share insights gained from your troubleshooting adventures. Thoroughness and patience are virtues when tackling complex orchestration issues. Imagine you're an archaeologist carefully excavating a historical site, methodically uncovering artifacts one layer at a time. In orchestration troubleshooting, thoroughness means leaving no stone unturned, exploring all potential causes and solutions with patience and diligence.

Time management is essential in orchestration troubleshooting. Picture this: you're juggling multiple tasks, and you need to allocate your time wisely to meet deadlines. Effective time management in troubleshooting involves prioritizing issues based on their impact, urgency, and complexity, ensuring that you allocate your resources efficiently.

Continuous learning and skill development are the cornerstones of becoming a proficient troubleshooter. Think of it as embarking on a lifelong journey of acquiring new tools and techniques for your troubleshooting toolkit. Staying up-to-date with the latest orchestration technologies and best practices empowers you to tackle even the most challenging scenarios.

Automation can streamline repetitive troubleshooting tasks. Imagine you have a robotic assistant that can perform routine chores, leaving you more time to focus on complex problem-solving. In orchestration, automation can be employed to collect data, analyze logs, and execute predefined corrective actions, expediting troubleshooting processes.

In summary, troubleshooting complex orchestration scenarios is an art that combines detective work, technical expertise, collaboration, and persistence. It's about unraveling mysteries, solving puzzles, and continuously improving your orchestration environment.

As you embark on your troubleshooting journeys, remember that each challenge you encounter is an opportunity to enhance your skills and deepen your understanding of orchestration. With the right mindset, tools, and techniques, you can confidently navigate the intricate landscapes of orchestration troubleshooting, ensuring that your orchestrated workflows perform flawlessly and deliver exceptional results.

Chapter 6: Scaling Strategies for Growing Workloads

Welcome to the fascinating realm of horizontal scaling techniques, where we embark on a journey to explore strategies that empower your applications and services to handle increased workloads and traffic seamlessly. Picture this as expanding your team of chefs in a bustling kitchen to cater to a growing number of diners without compromising the quality of your dishes.

Horizontal scaling, often referred to as "scaling out," is the art of adding more identical resources, such as servers or instances, to your infrastructure to distribute the load evenly. It's akin to opening additional lanes on a highway during rush hour to ensure smooth traffic flow.

Load balancing is your trusty traffic cop in the world of horizontal scaling. Think of it as directing vehicles to the right lanes to prevent congestion. Load balancers distribute incoming requests across multiple servers, ensuring that each one receives a fair share of the workload and preventing any single server from becoming overwhelmed.

Stateless architecture is like cooking a dish without relying on any previous cooking steps. In a stateless architecture, each request from a client contains all the information needed to fulfill it, making it easier to distribute requests to any available server. This approach simplifies horizontal scaling because any server can handle any request without relying on shared state information.

Containerization is the art of packaging your application, along with its dependencies, into a portable container. Imagine placing each ingredient for a recipe in its own sealed container, ensuring freshness and consistency. Containerization allows you to create lightweight, isolated instances of your application that can be easily deployed and scaled horizontally.

Orchestration platforms, like conductors leading a symphony, manage the deployment and scaling of containerized applications. These platforms automate tasks such as container provisioning, load balancing, and scaling, making it more efficient to horizontally scale your applications.

Microservices architecture breaks down your application into smaller, independently deployable services. Think of it as preparing a meal by assembling various small dishes that can be served individually. Microservices enable fine-grained control over horizontal scaling by allowing you to scale specific components of your application independently based on their demand.

Serverless computing takes the idea of horizontal scaling to the extreme. In a serverless environment, you don't need to provision or manage servers at all. Instead, you focus on writing code (functions) that run in response to events. Serverless platforms automatically handle the scaling of these functions based on incoming requests.

Autoscaling policies are like having a thermostat that adjusts the heating or cooling in your home based on the current temperature. Autoscaling policies define the rules and conditions under which new resources are added or removed from your infrastructure automatically. These policies ensure that your application can adapt to varying workloads.

Elasticity is the ability of your infrastructure to automatically adjust its capacity to match the workload. Imagine a rubber band that stretches or contracts as needed. Elasticity ensures that your application can quickly scale up during traffic spikes and scale down during quieter periods, optimizing resource usage and costs.

Graceful degradation is your backup plan in case of unexpected scaling challenges. Picture this: if a restaurant runs out of a popular dish, they offer an alternative that still satisfies the diners. Graceful degradation involves designing your application to gracefully handle situations where horizontal scaling may not be immediately available, ensuring that it continues to function, albeit with reduced capabilities.

Chaos engineering is a proactive approach to testing the resilience of your horizontally scaled applications. Think of it as conducting fire drills to ensure that everyone knows what to do in case of an emergency. Chaos engineering involves intentionally injecting failures or disruptions into your system to identify weaknesses and improve its overall robustness.

Monitoring and analytics tools serve as your watchful guardians when horizontally scaling your applications. These tools provide real-time insights into the performance and health of your infrastructure, helping you detect issues early and make informed decisions about scaling.

Cost optimization is an essential consideration when implementing horizontal scaling techniques. Imagine you're managing a restaurant, and you want to ensure that you're not overordering ingredients that may go to waste. Cost optimization involves balancing the benefits of horizontal scaling with the associated costs, making informed choices about when and how to scale. Security should never be overlooked when horizontally scaling your applications. Think of it as ensuring that your restaurant's expanded dining area has secure locks and surveillance cameras. Security measures should be in place to protect your horizontally scaled infrastructure, including access controls, encryption, and vulnerability management.

Testing and deployment strategies play a crucial role in successfully implementing horizontal scaling techniques. Picture this: you're rolling out a new menu item in your restaurant, and you want to ensure a smooth launch. Testing strategies, such as canary deployments and blue-green deployments, allow you to introduce changes incrementally, minimizing the risk of disruptions during scaling activities.

Edge computing extends the reach of your horizontally scaled applications to the edge of the network. Imagine setting up mini-kitchens in various neighborhoods to prepare meals closer to your customers. Edge computing reduces latency and enhances the user experience by processing data and running applications closer to the end-users.

Multi-cloud and hybrid cloud approaches offer flexibility and redundancy when horizontally scaling your infrastructure. Think of it as having multiple suppliers for your restaurant's ingredients to ensure a continuous supply. Multi-cloud and hybrid cloud strategies allow you to distribute your resources across different cloud providers or a combination of on-premises and cloud environments, mitigating the risk of vendor lock-in and enhancing resilience.

In summary, horizontal scaling techniques are your toolkit for expanding your application's capacity and resilience. They involve adding more resources, optimizing workload distribution, and embracing modern architectural principles. By applying these techniques thoughtfully and considering factors like cost, security, and testing, you can ensure that your horizontally scaled applications deliver exceptional performance and reliability, even in the face of ever-increasing demands.

Welcome to the world of vertical scaling methods, where we dive into strategies that allow your applications and systems to grow in power and capacity by enhancing the resources of individual components. Think of vertical scaling as giving your car a bigger engine to accelerate faster and carry heavier loads without adding more cars to the road.

Vertical scaling, also known as "scaling up," is the practice of improving the performance and capabilities of a single server or instance. It's like upgrading your computer with a faster processor, more memory, or additional storage to handle more demanding tasks.

Upgrading hardware is one of the most straightforward vertical scaling methods. Picture this: you've been using a basic smartphone, and now you decide to upgrade to the latest model with a faster processor, more RAM, and better camera capabilities. Upgrading hardware components, such as CPU, RAM, storage, or network interfaces, can significantly boost the performance of your server or instance.

Vertical scaling is akin to building a skyscraper by adding more floors to a single building rather than constructing multiple shorter buildings. By adding more resources to a single instance, you consolidate your computing power and reduce the complexity of managing multiple servers.

Database optimization is a critical aspect of vertical scaling, especially when dealing with data-intensive applications. Think of it as reorganizing a vast library to make finding books quicker and more efficient. Database optimization involves fine-tuning queries, indexing, and data storage to improve the overall performance and responsiveness of your application.

Caching mechanisms act as your memory aid in vertical scaling. Imagine having a notepad to jot down important information, reducing the need to constantly fetch data from your brain. Caching involves storing frequently accessed data in a high-speed memory, such as RAM or a dedicated cache server, to speed up data retrieval and reduce the load on your primary resources.

Load balancing, which we discussed earlier in the context of horizontal scaling, is equally important for vertical scaling. Load balancers distribute incoming requests across multiple instances or servers, ensuring that each one handles a manageable share of the workload. In vertical scaling, load balancing can be used to distribute requests to upgraded instances, ensuring optimal resource utilization.

Vertical scaling provides a straightforward approach to handling increased workloads and resource demands. It's like adding more horsepower to a vehicle to accommodate a heavier payload or faster acceleration. When your application experiences spikes in traffic or requires additional computational power, vertical scaling allows you to respond quickly by upgrading the existing resources.

Scaling vertically can be a cost-effective solution, particularly when you're dealing with applications that have variable resource requirements. Instead of maintaining a fleet of servers with varying levels of utilization, you can adjust the resources of individual instances to match the demand, potentially reducing operational costs.

Vertical scaling also simplifies management and maintenance. Think of it as owning a single, high-performance car instead of maintaining a fleet of smaller vehicles. With fewer instances to monitor and maintain, your administrative overhead is reduced, allowing your team to focus on optimizing the performance and security of a smaller, more powerful set of resources.

However, vertical scaling does have its limitations. There's a finite point at which you can no longer upgrade the hardware components of a single server. It's like trying to make a compact car as fast as a sports car—it reaches a performance ceiling.

Another challenge with vertical scaling is the risk of a single point of failure. When all your resources are concentrated in a single instance, any hardware or software failure can have a significant impact on your application's availability. To mitigate this risk, you may need to implement redundancy and failover mechanisms.

Resource allocation can also be less granular in vertical scaling. Upgrading the entire server or instance may lead to overprovisioning, where you're paying for resources that are not fully utilized. To address this, you'll need careful capacity planning and monitoring to ensure efficient resource utilization.

Vertical scaling is best suited for applications with specific resource-intensive tasks or those that require significant computing power for short bursts of activity. For example, running complex simulations, processing large datasets, or handling computationally intensive workloads can benefit from vertical scaling.

In summary, vertical scaling methods offer a powerful approach to meet the growing demands of your applications and services by enhancing the resources of individual instances. Whether you're upgrading hardware components, optimizing databases, implementing caching, or load balancing, vertical scaling allows you to boost performance and capacity without the complexities of managing a large number of servers. It's like giving your trusted vehicle a turbocharger to handle the challenges of the road ahead. By understanding when and how to apply vertical scaling, you can ensure that your applications continue to deliver high-performance experiences to your users while maintaining cost efficiency and reliability.

Chapter 7: Cost Optimization and Budget Management

Welcome to the world of cost analysis and optimization tools, where we'll explore the valuable resources and strategies that help you manage and optimize the expenses of your cloud-based infrastructure. Think of these tools as your financial advisors, guiding you toward efficient resource usage and cost savings in the cloud.

Cost analysis is the process of dissecting your cloud spending to understand where your resources are allocated and how they impact your budget. Imagine opening your monthly bank statement and categorizing your expenses to identify areas where you can cut back or reallocate funds. Cost analysis tools provide visibility into your cloud expenditures, helping you track spending patterns and make informed decisions.

Budgeting tools are like your personal finance apps, helping you set spending limits and financial goals. In the world of cloud computing, budgeting tools allow you to define spending thresholds for different aspects of your cloud infrastructure, ensuring that you stay within your allocated budget.

Resource tagging is akin to labeling your belongings to keep them organized and easily identifiable. In cloud environments, resource tagging involves attaching labels or metadata to your resources, such as virtual machines, databases, or storage buckets. These tags help you categorize resources based on their purpose, department, project, or any other criteria, making it easier to track spending and allocate costs accurately.

Cost allocation tools act as your financial detectives, attributing expenses to specific projects, teams, or departments. Imagine a detective unraveling a complex case by following the evidence trail. Cost allocation tools use resource tagging and usage data to allocate costs accurately, allowing you to charge back expenses to the responsible parties or departments.

Usage and performance monitoring tools are like the gauges on your car's dashboard, providing real-time insights into how your cloud resources are performing. These tools help you understand resource utilization, identify underutilized or overprovisioned instances, and detect performance bottlenecks that can impact costs.

Rightsizing tools are your guides to finding the right-sized resources for your workloads. Think of it as choosing the right-sized clothing—neither too loose nor too tight. Rightsizing tools analyze resource usage data and recommend resizing or reconfiguring instances to match the actual workload requirements, helping you eliminate unnecessary costs.

Savings plans and reserved instances are your tickets to cost savings in the cloud. Imagine buying tickets for future flights at a discounted price. Savings plans and reserved instances allow you to commit to a specific amount of cloud usage in exchange for substantial cost savings compared to on-demand pricing.

Spot instances are like bargain hunting in the cloud. They offer significant cost savings by allowing you to use spare capacity at a lower price. However, spot instances come with a catch—they can be terminated by the cloud provider with very little notice. They're best suited for fault-tolerant workloads that can handle interruptions.

Cost forecasting tools act as your financial crystal ball, predicting future spending based on historical data and trends. Imagine consulting a fortune teller to plan your financial decisions. Cost forecasting tools help you anticipate how changes in your infrastructure or usage patterns will impact your budget, allowing you to make proactive adjustments.

Cost anomaly detection tools are like security alarms for your budget, alerting you to unusual spending patterns or unexpected expenses. These tools use machine learning and statistical analysis to identify deviations from your expected spending, helping you catch cost anomalies early and take corrective actions.

Cost optimization recommendations are your trusted advisors, providing actionable insights on how to reduce cloud spending. Think of it as receiving personalized advice on how to cut back on unnecessary expenses. Cost optimization tools analyze your infrastructure and usage data to suggest specific actions, such as resizing instances, terminating idle resources, or choosing cost-effective storage options.

Lifecycle management tools are your timekeepers, helping you enforce policies for resource retirement and expiration. Imagine a library that automatically checks out books that haven't been read in a while. Lifecycle management tools automate the process of decommissioning or archiving resources that are no longer needed, reducing ongoing costs.

Container cost management tools cater to containerized applications, allowing you to monitor and optimize costs in a containerized environment. Think of it as tracking the cost of individual ingredients in a recipe. Container cost management tools provide insights into container resource usage, helping you rightsize containers, manage container sprawl, and optimize container-based workloads.

Serverless cost management tools are designed for serverless architectures, where you pay only for the execution of functions. These tools help you monitor and control serverless costs by tracking function invocations, execution duration, and resource consumption, enabling you to optimize the efficiency of your serverless applications.

Cloud cost governance is your playbook for establishing and enforcing cost management policies within your organization. Think of it as setting the rules of the game to ensure fair play. Cloud cost governance involves defining spending limits, cost allocation strategies, and resource tagging standards, as well as establishing roles and responsibilities for cost management.

Cost analysis and optimization tools are your allies in the quest for efficient cloud spending. They empower you to gain visibility into your expenses, set budgetary boundaries, allocate costs accurately, and optimize resource usage. By leveraging these tools and strategies, you can navigate the complex landscape of cloud economics with confidence, ensuring that your cloud infrastructure remains both cost-effective and performance-oriented.

Welcome to the realm of budgeting and cost control strategies, where we'll delve into the essential practices that help you manage your finances effectively and keep your projects on track within the dynamic landscape of cloud computing. Think of this as crafting a financial plan for your cloud endeavors, much like managing your household budget to ensure your expenses align with your income.

Budgeting in the cloud is a lot like creating a budget for your household expenses. It starts with setting clear financial goals and identifying how much you're willing to spend on your cloud resources. This initial step is crucial, as it provides a framework for your spending decisions and helps you avoid unplanned expenditures.

One fundamental principle of budgeting is defining your budget categories. These categories act as buckets to allocate your cloud spending effectively. Just as you might categorize your personal expenses into groceries, utilities, and entertainment, you categorize your cloud expenses into areas such as compute, storage, networking, and services.

Budget allocation is like dividing your income into different spending categories based on your priorities. In cloud budgeting, you allocate a portion of your overall budget to each category, ensuring that you have enough resources available to meet your project's requirements without overspending.

Tracking your expenses is a crucial aspect of budgeting. It's like keeping a ledger of your daily expenses to ensure you stay within your budget. In the cloud, tracking involves monitoring your resource usage, analyzing cost reports, and comparing your actual spending against your budgeted amounts.

Resource tagging plays a significant role in budgeting by helping you categorize your cloud resources effectively. Think of resource tags as labels that you attach to each resource, indicating its purpose, owner, department, or project. These tags provide clarity in tracking expenses, allowing you to see which resources belong to each budget category.

Cost monitoring tools are your allies in tracking your cloud expenses. These tools provide real-time insights into your spending, enabling you to see how much you've used in each budget category and whether you're on track to meet your financial goals.

Budget alerts act as your financial alarm system. Just as your bank might notify you when you're approaching your spending limit, budget alerts notify you when your cloud spending is about to exceed your predefined thresholds. This allows you to take corrective actions promptly.

Cost forecasting is like predicting your future expenses based on your past spending patterns. Just as you might forecast your annual vacation costs, cost forecasting in the cloud involves using historical data to estimate your future spending. This helps you plan your budget more effectively and anticipate potential challenges.

Cloud providers offer tools and services that simplify budgeting and cost control. For example, AWS Budgets, Azure Cost Management, and Google Cloud Cost Management provide comprehensive features to set budgets, track expenses, and gain insights into your spending patterns.

Reserved instances and savings plans are budgeting strategies that offer significant cost savings. They're like buying items in bulk to get a discount. With reserved instances and savings plans, you commit to using specific resources for a fixed duration, which results in lower costs compared to on-demand pricing.

Rightsizing is another cost control strategy that aligns your resources with your actual needs. Think of it as adjusting your utility plan to match your household's energy consumption. Rightsizing involves reviewing your cloud resources and scaling them up or down to match your workloads, ensuring that you don't pay for unused capacity.

Spot instances are budget-friendly options that offer substantial savings, similar to finding discounted items in a clearance sale. These instances allow you to access spare cloud capacity at a lower cost, making them ideal for workloads that can tolerate interruptions and sudden terminations.

Automation tools can be your budget's best friend. Just as automatic transfers help you save money in a separate savings account, automation tools in the cloud can help you optimize costs by automatically shutting down idle resources, scaling instances based on demand, and implementing cost control policies.

Budget optimization is a continuous process. It's like maintaining a healthy diet and exercise routine to stay in shape. In the cloud, optimizing your budget involves regularly reviewing your spending patterns, identifying areas for improvement, and implementing changes to reduce costs while maintaining performance.

Cost control policies are your budget's guardians, ensuring that your spending aligns with your financial goals. These policies define rules and restrictions on resource provisioning, usage, and allocation, helping you enforce budget constraints and prevent unexpected expenses.

Resource lifecycle management is akin to decluttering your home to free up space and reduce unnecessary expenses. In the cloud, managing the lifecycle of your resources involves identifying and decommissioning unused or outdated resources, reducing ongoing costs.

Budgeting and cost control strategies are essential for maintaining financial discipline and optimizing your cloud spending. Just as you carefully manage your personal budget to achieve your financial goals, effective budgeting and cost control in the cloud allow you to allocate resources wisely, prevent overspending, and ensure that your projects remain within budget constraints. By embracing these practices and utilizing cloud provider tools, you can navigate the dynamic world of cloud finance with confidence, making informed decisions that align with your organization's financial objectives.

Chapter 8: High Availability and Disaster Recovery

Welcome to the exciting realm of high availability solutions, where we'll explore the strategies and technologies that ensure your systems and applications remain accessible and operational even in the face of unexpected challenges. Think of this as fortifying your digital fortress to withstand any storm that may come your way.

High availability is a bit like having a backup generator for your home. Just as a generator kicks in when the power goes out, high availability solutions ensure that your services continue running smoothly even when primary components fail.

Redundancy is a cornerstone of high availability. It's like having spare keys for your car or a backup phone charger. Redundant systems involve duplicating critical components and resources, creating failover mechanisms that seamlessly switch over to backups when primary resources experience issues.

Load balancing is akin to a traffic cop directing vehicles on a busy intersection. In the digital world, load balancers distribute incoming requests across multiple servers or instances, ensuring that no single component is overwhelmed with traffic. This not only improves performance but also enhances fault tolerance.

Fault tolerance is your safety net in high availability. Imagine a trapeze artist with a safety harness. Fault-tolerant systems are designed to continue functioning even when individual components fail, reducing the risk of downtime and service interruptions.

Automatic failover is like having a backup driver ready to take the wheel when the primary driver needs a break. In high availability solutions, automatic failover mechanisms detect when a primary component becomes unavailable and seamlessly switch to a backup component, ensuring uninterrupted service.

Data replication is similar to making photocopies of important documents. In high availability, data replication involves creating copies of data in multiple locations, ensuring that if one copy becomes inaccessible, the others can be used to maintain operations.

Geographic redundancy extends your high availability net across different physical locations. Think of it as having a second home in a different city. Geographic redundancy involves replicating your resources and data in geographically distant data centers, providing resilience against regional outages or disasters.

Clustering is like forming a team of superheroes with unique abilities. In high availability, clustering involves grouping multiple servers or instances into a single unit that works together to provide redundancy and load balancing. If one member of the cluster falters, others step in to maintain service.

Failback mechanisms are your bounce-back strategy. Just as a gymnast gets back on the balance beam after a fall, failback mechanisms ensure that once a primary component is restored, it resumes its role as the primary resource, seamlessly taking over from the backup.

High availability is not just about technology; it's also about processes and procedures. Think of it as having a well-rehearsed emergency response plan. High availability planning involves defining clear roles and responsibilities, conducting regular drills, and establishing communication protocols to respond to incidents effectively.

Business continuity is your insurance policy for high availability. It's like having a backup plan for your business operations. Business continuity planning extends beyond technology and encompasses strategies to ensure that critical business functions can continue even in the face of disruptions.

Disaster recovery is like having a comprehensive emergency kit for your digital assets. In high availability, disaster recovery plans outline how to recover from catastrophic events. They include strategies for data backup, offsite storage, and procedures for restoring services.

Cloud-based high availability leverages the power of cloud providers to enhance redundancy and fault tolerance. It's like having access to an entire network of backup generators. Cloud services offer built-in redundancy, geographic distribution, and automatic failover, making high availability more accessible and cost-effective.

Distributed architectures are like building a city with multiple interconnected neighborhoods. In high availability, distributed architectures involve designing systems that are spread across different regions or data centers, reducing the risk of single-point failures.

Microservices and containerization are your toolkit for modular high availability. Think of them as LEGO blocks that you can assemble to build resilient applications. Microservices and containers allow you to design applications as a collection of smaller, independent components, making it easier to scale and recover individual parts without affecting the entire system.

Hybrid cloud solutions combine the strengths of on-premises infrastructure and cloud services. It's like having a combination of a personal vehicle and public transportation. Hybrid cloud allows you to balance cost-effectiveness and flexibility by using cloud resources while maintaining critical components on-premises.

Monitoring and alerting are your high availability watchdogs. Just as a guard dog watches over your property, monitoring tools keep an eye on your systems and applications, alerting you to potential issues or performance anomalies so you can take proactive measures.

High availability is not one-size-fits-all; it requires careful consideration of your specific needs and priorities. Think of it as tailoring a suit to fit your unique measurements. High availability solutions should be designed based on your business objectives, risk tolerance, and the criticality of your services.

High availability is an ongoing journey, not a one-time destination. It's like maintaining a vehicle to keep it running smoothly. Regular testing, updates, and reviews of your high availability strategies are essential to ensure that they remain effective in the ever-changing landscape of technology and business.

By embracing high availability solutions and best practices, you're building a resilient foundation for your digital endeavors. Just as a well-constructed building can withstand earthquakes and storms, your high availability measures ensure that your systems and services remain robust and reliable, no matter what challenges come your way. So, let's embark on this journey together and explore the world of high availability solutions to safeguard your digital kingdom.

Welcome to the world of disaster recovery planning and orchestration, where we'll explore the strategies and techniques that ensure your organization can effectively recover from unexpected disasters and disruptions. Think of this as preparing for the worst while hoping for the best, much like having a well-thought-out emergency plan for your home.

Disasters can take many forms, from natural calamities like hurricanes and earthquakes to human-made incidents such as cyberattacks or system failures. Disaster recovery planning is your shield against these uncertainties, much like having a sturdy umbrella ready for unexpected rain.

Business Impact Analysis (BIA) is your starting point in disaster recovery planning. It's like assessing your financial situation before making a major investment. BIA involves analyzing the potential impact of disasters on your organization, identifying critical business functions, and determining recovery priorities.

Risk assessment is similar to evaluating the safety features of a new car before buying it. In disaster recovery planning, risk assessment involves identifying potential threats, vulnerabilities, and risks that could disrupt your operations. This information helps you prioritize your disaster recovery efforts.

Recovery Time Objective (RTO) is your recovery deadline. Think of it as a countdown timer in a race. RTO specifies the maximum acceptable downtime for each critical business function, ensuring that you can resume operations within a defined timeframe after a disaster.

Recovery Point Objective (RPO) is like setting up a checkpoint in a video game. RPO defines the maximum data loss your organization can tolerate in the event of a disaster. It helps determine how frequently you should back up your data to ensure minimal data loss during recovery.

Backup and data replication are your safety nets in disaster recovery. They're like keeping copies of important documents in a secure vault. Backups involve creating copies of your data, applications, and configurations, while data replication ensures that data is synchronized between different locations.

Disaster recovery sites are your alternate command centers. Think of them as backup offices where you can continue operations if your primary location becomes inaccessible.

These sites are equipped with the necessary infrastructure and resources to support your recovery efforts.

Cloud-based disaster recovery is like having a remote backup generator. Cloud services offer scalable and cost-effective disaster recovery solutions, allowing you to replicate your data and applications in the cloud, reducing the need for dedicated recovery sites.

Testing and simulation exercises are your practice sessions for disaster recovery. Just as athletes train to perform at their best, organizations conduct disaster recovery drills to ensure that their plans and procedures are effective and their teams are prepared.

Documentation is your playbook for disaster recovery. Think of it as a detailed instruction manual for a complex piece of machinery. Comprehensive documentation includes step-by-step procedures, contact lists, recovery plans, and configuration details.

Communication is your lifeline during a disaster. It's like having a reliable phone line to call for help. Effective communication plans ensure that your teams can stay in touch, coordinate recovery efforts, and provide updates to stakeholders, customers, and partners.

Incident response teams are your first responders in a disaster. They're like firefighters rushing to extinguish a blaze. These teams are trained and equipped to assess the situation, initiate recovery procedures, and make critical decisions during a crisis.

Vendor relationships are your support network in disaster recovery. Just as you rely on your network of friends for help, maintaining strong relationships with vendors ensures that you can access essential resources and support when needed.

Business continuity planning extends beyond disaster recovery. It's like having a backup plan for your backup plan.

Business continuity planning encompasses strategies to maintain essential business functions, even in the face of disruptions, ensuring that your organization can continue to deliver value to customers.

Disaster recovery as a service (DRaaS) is like having an insurance policy that covers both your home and your car. DRaaS providers offer comprehensive disaster recovery solutions, including backup, replication, and recovery services, often with the flexibility to scale resources as needed.

Hybrid cloud disaster recovery leverages both on-premises and cloud resources. Think of it as having a combination of home security systems and professional monitoring services. Hybrid cloud allows you to design disaster recovery solutions that balance cost-effectiveness and performance.

Automated orchestration is your conductor in disaster recovery. It's like having a maestro directing a symphony. Automated orchestration tools streamline the recovery process, coordinating the execution of recovery plans and ensuring that everything runs smoothly.

Geographic diversity is your insurance against localized disasters. Just as diversifying your investments reduces risk, geographic diversity involves spreading your data centers and recovery sites across different regions, minimizing the impact of regional disasters.

Disaster recovery planning is an ongoing effort, not a one-time task. It's like maintaining your health through regular exercise and check-ups. Regular reviews, updates, and testing of your disaster recovery plans are essential to ensure their effectiveness in an ever-changing environment.

By embracing disaster recovery planning and orchestration, you're not just preparing for the worst; you're building resilience and confidence in your organization's ability to weather any storm. Just as a well-prepared ship can navigate through turbulent waters, your disaster recovery efforts ensure that your organization can navigate through disruptions with minimal impact. So, let's embark on this journey together and explore the world of disaster recovery planning and orchestration to safeguard your organization's future.

Chapter 9: Integration and Orchestration with Containers

Welcome to the world of orchestrating containerized workloads, where we'll dive into the exciting realm of container technology and how orchestration tools can help manage and streamline your containerized applications. Think of this as orchestrating a symphony of containers, each playing its unique role in your digital orchestra.

Containers are like digital parcels, containing everything needed to run an application, from code and dependencies to libraries and configurations. They provide a consistent environment, ensuring that applications run reliably across different platforms and environments.

Docker, one of the most popular containerization platforms, is like a magic box for developers. With Docker, you can package your application and its dependencies into a container image, making it easily transportable and deployable.

Kubernetes, often referred to as K8s, is like the conductor of your container orchestra. It's an open-source container orchestration platform that automates the deployment, scaling, and management of containerized applications. Kubernetes acts as the brain that coordinates and manages the lifecycle of containers.

Container orchestration, in essence, is the art of managing and coordinating containers at scale. It's like directing a synchronized dance performance, ensuring that each container knows when to start, stop, and perform its role harmoniously.

Scaling containers can be compared to adding more musicians to your orchestra when the audience demands an encore. Container orchestration tools like Kubernetes enable auto-scaling, which automatically adjusts the number of containers based on demand, ensuring that your application can handle traffic spikes.

Service discovery is like providing a map to your orchestra members, allowing them to find and communicate with each other. In container orchestration, service discovery mechanisms enable containers to locate and interact with one another, facilitating seamless communication within your application.

Load balancing is akin to ensuring that the workload is distributed evenly among your orchestra members. Container orchestration platforms often include load balancing features, distributing incoming requests to containers to prevent overload on any one instance.

Rolling updates are like rehearsing new parts in your orchestra. Container orchestration tools allow you to perform updates and upgrades to your application without causing downtime. Containers are gradually replaced with new versions, ensuring a smooth transition.

Health checks are your way of ensuring that each musician in your orchestra is in good shape. In container orchestration, health checks monitor the status of containers, automatically replacing or restarting unhealthy instances to maintain application reliability.

Immutable infrastructure is like having a set of pristine musical instruments for each performance. It involves treating containers as disposable entities, replacing them entirely when updates or changes are needed, rather than modifying existing containers.

Stateful and stateless containers are like different types of instruments in your orchestra. Stateful containers maintain data and state between restarts, while stateless containers are ephemeral, not storing any data. Container orchestration platforms accommodate both types, allowing you to choose the right tool for the job.

Container registries are like libraries where you store your musical compositions. They are repositories for container images, enabling you to store, share, and version your containerized applications.

Continuous integration and continuous deployment (CI/CD) pipelines are your backstage crew, ensuring that your orchestra is always ready to perform. CI/CD processes automate the building, testing, and deployment of container images, streamlining the development workflow.

Microservices architecture is like composing a symphony with modular movements. It involves breaking down applications into smaller, independent services, each running in its container. Container orchestration tools excel at managing complex microservices environments.

Pods in Kubernetes are like duets, where two or more containers share the same network and storage resources. Pods enable containers that need to work closely together to be scheduled on the same host.

Persistent storage is like providing your orchestra with dedicated lockers to store their instruments. In container orchestration, you can attach persistent storage volumes to containers, ensuring that data remains intact even when containers are replaced.

Namespaces in Kubernetes are like separate concert halls within the same venue. They provide a way to partition and isolate resources within a Kubernetes cluster, making it easier to manage applications with different requirements.

Helm, a package manager for Kubernetes, is like having a music sheet for your entire orchestra. Helm allows you to define, install, and upgrade complex applications in Kubernetes using charts, simplifying the deployment process.

Operators in Kubernetes are like hiring experienced conductors for your orchestra. Kubernetes Operators are software extensions that automate operational tasks, making it easier to manage and maintain applications in a Kubernetes environment.

Container security is your vigilant security guard ensuring the safety of your orchestra. Container orchestration platforms provide security features like role-based access control (RBAC), image scanning, and network policies to protect your containers from threats.

Observability is like having a clear view of your orchestra performance. Container orchestration platforms offer monitoring and logging capabilities, allowing you to gain insights into the behavior and performance of your containers and applications.

Challenges in orchestrating containerized workloads include managing the complexity of microservices, ensuring data persistence, and handling network configurations. Container orchestration tools aim to address these challenges and provide a cohesive solution.

Hybrid cloud and multi-cloud environments are like having different concert venues for your orchestra's world tour. Container orchestration platforms can be used across various cloud providers and on-premises infrastructure, offering flexibility and portability.

Container orchestration is a dynamic field with continuous development and innovation. Staying up-to-date with the latest features and best practices is essential to harness the full potential of containerization and orchestration.

In summary, orchestrating containerized workloads is about bringing harmony to the world of container technology. With the right orchestration tools and practices, you can ensure that your containerized applications perform like a well-coordinated orchestra, delivering reliability, scalability, and agility to your digital endeavors. So, let's embark on this journey together and explore the art of orchestrating containerized workloads to create beautiful digital symphonies.

Welcome to the world of Kubernetes and container orchestration, where we'll unravel the intricacies of managing containers at scale using one of the most powerful orchestration platforms available. Imagine Kubernetes as your trusty co-pilot, helping you navigate the vast and ever-expanding landscape of containerized applications.

Containers, those lightweight and portable units, are like the versatile building blocks of modern software development. They package everything an application needs to run, from code and dependencies to configurations, in a consistent and isolated environment. Think of them as self-contained boxes, each with its own set of tools and resources.

Docker, the poster child of containerization, is your go-to toolbox for creating and managing containers. It simplifies the process of packaging applications into containers, making them easy to build, share, and deploy. Just like a well-organized workshop, Docker provides the tools you need to craft your containerized applications.

Now, let's introduce Kubernetes, often fondly referred to as K8s, as the conductor of your container orchestra. Kubernetes is an open-source container orchestration platform, developed by Google, that takes container management to a whole new level. It's like having a conductor who ensures that each musician (container) plays its part harmoniously.

Container orchestration, at its core, is the art of managing containers across a cluster of machines. Picture it as choreographing a dance where each container knows its steps and timing, creating a seamless performance.

Kubernetes is your choreographer, orchestrating containers to ensure they start, stop, scale, and communicate effectively.

Scaling in Kubernetes is like adding more dancers to your routine when the audience demands an encore. Kubernetes offers automated scaling, allowing you to adjust the number of containers based on demand. It's as if the dance floor expands to accommodate the growing crowd.

Service discovery in Kubernetes is akin to dancers finding their partners on the ballroom floor. Containers need to locate and communicate with each other, and Kubernetes provides mechanisms to do just that. Think of it as assigning dance partners, ensuring smooth coordination.

Load balancing, an essential feature in Kubernetes, is like making sure your dance performance is evenly distributed across the stage. It ensures that incoming requests are distributed among the available containers, preventing any one container from being overwhelmed.

Rolling updates in Kubernetes are like introducing new dance moves into your routine without disrupting the performance. Kubernetes allows you to update your application without downtime. Old containers are gracefully replaced with new ones, ensuring a seamless transition.

Health checks are your way of making sure each dancer is in good shape throughout the performance. Kubernetes continuously monitors the health of containers and automatically replaces or repairs any that become unhealthy. It's like having a backstage medical team on standby.

Immutable infrastructure is like having a fresh set of costumes for every performance. In Kubernetes, containers are treated as immutable, meaning that when changes are needed, new containers are created rather than modifying existing ones. This practice ensures consistency and reliability.

Stateful and stateless containers are like having both solo and duet performances in your show. Stateful containers maintain data and state between restarts, while stateless containers don't store any data. Kubernetes supports both types, giving you flexibility in your choreography.

Container registries are like libraries where you store your dance routines. They house container images, allowing you to catalog, version, and share your containerized applications. Just like a choreographer keeps track of routines, a container registry keeps your images organized.

Continuous integration and continuous deployment (CI/CD) pipelines are like the rehearsal process for your dance troupe. CI/CD automates the building, testing, and deployment of container images, ensuring that your applications are always performance-ready.

Microservices architecture is akin to creating a dance with modular movements. It involves breaking down applications into smaller, independent services, each running in its container. Kubernetes excels at managing complex microservices environments, ensuring that each service can shine on its own.

Pods in Kubernetes are like dance partners who share the same stage. A pod is the smallest deployable unit in Kubernetes and can host one or more containers that work together. It's like having synchronized partners who complement each other's moves.

Persistent storage in Kubernetes is like having dedicated lockers for dancers to store their props and costumes. Containers can attach to persistent storage volumes, ensuring data persistence even when containers are replaced.

Namespaces in Kubernetes are like different sections of the theater where multiple performances are happening simultaneously. They provide a way to partition and isolate resources within a Kubernetes cluster, making it easier to manage applications with different requirements.

Helm, the package manager for Kubernetes, is like having a playbook for your entire dance performance. Helm simplifies application deployment in Kubernetes by defining, installing, and upgrading applications using charts, making it easier to manage complex setups.

Operators in Kubernetes are like hiring seasoned choreographers to fine-tune your dance routines. Kubernetes Operators are software extensions that automate operational tasks, making it easier to manage and maintain applications within a Kubernetes environment.

Container security is your vigilant stage manager, ensuring the safety and integrity of your dance performance. Kubernetes provides security features like role-based access control (RBAC), image scanning, and network policies to protect your containers from vulnerabilities.

Observability in Kubernetes is like having a front-row seat to the performance. Kubernetes offers monitoring and logging capabilities that provide insights into container behavior and performance, allowing you to fine-tune your choreography.

The challenges in orchestrating containers with Kubernetes include managing the complexity of microservices, handling data storage, and configuring networking effectively. Kubernetes offers solutions to these challenges, making it a versatile platform for modern containerized applications.

Hybrid cloud and multi-cloud deployments are like touring your dance troupe in different cities and venues. Kubernetes can be used across various cloud providers and on-premises infrastructure, offering flexibility and portability for your applications.

In this ever-evolving landscape of container orchestration, staying informed about the latest features and best practices is crucial to ensuring your containerized applications perform flawlessly. Kubernetes is your partner in this journey, providing the tools and capabilities needed to create memorable performances.

So, whether you're a seasoned choreographer or a newcomer to the world of container orchestration, Kubernetes is here to help you create dazzling containerized performances. Together, let's explore the art of orchestrating containers and dance to the rhythm of modern software development.

Chapter 10: Best Practices for Complex Orchestration Environments

Welcome to the realm of complex workflow design and management, where we'll embark on a journey to explore the intricacies of orchestrating intricate processes in the digital landscape. Think of it as orchestrating a grand symphony with multiple movements, each requiring careful planning and coordination.

Workflows are the heartbeats of any organization, defining how tasks and activities flow from one step to another. They're like the choreography that guides dancers through a performance, ensuring that everything happens in the right order and with precision.

Complex workflows, as the name suggests, are intricate and multifaceted. They involve numerous steps, decision points, and dependencies. It's as if you're choreographing a ballet with a large ensemble cast, each dancer playing a crucial role in the overall performance.

Automation is your trusty assistant in managing complex workflows. It's like having a team of stagehands who handle props and set changes behind the scenes. Automation tools streamline and optimize the execution of tasks, reducing manual effort and the risk of errors.

Workflow design is the process of defining the sequence of steps and decisions in a workflow. It's like creating a script for a play, outlining the actions and dialogues of each character. Well-designed workflows ensure efficiency and clarity in how work is carried out.

Visualization tools are like the blueprints that help you map out the intricate dance routines in your ballet. They provide a visual representation of your workflow, making it easier to understand and communicate with others involved in the process.

Human-centric design is your way of ensuring that the dancers (your team members) are comfortable and can perform at their best. Complex workflows often involve human tasks, and designing them with the end-user in mind ensures a smoother and more efficient process.

Decision points in workflows are like dramatic pauses in a theatrical performance. They're moments when a choice must be made, and the flow of the workflow depends on that decision. Effective decision-making is critical for successful workflow execution.

Integration with external systems is akin to collaborating with other performance groups in a grand theater production. Complex workflows often require interaction with external applications and data sources. Integration ensures that all parts of the performance work seamlessly together.

Conditional branching in workflows is like giving dancers the flexibility to adapt their steps based on the music's tempo. It allows workflows to take different paths depending on certain conditions, accommodating variations in the process.

Error handling in workflows is your safety net for when a dancer misses a step. It involves defining how the workflow responds to unexpected situations or errors, ensuring that the performance can continue even when things don't go as planned.

Monitoring and tracking are your backstage crew, keeping an eye on the performance and making sure everything runs smoothly. Workflow management tools provide real-time visibility into the progress of workflows, allowing you to identify bottlenecks and areas for improvement.

Audit trails in workflows are like documenting every rehearsal and performance. They provide a record of all actions taken within the workflow, helping you trace the history of a process and maintain compliance with regulations.

Complex workflows often involve collaboration among team members, much like a ballet ensemble working together to create a stunning performance. Workflow collaboration tools facilitate communication and coordination among team members, ensuring that everyone is in sync.

Data-driven workflows are like choreographing a dance that responds to the audience's reactions. They use data and analytics to make decisions and adapt the workflow in real-time, optimizing the process based on performance metrics.

Role-based access control (RBAC) is like assigning specific roles to dancers in your ballet. It ensures that only authorized individuals can perform certain actions within the workflow, maintaining security and compliance.

Scaling workflows to handle increasing demands is like preparing for a sold-out show. Workflow management tools offer scalability, allowing you to handle larger volumes of work without compromising performance.

Optimization of workflows is akin to fine-tuning the choreography to make every movement more efficient and graceful. It involves analyzing the workflow's performance and making adjustments to improve its execution.

Workflow templates are like pre-designed dance routines that can be customized for different performances. They provide a starting point for creating new workflows, saving time and effort in designing complex processes from scratch.

Orchestration of multiple workflows is like coordinating different acts in a theatrical production. Complex organizations often have multiple workflows running concurrently, and workflow orchestration tools help manage and synchronize them.

Machine learning and artificial intelligence (AI) can be compared to having a choreographer who can adapt the dance routines based on audience feedback in real-time. These technologies enable intelligent decision-making within workflows, optimizing them for better results.

Challenges in complex workflow design and management include balancing automation with human tasks, ensuring data accuracy, and handling exceptions gracefully. Overcoming these challenges requires careful planning and the right tools and techniques.

In a rapidly evolving digital landscape, staying agile and adaptable is essential for effective workflow management. Continuous improvement and innovation in workflow design and execution are keys to success in today's dynamic business environment.

Complex workflow design and management is not just about orchestrating processes; it's about creating a harmonious and efficient performance that delivers value to your organization and its customers. With the right tools and practices, you can turn intricate workflows into well-executed masterpieces.

So, as we journey through the world of complex workflow design and management, remember that every step, decision, and coordination effort contributes to the overall success of your performance. Together, let's explore the art of orchestrating complex workflows and creating seamless digital experiences.

Welcome to the exciting realm of orchestrating multicloud environments, where we'll delve into the art of managing workloads, resources, and services across multiple cloud platforms. Think of it as conducting a symphony with various instruments, each contributing to the overall harmony of your cloud ecosystem.

Multicloud, as the name implies, involves utilizing more than one cloud provider to meet your organization's computing needs. It's like having a diverse orchestra with musicians who specialize in different instruments, coming together to create a masterpiece.

Cloud providers, such as AWS, Azure, Google Cloud, and others, offer a range of services and capabilities. Orchestrating multicloud environments means leveraging the strengths of each provider to optimize performance, cost, and resilience. It's akin to composing a symphony that incorporates various musical elements to create a rich and dynamic composition.

Hybrid cloud, a subset of multicloud, involves integrating on-premises infrastructure with cloud resources. This integration is like blending traditional instruments with modern ones in your orchestra, allowing you to maintain existing investments while harnessing the benefits of the cloud.

Interoperability is your conductor's baton, guiding the various cloud services and platforms to work seamlessly together. It ensures that data, applications, and services can move freely across cloud boundaries, much like different sections of an orchestra playing in harmony.

Orchestration platforms are your maestros, directing the flow of resources and workloads across multicloud environments. These platforms automate and optimize tasks, ensuring that your cloud symphony plays without missing a beat.

Containerization, using technologies like Docker and Kubernetes, is like providing each musician with their individual sheet music. Containers encapsulate applications and their dependencies, making them portable and consistent across different cloud providers.

Serverless computing, such as AWS Lambda and Azure Functions, is akin to having guest performers join your orchestra for specific pieces. Serverless platforms allow you to run code without managing servers, enabling efficient execution of event-driven tasks.

Load balancing and traffic management are your ushers, ensuring that the audience (users) experiences a smooth and enjoyable performance. Load balancers distribute incoming requests across cloud resources, optimizing performance and ensuring high availability.

Data management in multicloud environments is like orchestrating a harmonious duet between different instruments. It involves ensuring data consistency, security, and accessibility across cloud providers while adhering to data governance and compliance standards.

Security and compliance are your vigilant stage managers, safeguarding your cloud symphony from potential threats and ensuring that it complies with industry regulations. Multicloud environments require robust security measures to protect data and resources.

Cost optimization in multicloud is like managing the budget for your orchestra, ensuring that you get the most value from your cloud investments. It involves monitoring and controlling cloud spending across multiple providers and services.

Monitoring and observability tools act as your keen-eared audience, providing real-time feedback on the performance of your multicloud environment. These tools offer insights into resource utilization, application performance, and potential issues.

Networking in multicloud environments is like orchestrating the flow of sound in a concert hall. It involves configuring and managing network connections, ensuring that data can travel seamlessly between cloud providers and on-premises infrastructure.

Disaster recovery and business continuity planning are your contingency composers, ensuring that your cloud symphony can continue even in the face of unexpected disruptions. Multicloud environments provide redundancy and failover options to minimize downtime.

Resource scaling in multicloud is like adjusting the volume of different instruments to maintain the right balance in your orchestra. It involves dynamically adding or removing resources to meet changing workload demands.

Service-level agreements (SLAs) with cloud providers are like the performance contracts between musicians and an orchestra. SLAs define the level of service, availability, and support you can expect from each cloud provider.

Governance and policy management in multicloud environments are like setting the rules for your orchestra's performance. These policies define how resources are allocated, accessed, and secured, ensuring that your cloud symphony operates within established guidelines.

Automation and scripting are your musical notes, allowing you to compose intricate melodies of cloud management. Automation simplifies repetitive tasks, accelerates deployments, and enhances the overall efficiency of your multicloud environment.

Cross-cloud application deployment is like arranging different sections of your orchestra on different stages, each contributing to the overall performance. Deploying applications across multiple cloud providers enables you to harness the unique capabilities of each.

Data migration and synchronization between cloud providers is like ensuring that musicians playing different instruments stay in perfect sync. Data movement tools facilitate the transfer of data between clouds, ensuring consistency and availability.

Hybrid cloud management platforms are like your conductor's podium, offering a centralized view and control of your entire multicloud orchestra. These platforms simplify the orchestration of resources and workloads across various cloud providers and on-premises infrastructure.

Vendor lock-in mitigation is your escape plan, ensuring that you're not tied to a single cloud provider. Strategies like using open standards and containerization enable you to maintain flexibility and portability in your multicloud environment.

Challenges in orchestrating multicloud environments include managing complexity, ensuring data consistency, optimizing costs, and maintaining security and compliance. Overcoming these challenges requires a strategic approach and the right set of tools and practices.

In a world where flexibility, scalability, and resilience are paramount, orchestrating multicloud environments is like conducting a symphony that adapts to ever-changing dynamics. It allows organizations to leverage the strengths of different cloud providers while delivering a seamless and harmonious experience to their users.

So, as we journey through the landscape of multicloud orchestration, remember that each cloud provider and service is like a unique instrument in your orchestra. By skillfully orchestrating these elements, you can create a cloud symphony that resonates with your organization's goals and aspirations. Together, let's explore the art of orchestrating multicloud environments and compose a digital masterpiece.

BOOK 3
CLOUD ORCHESTRATION FOR ENTERPRIS
ADVANCED STRATEGIES AND CASE STUDIES

ROB BOTWRIGHT

Chapter 1: Evolving Role of Cloud Orchestration in Enterprises

Welcome to the exciting world of digital transformation and the profound impact it has on businesses and society. Imagine it as a journey where organizations harness the power of technology to fundamentally change how they operate and deliver value.

In the digital age, businesses are undergoing a metamorphosis, transitioning from traditional, manual processes to digital ones. It's akin to upgrading from a manual typewriter to a sleek and efficient computer, vastly improving productivity and capabilities.

Digital transformation is driven by the relentless advancement of technology, where innovation serves as the engine propelling organizations forward. Think of it as the constant evolution of musical instruments, each iteration more sophisticated and capable than the last.

Data is the lifeblood of digital transformation, much like sheet music guides a musician through a composition. Organizations collect and analyze vast amounts of data to gain insights, make informed decisions, and create personalized experiences.

Cloud computing is the foundation of digital transformation, offering the flexibility and scalability required for modern businesses. It's like having a virtual orchestra, enabling organizations to access computing resources on-demand and from anywhere.

Artificial intelligence and machine learning are the virtuoso performers in this digital orchestra, enabling automation, predictive analytics, and intelligent decision-making. These technologies enhance efficiency and drive innovation across industries.

Customer-centricity is the melody that resonates through digital transformation efforts. Organizations are tuning their strategies to align with customer needs, preferences, and expectations, much like a musician tailors their performance to captivate an audience.

Agility is the key tempo of digital transformation, allowing organizations to adapt and respond rapidly to changing market dynamics. Agile practices enable businesses to pivot quickly, like a jazz ensemble improvising in real-time.

User experience design is the art of crafting delightful interactions, ensuring that customers and employees enjoy seamless and intuitive digital journeys. It's like composing a symphony that captivates and engages the audience from start to finish.

Cybersecurity is the vigilant guardian of digital transformation, protecting organizations from the ever-present threats in the digital landscape. It's akin to a security detail ensuring the safety of a high-profile event.

Collaboration tools and platforms are the virtual stages where teams come together to create, innovate, and perform. These tools enable remote work, global partnerships, and real-time communication, much like musicians collaborating from different corners of the world.

E-commerce and online marketplaces are the bustling market squares of the digital world, where transactions occur at the speed of light. They provide convenient access to products and services, transforming how consumers shop.

IoT devices and sensors are the instruments that orchestrate the symphony of data in the physical world. They collect and transmit real-time information, empowering organizations to make data-driven decisions, much like a conductor directing an orchestra.

Blockchain technology is the conductor's baton that ensures transparency and trust in digital transactions. It's like a musical score that records every note played, creating an unalterable ledger of events.

Digital marketing is the art of promoting and engaging audiences in the digital realm, using targeted campaigns and analytics to measure success. It's akin to a composer crafting melodies that resonate with specific audience segments.

Robotic process automation (RPA) is the diligent assistant automating repetitive tasks, allowing employees to focus on more meaningful work. It's like having a diligent page-turner for a musician, ensuring seamless transitions in a performance.

Supply chain digitization is the backbone of efficient logistics and operations, optimizing inventory management and distribution. It's like a synchronized ballet of goods moving seamlessly from production to delivery.

Data analytics tools are the maestros that transform raw data into actionable insights, guiding strategic decisions. They're like music arrangers who take individual notes and arrange them into a harmonious composition.

Digital twins are the mirrors reflecting the real world in the digital realm, enabling simulations and predictive modeling. They're akin to rehearsing a performance before taking the stage, minimizing errors and maximizing precision.

Edge computing brings processing power closer to where data is generated, reducing latency and enhancing real-time decision-making. It's like having a conductor's podium on stage, directing the orchestra without delay.

Augmented reality (AR) and virtual reality (VR) create immersive experiences that transport users to different worlds. They're like transporting an audience to a magical realm during a live performance.

5G connectivity is the high-speed highway that enables rapid data transfer and low latency, unlocking new possibilities for digital experiences. It's like upgrading from dial-up internet to fiber optic, unleashing lightning-fast capabilities.

Digital transformation journeys vary across industries and organizations, much like musical genres range from classical to rock. Each journey is unique, tailored to the specific needs, goals, and constraints of the organization.

Change management is the conductor's score, guiding employees and stakeholders through the transitions that digital transformation brings. It's like orchestrating a smooth transition between movements in a symphony.

Cultural transformation is the ensemble of behaviors, attitudes, and beliefs that shape an organization's identity. Much like a musical culture defines a genre, organizational culture sets the tone for digital transformation success.

Measuring the impact of digital transformation involves evaluating performance metrics, customer satisfaction, revenue growth, and more. It's like assessing the success of a concert through ticket sales, audience applause, and critical reviews.

The challenges of digital transformation include resistance to change, integration complexities, and the need for continuous innovation. Overcoming these challenges requires strong leadership, adaptability, and a commitment to the journey.

In the digital era, continuous transformation is the new normal, much like musicians constantly honing their skills and exploring new musical landscapes. Organizations must embrace change as an ongoing process, staying attuned to emerging technologies and evolving customer expectations.

The digital transformation impact extends far beyond individual organizations; it shapes economies, societies, and global dynamics. It's like a symphony that resonates across borders, bringing people together through shared experiences.

As we delve deeper into the realm of digital transformation, remember that it's not a destination but an ever-evolving journey. Just as a musician's mastery grows with practice and performance, organizations grow and thrive by embracing the opportunities and challenges of the digital age.

So, let's embark on this journey together, exploring the transformative power of technology and its profound impact on the world. Like skilled musicians in a grand orchestra, we'll harmonize the digital notes of innovation, collaboration, and agility to create a symphony of progress and prosperity.

Welcome to the exploration of the strategic importance of orchestration in the modern business landscape. Imagine orchestration as the conductor of an intricate symphony, harmonizing various elements to create a seamless and efficient performance.

In today's rapidly evolving digital world, businesses face a complex landscape filled with diverse technologies, platforms, and processes. Orchestration serves as the guiding hand, ensuring that these components work together harmoniously to achieve organizational goals.

Orchestration is more than just automation; it's the art of coordinating and optimizing workflows, resources, and data across an organization. It's like having a seasoned conductor who leads a diverse orchestra, transforming a cacophony of sounds into a beautiful composition.

Strategic planning is the foundation of effective orchestration. Organizations must define clear objectives, identify key performance indicators, and chart a course for success. Think of it as the conductor's score, which outlines the musical journey and sets the tempo for the orchestra.

Orchestration empowers businesses to streamline operations, reduce manual effort, and eliminate bottlenecks. It's akin to optimizing the flow of musicians on stage, ensuring they play their parts precisely and without interruption.

In the digital age, data is the fuel that powers organizations forward. Orchestration enables data integration and flow, much like the conductor guiding musicians through various musical sections, seamlessly transitioning from one to another.

Cloud computing is the stage where modern businesses perform. Orchestration allows organizations to leverage the cloud's scalability and flexibility, ensuring that applications and services can be deployed and managed effortlessly.

Security and compliance are paramount in today's business landscape. Orchestration includes robust security measures, acting as a vigilant guardian to protect against threats and ensure adherence to industry regulations.

Customer experience is the melody that resonates with modern consumers. Orchestration helps businesses create personalized, consistent, and engaging experiences, much like a well-composed piece that captivates an audience.

Agility is the tempo at which businesses must operate to remain competitive. Orchestration enables organizations to adapt quickly to changing market dynamics, like a conductor guiding the orchestra through tempo changes and improvisations.

Innovation is the creative spark that propels organizations forward. Orchestration fosters an environment where innovation can flourish, much like a conductor encouraging musicians to explore new musical territories.

Interoperability is the ability of systems and technologies to work together seamlessly. Orchestration ensures that different components and platforms can communicate and collaborate effectively, just as a conductor coordinates musicians playing different instruments.

Automation is the key instrument in the orchestration toolkit. It allows businesses to streamline repetitive tasks and processes, much like a musician practicing scales to achieve precision and efficiency.

Collaboration is the ensemble of talents working together to create something greater than the sum of its parts. Orchestration facilitates cross-functional collaboration, ensuring that teams across the organization can work in harmony.

Data analytics are the notes that reveal insights and guide decision-making. Orchestration integrates data from various sources, enabling organizations to make data-driven choices, much like a conductor interpreting musical notes to craft a beautiful performance.

Cost management is the financial conductor that ensures resources are allocated efficiently. Orchestration helps organizations optimize spending and resource allocation, like a conductor managing the budget for a grand symphony.

Change management is the choreographer of organizational transitions. Orchestration includes change management practices to ensure that shifts in processes or technologies are smoothly executed, much like a choreographer rehearses dancers for a flawless performance.

In a world where businesses are constantly evolving, orchestration is the conductor who keeps the performance running smoothly. It's about aligning technology, processes, and people to create a cohesive and adaptable organization.

Orchestration is not a one-size-fits-all solution. It must be tailored to the unique needs and objectives of each organization. Think of it as a conductor adapting their approach to the nuances of different musical compositions.

The benefits of orchestration extend beyond efficiency; they encompass agility, innovation, and resilience. It's like discovering that a well-conducted orchestra not only plays beautifully but also adapts to new musical genres with ease.

Orchestration is not a one-time effort but an ongoing process. Organizations must continuously refine and optimize their orchestration strategies, much like a conductor fine-tuning their interpretation of a musical masterpiece.

Competitive advantage in today's business landscape often hinges on the ability to orchestrate effectively. It's like being the conductor of a world-class orchestra, leading with precision and creating a performance that captivates and inspires.

Strategic orchestration is not a luxury but a necessity in the digital era. It's the conductor's baton that guides organizations through the complex symphony of modern business, ensuring that every note is played with precision and purpose.

As we delve deeper into the strategic importance of orchestration, remember that it's not just a business practice; it's an art form. Like a skilled conductor leading an orchestra to greatness, effective orchestration can elevate an organization to new heights of success and innovation. Together, let's explore the orchestration journey and uncover the strategies and principles that can drive business excellence in the digital age.

Chapter 2: Advanced Orchestration Frameworks and Tools

Welcome to the fascinating world of next-generation orchestration technologies, where innovation and automation converge to reshape how businesses operate and deliver value. Imagine it as the cutting-edge evolution of orchestration, akin to a modern-day symphony that blends traditional instruments with futuristic electronic sounds.

The rapid pace of technological advancement drives the need for next-generation orchestration. Think of it as composing a symphony for a digital orchestra, where each instrument represents a different technology, seamlessly integrated to create a harmonious composition.

Artificial intelligence (AI) and machine learning (ML) are the virtuoso performers in this digital orchestra, enabling predictive analytics, automation, and intelligent decision-making. They're like musicians who can adapt to the nuances of a composition, improvising and responding in real-time.

Next-generation orchestration goes beyond automating routine tasks; it encompasses cognitive capabilities that allow systems to learn and evolve, much like a musician who continually refines their technique. It's about systems that can adapt and respond intelligently to changing circumstances.

Robotic process automation (RPA) is the diligent assistant that automates repetitive tasks and processes, freeing up human talent for more creative and strategic work. Think of it as having a robotic musician who can flawlessly execute complex musical passages, leaving the human performers to focus on interpretation and emotion.

Microservices architecture is the blueprint for breaking down complex applications into smaller, more manageable components, like a musical composition divided into individual movements. Next-generation orchestration excels in managing these microservices, ensuring they work in harmony.

Serverless computing is the conductor's baton that allows organizations to execute code without the need for managing servers. It's like having an invisible conductor guiding an orchestra of invisible musicians, with the audience experiencing a flawless performance.

Containerization, particularly with technologies like Docker and Kubernetes, provides the flexibility and portability required for modern applications. Next-generation orchestration seamlessly manages containers, allowing them to be orchestrated like a symphony of individual instruments.

Edge computing is the stage where next-generation orchestration technologies shine. It brings processing power closer to where data is generated, reducing latency and enabling real-time decision-making, much like a live performance where musicians respond to the audience's reactions in real-time.

Multi-cloud and hybrid cloud environments are the expansive concert halls where orchestration must navigate complex landscapes. Next-generation orchestration thrives in these environments, ensuring that applications run seamlessly across multiple clouds, much like a versatile orchestra that can play in different venues.

Integration and interoperability are the keynotes of next-generation orchestration. It's about ensuring that different technologies, platforms, and data sources can communicate and collaborate effortlessly, much like a conductor who brings together musicians from diverse backgrounds to create a unified performance.

Security and compliance are paramount in the digital landscape, and next-generation orchestration includes advanced security measures. It's like having a highly skilled security team that protects the orchestra from any potential disruptions or threats.

Real-time analytics and monitoring are the watchful eyes and ears of next-generation orchestration. They continuously gather data and provide insights that enable organizations to make informed decisions, much like a conductor who listens to the orchestra and adjusts their direction in response.

Machine-to-machine communication is the secret language of next-generation orchestration. Devices and systems communicate seamlessly to execute tasks and optimize processes, like musicians who communicate through subtle cues and gestures during a live performance.

Continuous deployment and continuous integration (CI/CD) pipelines are the backstage crew that ensures code is tested, integrated, and deployed smoothly. Next-generation orchestration manages these pipelines efficiently, ensuring a flawless performance every time.

DevOps practices are the collaborative spirit that underlies next-generation orchestration. It's about breaking down silos between development and operations, much like musicians and conductors working together to bring a composition to life.

Data lakes and data warehouses are the repositories of information that fuel next-generation orchestration. They store and provide access to vast amounts of data, allowing organizations to make data-driven decisions, much like a library of sheet music that guides musicians through a performance.

Quantum computing, though still in its infancy, holds promise for solving complex problems that are currently beyond the reach of classical computing. Next-generation orchestration is ready to embrace quantum capabilities, like a conductor who eagerly anticipates the arrival of a new and unique instrument in the orchestra.

Next-generation orchestration technologies are not a distant future but a reality that organizations are adopting today. They empower businesses to navigate the ever-changing digital landscape with agility, precision, and innovation.

The benefits of next-generation orchestration extend beyond efficiency and cost savings; they encompass resilience, adaptability, and the ability to seize new opportunities. It's like having an orchestra that not only plays well but also thrives in different musical genres, seamlessly transitioning from classical to electronic sounds.

As we journey deeper into the world of next-generation orchestration technologies, remember that it's not just about automation; it's about creating symphonies of innovation and efficiency that resonate throughout organizations. Together, let's explore the possibilities and principles that drive success in this exciting era of orchestration evolution.

Welcome to the world of tools for enterprise-scale orchestration, where technology and strategy unite to empower organizations with the capability to orchestrate complex workflows and processes on a grand scale. Imagine this as a toolkit filled with specialized instruments, each contributing to the symphony of efficient operations in large enterprises.

At the heart of enterprise-scale orchestration is a robust orchestration platform that serves as the conductor, coordinating and synchronizing the various components of a business's operations. Think of it as the maestro who directs the entire orchestra, ensuring that every section plays in harmony.

Workflow automation tools are the virtuosos that automate repetitive and manual tasks, much like musicians who practice tirelessly to achieve precision in their performances. These tools streamline processes, reducing the need for human intervention and minimizing the risk of errors.

Integration platforms are the connectors that facilitate seamless communication between different applications, systems, and databases within an enterprise. They are like interpreters who help musicians from different backgrounds understand and play together cohesively.

Business process management (BPM) software acts as the score, outlining the choreography of enterprise processes. BPM tools allow organizations to model, optimize, and monitor their workflows, ensuring that each step is executed with precision.

Artificial intelligence (AI) and machine learning (ML) are the soloists who bring intelligence to enterprise-scale orchestration. They analyze data, make predictions, and optimize processes, akin to musicians who improvise and adapt during a live performance.

Enterprise service bus (ESB) solutions are the conduits that facilitate communication between different services and applications within an organization. They act like the sound engineers who ensure that the sound travels seamlessly from one part of the orchestra to another.

Data analytics and business intelligence tools are the critics who scrutinize the performance and provide insights for improvement. They analyze data generated by enterprise operations, offering valuable feedback and guidance for optimization.

Security orchestration, automation, and response (SOAR) platforms are the security guards who protect enterprise-scale orchestration from threats and vulnerabilities. They identify and respond to security incidents, ensuring that the orchestration process remains secure.

Container orchestration platforms like Kubernetes are the stage managers who oversee the deployment and management of containerized applications at scale. They ensure that containers run smoothly and efficiently, much like a stage manager who ensures that the set changes happen seamlessly during a theater production.

Cloud management platforms are the meteorologists who monitor and manage cloud resources, ensuring that they are used optimally and cost-effectively. They provide visibility into cloud spending and performance, helping organizations make informed decisions.

Enterprise-scale orchestration also relies on enterprise resource planning (ERP) systems that serve as the administrative backbone of an organization. They manage everything from finances to human resources, providing a solid foundation for orchestration.

DevOps tools and practices bridge the gap between development and operations teams, much like conductors who ensure that the orchestra and choir perform in perfect harmony. They foster collaboration and automate the deployment of software.

Advanced analytics tools leverage big data to uncover insights and patterns that can inform decision-making. They are like detectives who sift through vast amounts of data to solve complex mysteries, helping organizations make data-driven choices.

API management platforms are the gatekeepers who control access to enterprise APIs (Application Programming Interfaces). They ensure that APIs are secure, well-documented, and used effectively by internal and external stakeholders.

Monitoring and observability tools provide real-time insights into the performance of enterprise systems and applications. They act as the audience, keenly observing the orchestra's every move and providing feedback for adjustments.

Identity and access management (IAM) solutions ensure that only authorized individuals have access to enterprise resources. They are like security personnel who verify credentials and grant access to performers backstage.

Collaboration and communication tools enable seamless interaction among employees, teams, and departments. They act as the communication network that ensures everyone is on the same page, much like a clear communication channel between the conductor and musicians.

Change management tools and methodologies help organizations navigate transitions and transformations smoothly. They are like choreographers who teach dancers new routines and ensure a seamless performance during transitions.

Service desk and incident management systems are the first responders who address and resolve issues and incidents within an enterprise. They are like paramedics who provide immediate assistance when a performer faces an unexpected challenge.

Intrusion detection and prevention systems (IDPS) are the vigilant security personnel who monitor network traffic for signs of malicious activity. They act swiftly to prevent security breaches, ensuring the integrity of the orchestration process.

Enterprise-scale orchestration also encompasses data governance and compliance tools that ensure data is managed responsibly and in accordance with regulations. These tools act like compliance officers who ensure that the orchestra adheres to performance regulations.

Orchestration tools for enterprise-scale operations are not just a collection of technologies; they are the enablers of efficiency, agility, and innovation in large organizations. Like a skilled conductor who directs a grand orchestra, these tools harmonize the diverse elements of an enterprise to create a symphony of success.

The benefits of employing these tools are vast, from streamlined operations and cost savings to enhanced security and compliance. They empower organizations to perform at their best, much like a well-equipped orchestra producing an awe-inspiring performance.

As we dive deeper into the world of tools for enterprise-scale orchestration, remember that they are not just tools; they are the architects of organizational excellence. Together, let's explore how these tools can shape the future of large enterprises, orchestrating success on a grand scale.

Chapter 3: Enterprise Orchestration Patterns and Architectures

Welcome to the exciting world of designing scalable orchestration architectures, where the art of orchestrating complex processes meets the science of scalability. Imagine this as the blueprints for a grand symphony hall, carefully designed to accommodate a full orchestra, while ensuring that every note resonates clearly to captivate the audience.

At the core of designing scalable orchestration architectures is the concept of modularity, much like building blocks that fit together seamlessly. Each module represents a specific task or function, and when combined, they form a coherent and scalable orchestration system.

Scalability is not just about handling increased workloads; it's about doing so efficiently and without compromising performance. It's like expanding the seating capacity of a concert hall to accommodate more attendees while maintaining excellent acoustics and comfort.

Horizontal scalability is akin to adding more musicians to an orchestra to enhance the sound and accommodate a larger audience. In the context of orchestration, it means adding more resources or instances to handle increased demand without overburdening the system.

Vertical scalability is like upgrading the skills of individual musicians in the orchestra, enabling them to play more complex pieces with ease. In orchestration, it involves enhancing the capabilities of individual components or nodes to handle more significant workloads.

Designing scalable orchestration architectures also involves fault tolerance and redundancy, much like having backup musicians who can seamlessly take over if a primary musician falls ill. This ensures that orchestration processes continue to run smoothly, even in the face of unexpected failures.

Load balancing plays a critical role in distributing workloads evenly across multiple resources, ensuring optimal performance. It's like a conductor who ensures that each musician contributes equally to the overall sound of the orchestra.

Caching mechanisms are like the musical memory of an orchestra, where musicians recall previously played notes to improve their performance. In orchestration, caching reduces the need to repeat certain processes, enhancing efficiency.

Scalable orchestration architectures embrace the principles of loose coupling, ensuring that individual components can function independently. It's like musicians who can play their parts without relying heavily on cues from the conductor, fostering independence and flexibility.

Microservices architecture is a key player in scalable orchestration, as it breaks down complex applications into smaller, manageable services. Think of it as composing a symphony by combining individual musical pieces, each played by a different musician.

Containerization, particularly with technologies like Docker and Kubernetes, enhances scalability by providing a consistent environment for applications to run. It's like having musicians who can quickly adapt to different stages and perform with ease.

Scalable orchestration architectures also leverage cloud computing, which is akin to having a portable orchestra that can perform in various locations with minimal setup time. Cloud resources can be scaled up or down as needed to accommodate changing demands.

Elasticity is a vital concept in scalability, allowing resources to automatically expand or contract based on workload fluctuations. It's like having an orchestra that seamlessly adjusts its size based on the size of the concert hall and the audience.

Scalable orchestration architectures incorporate monitoring and analytics tools that provide real-time insights into system performance. Think of it as having a dedicated team of sound engineers who fine-tune the orchestra's sound during a live performance.

Autoscaling is like having a dynamic conductor who adjusts the number of musicians on stage based on audience response, ensuring that the orchestra always delivers a captivating performance.

Designing scalable orchestration architectures also involves considering data storage and retrieval. It's like maintaining an extensive library of musical scores that musicians can access quickly to enhance their performance.

Distributed systems are at the heart of scalable orchestration, allowing tasks to be divided and conquered across multiple nodes. It's like having sections of the orchestra perform in different locations but still play in perfect harmony.

Scalable orchestration architectures must prioritize security, much like having vigilant ushers who ensure the safety of the concertgoers. Security measures protect against threats and vulnerabilities in the orchestration process.

Automation is a driving force behind scalability, enabling processes to adapt and expand without manual intervention. It's like having an automatic stage setup that adjusts the scenery based on the requirements of each performance.

Scalable orchestration architectures are designed with the future in mind, much like a concert hall that anticipates evolving musical tastes and technologies. They accommodate growth and innovation, ensuring that orchestration remains relevant and adaptable.

The benefits of designing scalable orchestration architectures are substantial. They include improved performance, cost efficiency, and the ability to handle growing workloads without significant disruptions. It's like having an orchestra that can perform flawlessly in small chamber settings or on grand stages with thousands of attendees.

As we delve deeper into the art and science of designing scalable orchestration architectures, remember that it's not just about handling more work; it's about doing so gracefully and efficiently. Together, let's explore the strategies and principles that underpin the orchestration of complex processes at any scale.

In the realm of enterprise orchestration, there exists a rich tapestry of common patterns that organizations often weave into their workflows to achieve specific goals and address unique challenges. These patterns are like familiar musical motifs that recur in different compositions, offering a sense of continuity and cohesion to the orchestration of enterprise processes.

One prevalent pattern is the "Approval Workflow," where a series of steps are orchestrated to ensure that certain actions or decisions receive the necessary approvals. Think of it as a formal review process where key stakeholders, much like conductors, ensure that the orchestration proceeds according to established guidelines.

Another widely used pattern is the "Data Integration Workflow," which involves the seamless exchange of data between various systems and applications within an enterprise. It's akin to orchestrating a symphony where different instruments contribute their unique sounds to create a harmonious whole.

The "Event-Driven Workflow" pattern is like composing a piece of music that responds to specific triggers or events. In this pattern, orchestration processes are initiated based on predefined events, ensuring that actions are taken when needed, just as musicians play their instruments when the conductor signals.

The "Error Handling Workflow" is essential for maintaining the integrity of orchestration processes. Similar to a safety net in a circus act, this pattern is designed to catch and address errors or exceptions that may occur during orchestration, preventing them from disrupting the performance.

For complex decision-making processes, the "Branching Workflow" pattern is employed. It's like composing a piece of music with multiple possible melodies, where the direction of the composition is determined by specific conditions or criteria.

The "Parallel Workflow" pattern allows multiple tasks or actions to be executed concurrently, speeding up processes and enhancing efficiency. It's akin to having multiple musicians playing different parts of a composition simultaneously, creating a rich and layered sound.

The "Choreography Workflow" pattern is like orchestrating a ballet, where individual performers follow predefined steps and cues to create a synchronized performance. In enterprise orchestration, this pattern is used to coordinate processes that involve multiple participants.

When orchestrating processes that span different departments or teams, the "Cross-Functional Workflow" pattern comes into play. It's like composing a symphony that requires musicians from various sections of the orchestra to collaborate seamlessly.

The "Human Interaction Workflow" pattern recognizes the importance of human input in certain processes. It's similar to a conductor who engages with musicians, providing guidance and feedback during a live performance.

In situations where multiple orchestrations need to be coordinated, the "Composite Workflow" pattern is employed. It's like conducting a complex musical piece where different sections of the orchestra, each with its conductor, come together under the guidance of a lead conductor to create a unified performance.

The "Escalation Workflow" pattern ensures that critical issues are escalated to higher levels of authority for resolution. It's akin to a conductor signaling to the principal musician to take a solo when a particular moment demands it.

For processes that involve long durations or waiting periods, the "Timer Workflow" pattern is used to initiate actions or reminders after a specified time has elapsed. It's like setting a metronome to ensure that the tempo of the composition remains consistent.

The "Reconciliation Workflow" pattern is essential for ensuring that data and records are consistent across different systems. It's akin to tuning musical instruments to the same pitch to create harmonious music.

In the world of enterprise orchestration, the "Retry Workflow" pattern acknowledges that sometimes, actions or tasks may fail initially but can be retried later. It's like musicians practicing a challenging passage repeatedly until they master it.

The "Rollback Workflow" pattern is akin to having an emergency brake in a musical performance, allowing for a graceful exit in case something goes awry. It's essential for undoing actions or processes that may have unintended consequences.

The "Notification Workflow" pattern is like sending invitations to a concert, ensuring that stakeholders are informed about important events or changes in the orchestration process.

The "Audit Trail Workflow" pattern serves as a record of all actions and events within an orchestration process, much like keeping a detailed score of a musical performance for future reference.

Lastly, the "Dynamic Workflow" pattern allows for flexibility and adaptability in orchestration processes. It's like having a conductor who can adjust the tempo and dynamics of a piece based on the mood of the audience.

Each of these common enterprise-specific patterns is a valuable tool in the orchestration of complex processes within organizations. They offer a structured and effective way to tackle various challenges and optimize workflows. Like the diverse instruments in an orchestra, these patterns can be combined and harmonized to create intricate and beautiful compositions of enterprise orchestration.

Chapter 4: Case Studies: Real-World Enterprise Orchestration

Let's delve into an intriguing case study that explores the complexities and triumphs of a large enterprise migration to the cloud. Picture this as an epic journey, where a colossal organization embarks on a quest to harness the power of the cloud to transform its operations and achieve new heights of efficiency and agility.

Our protagonist in this case study is a well-established multinational corporation with a vast network of offices, data centers, and a diverse range of applications and services. Like a seasoned orchestra with a wide array of instruments, this enterprise had accumulated an impressive portfolio of technologies over the years.

The organization's leadership recognized the need for a strategic shift towards cloud computing to stay competitive in an ever-evolving landscape. This decision was akin to a conductor choosing to transition from traditional instruments to state-of-the-art electronic ones, embracing innovation while preserving the essence of their music.

The migration journey began with a thorough assessment of the organization's existing infrastructure, applications, and workloads. Much like a musician tuning their instrument before a performance, this initial step ensured that the enterprise's systems were in harmony with the cloud environment they were about to enter.

One of the organization's primary goals was to achieve scalability, allowing them to handle increased workloads without missing a beat. It was like preparing for a grand concert where the audience size could vary greatly, and the orchestra needed to adapt effortlessly.

The migration strategy involved a phased approach, akin to composing a symphony with distinct movements. This allowed the organization to migrate critical workloads first, ensuring minimal disruption to ongoing operations.

As with any migration, there were challenges along the way. Some legacy applications required significant adjustments to function effectively in the cloud, similar to a musician learning a new technique to play their instrument better.

Security was paramount, much like safeguarding priceless musical instruments. The organization implemented robust security measures to protect sensitive data and ensure compliance with industry regulations.

Throughout the migration, constant monitoring and optimization were essential. It was akin to having a sound engineer fine-tune the orchestra's performance during a live concert, ensuring that everything ran smoothly.

One of the most significant benefits of the migration was cost savings. The organization no longer needed to maintain and upgrade its extensive on-premises infrastructure, much like reducing the overhead of maintaining a large orchestra with many instruments.

The flexibility of cloud computing allowed the enterprise to experiment with new services and applications rapidly. This was akin to a composer trying out different musical styles and arrangements to create fresh compositions.

The migration also improved collaboration and communication across the organization, much like musicians in an orchestra reading from the same score and coordinating their performance.

As the migration neared completion, the organization found itself in a new era of agility and innovation. It was like an orchestra that had embraced electronic instruments, allowing them to explore new genres and push the boundaries of their music.

This case study demonstrates the immense potential of large enterprise migrations to the cloud. Much like a symphony evolving with the times, organizations can harness the cloud's power to achieve greater flexibility, efficiency, and competitiveness. The journey may be challenging, but with the right strategy and orchestration, enterprises can orchestrate a harmonious transition to the cloud, where the music of innovation and growth can flourish.

Now, let's embark on an exciting journey through another captivating case study, one that explores the triumphs and strategies behind a successful multicloud integration effort. Imagine this as a thrilling expedition where a dynamic organization orchestrates a symphony of cloud services from different providers to achieve its goals with finesse.

In this case study, our protagonist is a forward-thinking technology company, much like a versatile orchestra that can seamlessly switch between classical and contemporary genres. This company had a vision to leverage the strengths of multiple cloud providers, creating a harmonious blend of services that would enable them to scale, innovate, and deliver exceptional value to their customers.

The organization's decision to adopt a multicloud strategy was akin to assembling a diverse ensemble of musicians, each skilled in a particular instrument, to create a symphony that transcends boundaries. They recognized that no single cloud provider could fulfill all their needs, and by embracing multicloud, they aimed to harness the unique capabilities of each cloud platform.

The journey began with a comprehensive assessment of their business objectives and technology requirements. This was akin to the conductor understanding the nuances of each instrument and selecting the right ones to create a balanced composition.

The organization carefully identified the strengths and weaknesses of different cloud providers, much like a composer choosing instruments based on their tonal qualities. This allowed them to allocate workloads to the cloud platforms that best suited their characteristics.

Much like a conductor guiding musicians through rehearsals, the organization developed a robust governance and management framework to ensure consistent performance across multiple clouds. They established clear guidelines for orchestration, security, compliance, and cost management.

The orchestration of multicloud services required a well-thought-out strategy, akin to composing a symphony with multiple movements that seamlessly transition from one to another. This ensured that workloads could move between clouds effortlessly, like a melody transitioning from one instrument to another.

Interoperability was key, similar to orchestrating a composition where different instruments need to synchronize their timing and notes. The organization invested in tools and technologies that facilitated seamless communication and data sharing between cloud providers.

Much like a conductor guiding musicians through complex passages, they implemented robust automation and orchestration tools to streamline workflows and reduce manual intervention. This not only improved efficiency but also minimized the risk of errors.

Security and compliance were paramount, much like protecting valuable musical instruments in a symphony orchestra. The organization implemented stringent security measures and monitoring tools to safeguard their data and ensure regulatory compliance across all cloud environments.

Cost management was an ongoing concern, similar to managing the budget for a grand orchestral performance. The organization constantly monitored resource usage and optimized their multicloud environment to control expenses while delivering outstanding performance.

The benefits of the multicloud integration strategy soon became evident. Just as an orchestra with diverse instruments can produce a rich and layered sound, the organization could leverage the unique strengths of each cloud provider to enhance their services and deliver exceptional value to their customers.

Scalability was no longer a concern, similar to an orchestra being able to adapt to different venues and audiences. With multicloud, the organization could easily scale resources up or down to meet changing demands.

Innovation flourished as the organization experimented with new services and technologies from different cloud providers. This was akin to a composer exploring novel musical styles and arrangements to create fresh compositions.

Collaboration across departments and teams improved significantly, much like musicians in an orchestra reading from the same score and coordinating their performance. The multicloud strategy fostered a culture of teamwork and innovation.

As this case study illustrates, successful multicloud integration is akin to orchestrating a symphony where each cloud provider plays a unique instrument, contributing to a harmonious and dynamic composition. With careful planning, governance, and orchestration, organizations can leverage the strengths of multiple clouds to achieve their strategic objectives and create a symphony of success in the modern digital landscape.

Chapter 5: Scalability and Performance Optimization in Enterprise Environments

In the ever-evolving landscape of technology and business, scaling strategies for enterprise workloads are akin to the conductor of a grand orchestra adapting to varying tempos and dynamics to create a harmonious symphony. It's a crucial aspect of managing the growth and demands of modern organizations, much like a conductor orchestrating a seamless performance that captivates the audience.

Enterprise workloads encompass a vast array of applications, services, and data that power an organization's daily operations. These workloads are dynamic, much like a piece of music that can range from soft and melodic to loud and dynamic. Scaling them effectively requires a deep understanding of the organization's needs and goals.

One of the key considerations in scaling enterprise workloads is anticipating growth, much like a conductor planning for a larger audience in the future. Organizations must assess their current infrastructure and capacity to ensure it can accommodate increased demands without missing a beat.

Scalability can take different forms, similar to a composer choosing various instruments to create different moods in a composition. Horizontal scaling involves adding more identical resources, such as servers, to distribute the workload. Vertical scaling, on the other hand, involves upgrading existing resources to handle more significant loads.

Automation plays a vital role in scaling strategies, much like the automation of musical instruments that allows musicians to focus on their artistry. By automating the provisioning and management of resources, organizations can respond to workload changes swiftly and efficiently.

Monitoring and analytics are crucial components of scaling, akin to a conductor using a keen ear to detect variations in the orchestra's performance. Organizations need real-time insights into their workloads to identify bottlenecks, trends, and performance issues.

The cloud has revolutionized scaling strategies, much like a modern composer using electronic instruments to create innovative sounds. Cloud computing offers elastic scalability, allowing organizations to scale up or down on-demand, paying only for the resources they use.

Hybrid and multicloud strategies have become popular, similar to a composer incorporating diverse instruments and styles to create a unique composition. Organizations can leverage multiple cloud providers to optimize costs, enhance performance, and ensure redundancy.

Scaling for high availability is paramount, much like a conductor ensuring that musicians are always ready to play their part. Organizations must design their workloads to be fault-tolerant and resilient to minimize downtime and disruptions.

Cost optimization is a significant consideration in scaling strategies, akin to a conductor managing the budget for an orchestra. Organizations must strike a balance between meeting performance demands and controlling expenses.

The DevOps culture and practices have a profound impact on scaling strategies, similar to musicians rehearsing tirelessly to achieve flawless performances. DevOps emphasizes collaboration, automation, and continuous improvement, enabling organizations to scale with agility.

Containerization and microservices architecture offer scalability benefits, much like a composer breaking down a symphony into smaller, manageable parts. These technologies enable organizations to scale individual components of their applications independently.

Serverless computing represents a paradigm shift in scaling, similar to a composer creating music without traditional instruments. With serverless, organizations can execute code in response to events, scaling automatically without managing servers.

Machine learning and AI are increasingly used in scaling strategies, akin to a conductor using technology to enhance the orchestra's performance. These technologies can predict workload patterns and automate scaling decisions.

The cultural aspect of scaling is vital, much like the camaraderie and teamwork among orchestra members. Organizations must foster a culture of adaptability and continuous improvement to effectively implement scaling strategies.

In summary, scaling strategies for enterprise workloads are a dynamic and essential aspect of modern business operations. They require careful planning, automation, monitoring, and a willingness to embrace new technologies and practices. Like a conductor guiding an orchestra through a complex composition, organizations must orchestrate their scaling efforts to create a harmonious and successful performance in the ever-changing world of technology and business.

When it comes to performance optimization for critical applications, it's akin to tuning a high-performance sports car for a race; every aspect must be finely tuned to achieve peak performance. These critical applications are the heart and soul of many businesses, serving as the engines that drive revenue, customer satisfaction, and competitive advantage.

Optimizing the performance of these applications is not merely a luxury; it's a necessity. Just as a race car driver seeks to shave milliseconds off their lap times, organizations must relentlessly pursue optimization to ensure that their critical applications perform at their best.

One of the foundational principles of performance optimization is understanding the specific requirements of the critical application, much like a race car engineer analyzes the track conditions to fine-tune the vehicle. This involves identifying the performance metrics that matter most, such as response time, throughput, and resource utilization.

Optimization begins with benchmarking, where the current performance of the application is measured and analyzed. This is akin to recording a race car's lap times and reviewing telemetry data to pinpoint areas for improvement.

Bottlenecks, similar to obstacles on a race track, are the primary focus of optimization efforts. These bottlenecks can occur at various points in the application stack, from the hardware and infrastructure to the code itself. Identifying and addressing these bottlenecks is paramount to achieving optimal performance.

For hardware and infrastructure optimization, organizations often invest in high-performance components, much like a race team invests in top-of-the-line tires, engines, and aerodynamics. This includes using the latest server hardware, storage solutions, and networking technologies to provide a solid foundation for the critical application.

In the software realm, code optimization is essential, much like a race car's engine must be finely tuned to maximize power and efficiency. This involves analyzing and refactoring code to eliminate inefficiencies, reduce resource consumption, and improve algorithmic performance.

Caching strategies play a critical role in performance optimization, similar to a race car driver strategically conserving tires for specific parts of the race. Caching can significantly reduce the load on backend systems by storing frequently accessed data in memory for rapid retrieval.

Load balancing is another key strategy, much like a skilled driver adjusts their racing line to distribute weight evenly. Load balancers distribute incoming requests across multiple servers to ensure even resource utilization and prevent overloading.

Scalability is a core principle of performance optimization, akin to a race team preparing multiple cars for different track conditions. Organizations should design their critical applications to scale horizontally by adding more resources or instances to handle increased load.

Monitoring and real-time performance analytics are essential, much like a race team relies on telemetry data to make split-second decisions during a race. Organizations must continuously monitor their critical applications, using tools and dashboards to gain insights into performance trends and anomalies.

Capacity planning is a crucial aspect of optimization, similar to a race team estimating fuel consumption and tire wear for a race. By forecasting future demands, organizations can proactively allocate resources and prevent performance degradation during peak usage.

Database optimization is often a focal point, much like a race car's engine undergoes meticulous tuning to deliver maximum power. This involves indexing, query optimization, and database design improvements to ensure efficient data retrieval.

Content delivery networks (CDNs) are invaluable, much like a race car driver relies on a well-maintained track for optimal performance. CDNs distribute content geographically, reducing latency and enhancing the delivery of web-based critical applications.

Security considerations should not be overlooked, similar to a race car driver ensuring that safety features are in place. Security measures must be implemented without compromising performance, protecting critical applications from threats and vulnerabilities.

Testing is an ongoing process, akin to a race car undergoing continuous testing and adjustments. Performance testing, load testing, and stress testing help organizations identify weaknesses and fine-tune their critical applications for peak performance.

In summary, performance optimization for critical applications is a multifaceted journey that requires a holistic approach. Organizations must align their hardware, software, and infrastructure to meet the specific demands of these applications. Just as a race car is meticulously prepared for a race, critical applications should be continuously optimized to deliver the speed, reliability, and efficiency that businesses rely on for success.

Chapter 6: Security and Compliance in Enterprise Orchestration

In the complex landscape of modern business operations, ensuring regulatory compliance is much like steering a ship through a maze of ever-changing navigational rules and regulations. Navigating the waters of compliance is a challenging task, but it is one that organizations must undertake with diligence and commitment to avoid pitfalls and potential legal consequences.

Regulatory compliance refers to adhering to the laws, regulations, and standards that govern an industry or a specific aspect of business operations. It encompasses a wide range of areas, including data privacy, financial reporting, environmental protection, and consumer protection, among others.

One of the foundational principles of ensuring regulatory compliance is understanding the specific regulations that apply to your organization, much like a navigator must be familiar with the navigational rules of a particular waterway. These regulations can vary significantly depending on the industry, location, and type of business.

Compliance begins with comprehensive risk assessment, similar to a ship's captain assessing weather conditions and potential hazards before setting sail. Organizations must identify the regulatory risks that apply to their operations and assess the potential impact of non-compliance.

A crucial aspect of compliance is developing and implementing policies and procedures, akin to a ship's crew following a well-defined set of navigational procedures. These policies outline how the organization will comply with relevant regulations and serve as a guide for employees and stakeholders.

Training and education are vital components of compliance, much like a ship's crew members must be trained in navigation and safety protocols. Employees should receive ongoing training to ensure they understand their roles and responsibilities in maintaining compliance.

Monitoring and auditing are essential to ensure ongoing compliance, similar to regular inspections and maintenance checks on a ship. Organizations should conduct internal audits and assessments to identify areas of non-compliance and take corrective actions.

Data protection regulations, such as the General Data Protection Regulation (GDPR) and the Health Insurance Portability and Accountability Act (HIPAA), require organizations to safeguard sensitive information, much like a ship's crew must protect valuable cargo. This involves implementing security measures, data encryption, and access controls.

Financial compliance involves adhering to accounting standards and financial reporting requirements, similar to keeping accurate records of a ship's finances and transactions. Organizations must maintain transparent and accurate financial records, often with the assistance of certified accountants or auditors.

Environmental regulations aim to minimize the impact of business operations on the environment, much like ships must comply with emissions standards and pollution prevention measures. Organizations may need to implement sustainable practices, reduce emissions, and manage waste responsibly.

Consumer protection regulations, such as the Consumer Protection Act, require businesses to ensure the safety and satisfaction of their customers, similar to a ship's crew prioritizing passenger safety and comfort. This involves providing clear product information, handling customer complaints, and adhering to quality standards.

Health and safety regulations mandate that organizations provide a safe working environment for employees, similar to ensuring that a ship is equipped with safety measures and life-saving equipment. This includes conducting safety assessments, providing training, and addressing potential hazards.

International regulations, such as trade agreements and sanctions, can impact businesses engaged in global operations, much like a ship navigating international waters must adhere to international maritime laws. Organizations must stay informed about global regulations and comply with trade restrictions.

Legal and regulatory compliance is an ongoing effort, akin to a ship continually adjusting its course to navigate changing waters and weather conditions. Organizations must stay vigilant, monitor regulatory changes, and adapt their compliance strategies accordingly.

Non-compliance with regulations can lead to legal penalties, fines, reputational damage, and operational disruptions, similar to a ship running aground or encountering a navigational hazard. Therefore, organizations must prioritize compliance as a fundamental aspect of their business strategy.

In summary, ensuring regulatory compliance is a complex but necessary endeavor for organizations across industries. Just as a skilled navigator safely guides a ship through challenging waters, businesses must navigate the intricate regulatory landscape with care, attention to detail, and a commitment to upholding the highest standards of legal and ethical conduct.

Securing data in enterprise orchestration is akin to

protecting a vault of valuable treasures, where the treasures represent sensitive information that must be safeguarded from potential threats. In today's digital age, data is the lifeblood of organizations, and its security is paramount to maintaining trust, complying with regulations, and mitigating risks.

Data security in enterprise orchestration encompasses a wide range of measures and practices, all designed to ensure the confidentiality, integrity, and availability of data. It's like building multiple layers of security around the vault, each one designed to thwart different types of threats.

One of the foundational principles of data security is access control, which is much like having a secure vault door that only authorized personnel can open. Access control involves defining who has access to specific data and what actions they can perform with it. This ensures that only individuals with the appropriate permissions can view, modify, or delete data.

Authentication and authorization are key components of access control, much like requiring both a key and a passcode to open a vault. Authentication verifies the identity of users, typically through methods like passwords, biometrics, or multi-factor authentication. Authorization, on the other hand, determines what users are allowed to do once their identity is verified.

Encryption is a critical aspect of data security, similar to placing treasures in locked, tamper-evident containers within the vault. Encryption transforms data into an unreadable format, which can only be deciphered with the appropriate decryption key. This ensures that even if unauthorized parties gain access to the data, they cannot make sense of it.

Network security is akin to the security measures protecting the perimeter of the vault. It involves implementing firewalls, intrusion detection systems, and encryption protocols to safeguard data as it travels across networks. Network security also includes measures to prevent unauthorized access to the network itself.

Data backup and disaster recovery are like having a backup vault in a secure location. In the event of data loss or a security breach, organizations can restore data from backups to ensure business continuity. This is crucial for mitigating the impact of data breaches or unforeseen disasters.

Regular security audits and assessments are akin to conducting regular security drills and inspections of the vault. Organizations must periodically evaluate their data security measures to identify vulnerabilities and weaknesses. This includes penetration testing, vulnerability scanning, and risk assessments.

Data masking and anonymization are techniques used to protect sensitive data, similar to disguising some treasures in plain sight within the vault. These methods involve replacing or obscuring sensitive information so that even those with access to the data cannot identify individuals or confidential details.

Security policies and employee training play a pivotal role in data security, much like having well-trained guards to protect the vault. Organizations must establish clear security policies and educate employees on best practices for data protection. This includes training on recognizing phishing attempts, using strong passwords, and reporting security incidents.

Monitoring and incident response are akin to having security cameras and alarms in the vault. Organizations must continuously monitor data access and network activity to detect suspicious behavior. In the event of a security incident, a well-defined incident response plan helps mitigate the impact and prevent further damage.

Data classification and labeling are similar to categorizing treasures within the vault based on their value and importance. Organizations should classify data into different categories (e.g., public, confidential, sensitive) and apply appropriate security measures based on these classifications. This ensures that sensitive data receives the highest level of protection.

Compliance with data protection regulations, such as the General Data Protection Regulation (GDPR) and the Health Insurance Portability and Accountability Act (HIPAA), is crucial for organizations, much like adhering to legal requirements for securing the vault. Compliance involves understanding the specific regulations that apply to the type of data being processed and implementing measures to meet those requirements.

Data security is an ongoing effort, similar to the continuous monitoring and maintenance of a vault's security systems. Threats and vulnerabilities evolve over time, and organizations must adapt their security measures accordingly.

Failure to secure data adequately can result in severe consequences, such as data breaches, financial losses, legal liabilities, and damage to reputation. Just as the loss of valuable treasures from a vault would be devastating, the loss of sensitive data can have far-reaching and costly implications.

In summary, securing data in enterprise orchestration is a multifaceted endeavor that requires a combination of technical measures, policies, and employee awareness. Much like protecting treasures in a vault, organizations must take a proactive and comprehensive approach to data security to safeguard their most valuable asset.

Chapter 7: Managing Multicloud and Hybrid Cloud Orchestration

Navigating the vast landscape of cloud computing, organizations are increasingly embracing multicloud strategies, akin to exploring multiple avenues to reach a destination. This approach involves using multiple cloud service providers, each with its own strengths and specialties, to harness a broader spectrum of services and capabilities.

Imagine multicloud strategy as a fleet of vehicles, each representing a different cloud provider, working together to transport your organization's workloads, data, and applications. Just as you might choose a sports car for speed, a van for cargo, and a luxury sedan for comfort on a road trip, multicloud allows you to select the right cloud for each specific task.

The primary motivation behind adopting a multicloud strategy is flexibility. It's akin to diversifying your investment portfolio to spread risk and increase the likelihood of returns. By leveraging multiple cloud providers, organizations can avoid vendor lock-in and capitalize on the best features and pricing structures of each provider.

Moreover, multicloud provides redundancy and resilience, much like having spare tires in different vehicles in case of a flat. If one cloud provider experiences downtime or an outage, your organization can seamlessly shift workloads to another provider to maintain business continuity. This high availability is especially crucial for critical applications that cannot afford interruptions.

However, managing a multicloud environment is not without its challenges. Picture it as driving multiple vehicles simultaneously on a complex highway system. Each cloud provider may have its management tools, billing processes, and security measures, making it challenging to maintain a unified view of your entire infrastructure.

This is where multicloud management comes into play, acting as a skilled traffic controller guiding your cloud fleet. Multicloud management platforms offer centralized control and visibility, allowing organizations to monitor, optimize, and secure their multicloud environments from a single dashboard.

Cloud management platforms are akin to the navigation systems in your vehicles, providing real-time data and insights to help you make informed decisions. They offer features like workload placement recommendations, cost optimization suggestions, and security alerts to streamline multicloud operations.

Cost optimization is a critical aspect of multicloud strategy, much like managing fuel efficiency across your vehicles. Multicloud environments can quickly become costly if not managed efficiently. Therefore, organizations must continuously assess their cloud usage, right-size resources, and leverage cost-saving options provided by each provider.

Security in a multicloud environment is paramount, similar to ensuring the safety of your passengers in each vehicle. Organizations must implement a robust security posture that spans all cloud providers, including identity and access management, encryption, and threat detection.

Moreover, compliance considerations are crucial when adopting a multicloud strategy. Organizations must adhere to industry-specific regulations and data protection laws across all cloud providers they utilize. Compliance is not just a destination; it's an ongoing journey, much like maintaining the roadworthiness of your vehicles.

Integration is another key challenge in multicloud environments, much like ensuring that all your vehicles communicate effectively. Organizations must establish seamless connections between different cloud services, on-premises data centers, and existing applications to achieve a cohesive and efficient ecosystem.

Hybrid cloud is a common component of multicloud strategies, much like having both electric and gasoline-powered vehicles in your fleet. Hybrid cloud combines public cloud services with on-premises infrastructure, offering the flexibility to run workloads where they make the most sense, whether in the cloud or on-premises.

A well-thought-out multicloud strategy involves aligning cloud usage with business goals, much like planning the routes for each vehicle to reach specific destinations efficiently. This entails assessing which workloads are suitable for each cloud provider based on factors like performance requirements, geographic location, and compliance needs.

Data management is a critical consideration in multicloud environments, akin to ensuring that each vehicle in your fleet has the right cargo securely stored. Organizations must define data governance policies, including data classification, encryption, and data lifecycle management, to maintain data consistency and security across all cloud providers.

Vendor management becomes more complex in a multicloud strategy, similar to coordinating maintenance schedules for multiple vehicles. Organizations must establish strong relationships with each cloud provider, negotiate service-level agreements (SLAs), and regularly review and update contracts to ensure they align with business objectives.

Monitoring and performance optimization are ongoing tasks in multicloud management, much like regular vehicle maintenance to keep them running smoothly. Organizations must continuously monitor the performance of their workloads and applications, using cloud-native tools and third-party solutions to identify and address performance bottlenecks.

As organizations embark on their multicloud journey, it's essential to recognize that multicloud strategy is not a one-size-fits-all solution. Much like selecting the right vehicles for a specific road trip, the choice of cloud providers and the design of the multicloud architecture should align with the organization's unique needs, goals, and constraints.

In summary, multicloud strategy and management offer organizations the ability to harness the full potential of cloud computing by combining the strengths of multiple cloud providers. While it brings benefits such as flexibility, redundancy, and resilience, it also poses challenges in terms of complexity, cost management, security, and integration. By carefully planning, adopting the right multicloud management tools, and adhering to best practices, organizations can navigate the multicloud landscape effectively and drive their digital transformation initiatives forward.

In the ever-evolving landscape of cloud computing, organizations often find themselves navigating the intricate terrain of hybrid cloud environments. These environments blend the capabilities of both public and private clouds, creating a flexible ecosystem where on-premises infrastructure coexists with cloud services from various providers.

Picture hybrid cloud as a bridge that connects two distinct islands—the private cloud on one side and the public cloud on the other. It enables seamless movement of workloads, data, and applications between these two worlds, allowing organizations to leverage the advantages of each while addressing specific business needs.

The motivation behind adopting a hybrid cloud approach lies in its ability to offer a balanced solution to complex IT challenges. Imagine it as a versatile toolkit that allows organizations to select the right tool for the job. Certain workloads and applications may thrive in the public cloud's elastic and scalable environment, while others may require the security and control of an on-premises private cloud.

Hybrid cloud also provides a pathway for organizations to modernize their IT infrastructure without the need for a complete overhaul. This modernization is akin to renovating an old building while preserving its historical charm. Legacy systems can coexist with cloud-native applications, ensuring a smooth transition to a more agile and scalable environment.

However, building and managing a hybrid cloud environment is not without its complexities. Consider it as constructing a bridge across a vast and ever-flowing river. Organizations must carefully plan, design, and implement their hybrid cloud architecture to ensure it meets their performance, security, and compliance requirements.

One of the key challenges in hybrid cloud environments is achieving seamless integration between on-premises infrastructure and cloud services. It's akin to ensuring that the bridge's pillars are solidly anchored on both sides of the river. Application and data integration, identity and access management, and network connectivity are crucial components of this integration effort.

Security is a paramount concern in hybrid cloud environments, much like ensuring the safety of travelers crossing a bridge. Organizations must implement robust security measures that span both their on-premises and cloud resources. This includes identity management, encryption, threat detection, and compliance enforcement.

Moreover, compliance considerations are essential when bridging gaps in hybrid cloud environments. Organizations must adhere to industry-specific regulations, data protection laws, and internal policies across both on-premises and cloud environments. Achieving compliance is not just a one-time effort but an ongoing commitment.

Cost management is another critical aspect of hybrid cloud. Organizations must carefully monitor and optimize their hybrid cloud usage to avoid unexpected expenses. This is akin to maintaining the bridge to ensure it remains cost-effective and efficient throughout its lifecycle.

Resource allocation in hybrid cloud environments is much like managing traffic on a busy bridge. Organizations must allocate resources effectively, scaling up or down as needed to meet changing demands. This requires a deep understanding of workload requirements and the ability to adapt quickly.

Hybrid cloud offers organizations the flexibility to choose where and how to run their workloads, much like travelers selecting their preferred mode of transportation. Organizations can leverage the scalability and cost-efficiency of the public cloud for certain workloads while keeping sensitive data and critical applications within the private cloud.

A well-designed hybrid cloud strategy aligns cloud usage with business goals, much like planning the bridge's construction to connect two vital locations efficiently. It entails identifying which workloads and applications are best suited for the public cloud and which should remain on-premises.

Data management is a pivotal consideration in hybrid cloud environments, akin to ensuring smooth traffic flow on the bridge. Organizations must establish data governance policies, including data classification, encryption, and data lifecycle management, to maintain data consistency and security across both on-premises and cloud environments.

Disaster recovery and business continuity planning are essential aspects of hybrid cloud strategy, much like having contingency plans in place for the bridge in case of emergencies. Organizations must ensure that critical data and applications are backed up and can be quickly restored in the event of a disaster.

Monitoring and performance optimization are ongoing tasks in hybrid cloud management, much like regular bridge maintenance to keep it operating smoothly. Organizations must continuously monitor the performance of their hybrid cloud workloads, using cloud-native tools and third-party solutions to identify and address performance bottlenecks.

In summary, bridging gaps in hybrid cloud environments presents organizations with opportunities to harness the strengths of both on-premises and cloud resources. While it offers flexibility, modernization, and cost-efficiency, it also poses challenges in terms of integration, security, compliance, and resource management. By carefully planning, implementing robust security measures, and adhering to best practices, organizations can build bridges that connect their on-premises and cloud environments effectively, facilitating a seamless and agile IT ecosystem.

Chapter 8: Data Governance and Orchestration

Data governance is like the conductor of an orchestra, ensuring that all the instruments (data) play harmoniously together to create beautiful music (insights and decisions). In the digital age, data is a precious resource, and effective data governance is the key to unlocking its full potential.

Imagine data governance as a set of guiding principles, rules, and practices that orchestrate how an organization collects, stores, manages, and uses data. It's the framework that ensures data is accurate, consistent, secure, and compliant with regulations.

At its core, data governance is about accountability and responsibility. It's the equivalent of assigning roles in a theater production, where each actor knows their part and the show runs smoothly. In the world of data, roles and responsibilities are clearly defined to ensure that data is treated with the care it deserves.

A critical component of data governance is data quality. Just as a director wouldn't allow an actor to deliver a subpar performance, data governance ensures that data is accurate, reliable, and free of errors. Data quality is maintained through validation processes, data cleansing, and error detection.

Data lineage is like the script of a play, detailing the journey of data from its source to its final destination. This is essential for understanding how data flows through an organization and how it's transformed along the way. Data lineage provides transparency and accountability.

Data security is a paramount concern in data governance. Think of it as the security team ensuring that no unauthorized individuals enter the theater during a performance. Data encryption, access controls, and security protocols safeguard data from breaches and unauthorized access.

Data privacy is a key component of data governance, especially in the era of regulations like GDPR and CCPA. It's akin to respecting the audience's privacy by not sharing their personal information without consent. Data governance policies ensure that data is handled in compliance with privacy laws.

Metadata management is the equivalent of program notes in a theater program, providing context and information about the data. It describes the data's origin, purpose, and structure. Metadata is essential for data discovery and understanding.

Data stewardship is like the stage manager, responsible for ensuring that everything runs smoothly behind the scenes. Data stewards are individuals or teams who oversee data assets, ensuring they align with governance policies and are used responsibly.

Data governance policies and standards are the script of the data governance playbook. They set the rules and guidelines for data management, ensuring that everyone follows the same script. Policies cover data retention, data classification, and data access.

Data governance tools are the equivalent of high-tech stage equipment that makes the performance seamless. These tools automate data governance tasks, providing a centralized platform for managing metadata, data lineage, and data quality.

Collaboration and communication are at the heart of data governance. Just as actors must communicate with each other to deliver a great performance, data stewards, data owners, and other stakeholders must collaborate to ensure data governance success.

Data governance is an ongoing effort, much like a long-running theater production. It's not a one-time event but a continuous practice that evolves with the organization's data needs and regulatory changes.

Governance extends to data lifecycle management, ensuring that data is retained, archived, and deleted in accordance with policies and regulations. This prevents data hoarding and helps manage storage costs.

Data governance also involves data cataloging, which is like creating a program brochure with details about each actor and their roles. A data catalog provides a searchable inventory of data assets, making it easier for users to discover and access data.

Data governance isn't a one-size-fits-all endeavor. Just as different plays require different sets and costumes, organizations must tailor their data governance approach to their unique needs and industry regulations.

In essence, data governance is the conductor that ensures data plays in harmony, producing valuable insights and driving informed decisions. It's a multifaceted discipline that encompasses data quality, security, privacy, metadata management, and collaboration. By implementing effective data governance best practices, organizations can unlock the true potential of their data, delivering a performance that resonates with success and compliance.

Imagine orchestrating data pipelines as choreographing a dance where different performers, each representing a unique data source or transformation, come together to create a seamless and captivating performance. In today's data-driven world, the ability to manage and orchestrate data pipelines efficiently is crucial for organizations seeking to harness the power of their data.

Data pipelines are the lifelines of data-driven organizations. They are the structured workflows that facilitate the movement of data from various sources to its destination, be it a data warehouse, analytics platform, or application. Just as a dance choreographer plans each move meticulously, data pipeline orchestrators carefully design and manage the flow of data.

The first step in orchestrating data pipelines is data ingestion, where data from diverse sources, such as databases, sensors, or external APIs, is collected and prepared for processing. Think of this as gathering the dancers for the performance; each one must be ready to step onto the stage.

Data transformation is the heart of the data pipeline, where raw data is refined, enriched, and cleaned. Just as dancers rehearse and refine their moves, data goes through a series of operations to ensure its quality and relevance.

Data enrichment, like adding costumes and props to the performance, enhances the data's context and usefulness. This may involve merging data from different sources or enriching it with external data sets.

Data validation is akin to checking the dancers' costumes and ensuring they are in perfect condition. It involves verifying the integrity and quality of data to prevent errors from propagating through the pipeline.

Data orchestration tools are the choreographers behind the scenes, managing the sequence and dependencies of data processing tasks. They ensure that data flows smoothly through the pipeline, just as a choreographer ensures that dancers move seamlessly on stage.

Data pipeline monitoring is crucial for keeping an eye on the performance in real-time. It's like having stage managers who ensure that the show runs smoothly and that any issues are addressed promptly.

Error handling is part of the pipeline orchestration, much like having a plan for when a dancer stumbles. It involves defining how to handle errors and exceptions gracefully to prevent data disruptions.

Data pipeline automation, similar to automating lighting and sound cues in a performance, streamlines the execution of data workflows. It reduces manual intervention and accelerates data processing.

Version control for data pipelines ensures that changes and updates are tracked and documented, allowing organizations to maintain a history of their data processing logic, much like recording the evolution of a dance routine.

Scalability is a critical consideration in data pipeline orchestration. Just as a dance performance may have to accommodate a larger audience, data pipelines must be able to handle increased data volumes efficiently.

Data pipeline security involves safeguarding data during its journey through the pipeline, ensuring that sensitive information is protected and compliant with data privacy regulations.

Data lineage, much like a choreographer's notes on a dance routine, provides a complete record of how data moves through the pipeline, making it easier to trace and understand.

Data pipeline optimization is an ongoing process, akin to fine-tuning a dance performance to make it more captivating and efficient. It involves identifying bottlenecks and optimizing data processing for better performance.

Data pipeline orchestration is not a one-size-fits-all approach; it varies depending on the organization's data needs and objectives. Just as different dances require distinct choreography, data pipelines must be tailored to meet specific data processing requirements.

Cloud-based data pipeline solutions offer flexibility and scalability, allowing organizations to adapt to changing data demands. They provide the stage and infrastructure needed to orchestrate data pipelines effectively.

Serverless computing, like a modern theater with state-of-the-art equipment, simplifies data pipeline orchestration by abstracting infrastructure management and allowing organizations to focus on data processing logic.

Real-time data processing, akin to a live dance performance, enables organizations to respond to data events as they happen. It's particularly valuable for applications requiring immediate insights.

Streaming data pipelines, much like live streaming a performance, allow organizations to process and analyze data in real-time, making it suitable for applications like fraud detection and monitoring.

Batch data pipelines, on the other hand, are like recorded performances that process data in predefined chunks or batches. They are suitable for scenarios where data can be processed periodically.

Hybrid data pipeline orchestration involves combining both batch and real-time processing to meet diverse data processing needs. It's like incorporating both live and recorded elements into a performance.

Data pipeline testing is akin to dress rehearsals before a big show, where the pipeline's functionality and performance are rigorously tested to ensure it meets expectations.

Data governance plays a vital role in data pipeline orchestration by defining policies and standards for data handling, ensuring data quality, and compliance with regulations.

Data ethics, much like the moral values upheld in a performance, are essential in data pipeline orchestration. Organizations must consider the ethical implications of data collection and use.

Data pipeline documentation, similar to program notes in a theater program, provides insights into the pipeline's design, logic, and dependencies, making it easier for teams to collaborate and troubleshoot.

Data lineage and auditing are essential for compliance and transparency. They allow organizations to trace the origin and history of data, ensuring accountability.

Data pipeline monitoring and alerting, like having ushers in a theater who address audience concerns, provide real-time visibility into pipeline health and notify teams of any issues that require attention.

Data pipeline orchestration is a continuous process of planning, designing, executing, and optimizing data workflows. It's a dynamic discipline that adapts to evolving data needs and technology advancements.

In summary, orchestrating data pipelines is like choreographing a captivating dance performance where data moves gracefully from source to destination, undergoing transformations, validations, and enrichments along the way. It requires careful planning, automation, monitoring, and optimization to ensure data flows seamlessly and delivers valuable insights to organizations. Just as a well-executed dance performance leaves a lasting impression, effective data pipeline orchestration empowers organizations to make informed decisions and thrive in the data-driven landscape.

Chapter 9: DevOps Integration and Continuous Delivery

DevOps principles are the guiding stars that illuminate the path to efficient and effective enterprise orchestration, much like the North Star guides sailors on their journeys. DevOps, short for Development and Operations, represents a cultural shift and set of practices that promote collaboration, automation, and the integration of development and IT operations teams. In the realm of enterprise orchestration, these principles play a pivotal role in streamlining processes, enhancing collaboration, and achieving a seamless flow of work.

At its core, DevOps is about breaking down silos, fostering collaboration, and promoting a culture of continuous improvement. It is the idea that development teams and operations teams should work together throughout the entire software development lifecycle. In the context of orchestration, this means that orchestration workflows should be designed and managed with the input and collaboration of both development and operations teams. This ensures that the needs and requirements of both groups are considered, leading to more efficient and effective orchestration processes.

One of the fundamental principles of DevOps is automation. Automation is like having a trusty assistant that takes care of repetitive and manual tasks, allowing orchestration teams to focus on higher-value activities. In enterprise orchestration, automation can be applied to various aspects of the workflow, from provisioning and deployment to monitoring and scaling. By automating these tasks, organizations can reduce the risk of human error, increase consistency, and accelerate the delivery of services.

Another key DevOps principle is continuous integration and continuous delivery (CI/CD). CI/CD is like having a well-oiled machine that ensures code changes are integrated smoothly and delivered to production without hiccups. In the context of orchestration, CI/CD practices can be applied to the development and deployment of orchestration workflows. This means that changes to workflows can be tested, integrated, and deployed quickly and with confidence, reducing the time it takes to respond to changing business needs.

Collaboration and communication are at the heart of DevOps, much like a well-coordinated team that communicates effectively on and off the field. In enterprise orchestration, this means that development and operations teams should work closely together to design, build, and maintain orchestration workflows. Effective communication between these teams ensures that everyone is on the same page, leading to better outcomes and fewer misunderstandings.

Monitoring and feedback are crucial components of DevOps, similar to coaches providing feedback to athletes. In the context of orchestration, this means that organizations should have robust monitoring and feedback mechanisms in place to track the performance of orchestration workflows and gather insights for improvement. This feedback loop helps orchestration teams identify bottlenecks, inefficiencies, and areas for optimization.

Scalability is another key consideration in DevOps, much like a sports team that can adapt to different opponents and game situations. In enterprise orchestration, scalability means that orchestration workflows should be designed to handle changes in workload and demand. This ensures that organizations can scale their operations up or down as needed, responding to changing business requirements effectively.

Security is a non-negotiable aspect of DevOps, akin to a team's commitment to safety. In enterprise orchestration, security should be integrated into every aspect of the workflow, from the provisioning of resources to the deployment of applications. This ensures that security is not an afterthought but an integral part of the process, protecting organizations from threats and vulnerabilities.

DevOps principles emphasize the importance of measuring performance and using data-driven insights to make informed decisions. In enterprise orchestration, this means that organizations should gather data on the performance of their workflows, such as response times, error rates, and resource utilization. This data can be used to identify areas for improvement and optimization.

Flexibility is a hallmark of DevOps, much like athletes who adapt their strategies based on the opponent's strengths and weaknesses. In enterprise orchestration, flexibility means that workflows should be designed to be adaptable and flexible, capable of handling changes in requirements and technologies. This ensures that organizations can pivot and adjust their orchestration processes as needed.

Ultimately, DevOps principles provide a framework for achieving efficient and effective enterprise orchestration. By embracing collaboration, automation, continuous integration, and other DevOps practices, organizations can streamline their orchestration workflows, deliver services faster, and respond more effectively to changing business needs. Just as a winning sports team follows a game plan, organizations that embrace DevOps principles in their orchestration efforts can gain a competitive edge in today's fast-paced digital landscape.

In the world of enterprise orchestration, streamlining continuous delivery pipelines is akin to fine-tuning a well-oiled machine. It's about optimizing the process through which software changes are delivered to production environments, ensuring efficiency, reliability, and speed in the delivery of applications and services.

At its core, a continuous delivery (CD) pipeline is a set of automated processes and tools that enable the rapid and reliable deployment of software updates. Think of it as a conveyer belt that moves code changes from development through testing and into production. In the context of orchestration, the CD pipeline plays a crucial role in automating the deployment and scaling of orchestrated workflows.

The journey of streamlining a CD pipeline begins with the design of the pipeline itself. It involves defining the stages and steps that code changes will go through before reaching production. This design phase is akin to planning the route for a road trip, ensuring that every stop along the way contributes to the overall goal of delivering high-quality software.

One of the foundational principles of a well-structured CD pipeline is automation. Automation is the driving force that ensures that code changes are consistently and reliably moved through the pipeline. It eliminates manual interventions, reduces the risk of human error, and accelerates the delivery process. In orchestration, this means automating the deployment of orchestrated workflows, ensuring that they can be rapidly and consistently provisioned and scaled.

Continuous integration (CI) is another essential component of streamlining a CD pipeline. CI involves regularly integrating code changes into a shared repository and running automated tests to detect issues early. It's like having a team of vigilant inspectors who examine every component of a car to ensure it meets quality standards before it hits the road. In orchestration, CI ensures that changes to workflows are thoroughly tested before being deployed, reducing the likelihood of errors in production.

Testing is a critical aspect of any CD pipeline, much like safety checks before a flight. In enterprise orchestration, testing involves validating the functionality and performance of orchestrated workflows. This includes unit tests, integration tests, and performance tests to ensure that workflows meet their intended goals and can handle the expected load.

Visibility and monitoring are key elements of streamlining a CD pipeline. Just as a pilot relies on instruments to navigate through different weather conditions, organizations depend on monitoring tools to track the progress of code changes as they move through the pipeline. In orchestration, monitoring provides real-time insights into the performance of orchestrated workflows, helping teams detect and address issues promptly.

Feedback loops are vital for continuous improvement in a CD pipeline. Feedback helps teams identify bottlenecks, pain points, and areas for optimization. It's like receiving feedback from passengers after a flight to enhance the overall travel experience. In orchestration, feedback loops can lead to refinements in the design and automation of workflows, making them more efficient and effective.

Security is a non-negotiable aspect of a streamlined CD pipeline, akin to airport security checks before boarding a plane. In orchestration, security measures must be integrated into every stage of the pipeline to protect sensitive data and ensure compliance with security standards.

Scalability is a crucial consideration in enterprise orchestration, much like expanding an airport to accommodate more travelers. A streamlined CD pipeline should be designed to handle changes in workload and demand, ensuring that orchestrated workflows can scale seamlessly to meet business needs.

Flexibility is another hallmark of a well-optimized CD pipeline. It's like having the ability to switch routes during a road trip to avoid traffic. In orchestration, flexibility means that the pipeline can adapt to changes in requirements and technologies, accommodating evolving business needs.

The role of collaboration in streamlining a CD pipeline cannot be overstated. Collaboration ensures that development, operations, and other stakeholders work together seamlessly to achieve the common goal of efficient software delivery. It's like a well-coordinated team working together to win a game. In orchestration, collaboration means that teams responsible for creating and maintaining orchestrated workflows must collaborate closely to ensure the smooth operation of the CD pipeline.

Documentation is the roadmap that guides teams through the CD pipeline, much like a travel itinerary. It provides clear instructions and guidelines for all stages of the pipeline, ensuring that everyone knows their roles and responsibilities. In orchestration, documentation is essential for maintaining and evolving orchestrated workflows over time.

Continuous improvement is the driving force behind a streamlined CD pipeline. It's like a commitment to ongoing training and development to become a better athlete. In orchestration, continuous improvement means regularly reviewing and refining the CD pipeline to enhance efficiency and effectiveness.

In summary, streamlining a continuous delivery pipeline in enterprise orchestration is a journey that involves designing, automating, testing, monitoring, securing, and continuously improving the process of delivering orchestrated workflows to production environments. It requires a collaborative effort, a commitment to automation, and a focus on quality and security. Just as a well-tuned engine powers a vehicle, a streamlined CD pipeline powers efficient and reliable orchestration in the modern enterprise landscape.

Chapter 10: Future Trends in Enterprise Cloud Orchestration

Emerging technologies in enterprise orchestration are like the sunrise on the horizon of the digital landscape, promising new possibilities and opportunities for businesses seeking to streamline their operations and stay competitive in a rapidly evolving world. These technologies represent the cutting edge of innovation, and they have the potential to transform the way organizations orchestrate and manage their processes.

One of the most exciting emerging technologies in enterprise orchestration is artificial intelligence (AI). AI is like a digital brain that can analyze vast amounts of data, make predictions, and even take actions autonomously. In the context of orchestration, AI can be harnessed to optimize workflows, automate decision-making, and enhance the overall efficiency of orchestrated processes. Imagine having an intelligent assistant that can learn from past performance and continuously fine-tune orchestration strategies to achieve better outcomes.

Machine learning, a subset of AI, is another technology making waves in enterprise orchestration. Machine learning algorithms can sift through historical data to identify patterns and trends, allowing organizations to make data-driven decisions. In orchestration, machine learning can be applied to resource allocation, workload management, and predictive maintenance, ensuring that workflows run smoothly and cost-effectively.

Blockchain technology, known primarily for its role in cryptocurrencies, is also finding its way into enterprise orchestration. Blockchain is like a tamper-proof digital ledger that records transactions in a transparent and secure manner. In orchestration, blockchain can be used to create trust and transparency in complex supply chains, ensuring that data related to the movement of goods and services is accurate and immutable.

Internet of Things (IoT) devices are becoming increasingly prevalent in enterprise environments. These devices, ranging from sensors to smart appliances, can generate a wealth of data that can be leveraged for orchestration purposes. Imagine a manufacturing plant where IoT sensors detect equipment failures in real time and trigger automated maintenance workflows, minimizing downtime and optimizing production.

Edge computing is a technology that brings computing power closer to the data source, reducing latency and enabling real-time decision-making. In orchestration, edge computing can be applied to scenarios where split-second responses are critical, such as autonomous vehicles or industrial automation. It ensures that orchestration decisions can be made swiftly and efficiently at the edge of the network.

Robotic Process Automation (RPA) is another technology making its mark in enterprise orchestration. RPA involves the use of software robots to automate repetitive and rule-based tasks. In orchestration, RPA can streamline manual processes, such as data entry or invoice processing, freeing up human resources for more strategic and creative tasks.

Quantum computing, though still in its infancy, holds immense promise for enterprise orchestration. Quantum computers have the potential to perform complex calculations at speeds unimaginable with classical computers. In orchestration, quantum computing can be applied to optimization problems, such as route planning or resource allocation, where the sheer computational power of quantum machines can unlock new levels of efficiency.

5G technology is set to revolutionize connectivity and communication in the business world. With its ultra-fast speeds and low latency, 5G can enable real-time orchestration of processes and services that were previously constrained by network limitations. Imagine a remote healthcare service that relies on 5G connectivity to orchestrate telemedicine consultations with minimal lag.

Augmented Reality (AR) and Virtual Reality (VR) are technologies that are finding applications beyond gaming and entertainment. In enterprise orchestration, AR and VR can be used for training and remote assistance. Employees can use AR glasses to receive real-time instructions and visual cues while performing complex tasks, improving accuracy and efficiency.

Cybersecurity, while not a new technology, is an ever-evolving field in enterprise orchestration. As orchestration becomes more reliant on digital systems and data, the need for robust cybersecurity measures becomes paramount. Technologies like zero-trust security architectures and AI-driven threat detection are essential for safeguarding orchestrated workflows from cyber threats.

Quantum computing, though still in its infancy, holds immense promise for enterprise orchestration. Quantum computers have the potential to perform complex calculations at speeds unimaginable with classical computers. In orchestration, quantum computing can be applied to optimization problems, such as route planning or resource allocation, where the sheer computational power of quantum machines can unlock new levels of efficiency.

5G technology is set to revolutionize connectivity and communication in the business world. With its ultra-fast speeds and low latency, 5G can enable real-time orchestration of processes and services that were previously constrained by network limitations. Imagine a remote healthcare service that relies on 5G connectivity to orchestrate telemedicine consultations with minimal lag.

Augmented Reality (AR) and Virtual Reality (VR) are technologies that are finding applications beyond gaming and entertainment. In enterprise orchestration, AR and VR can be used for training and remote assistance. Employees can use AR glasses to receive real-time instructions and visual cues while performing complex tasks, improving accuracy and efficiency.

Cybersecurity, while not a new technology, is an ever-evolving field in enterprise orchestration. As orchestration becomes more reliant on digital systems and data, the need for robust cybersecurity measures becomes paramount. Technologies like zero-trust security architectures and AI-driven threat detection are essential for safeguarding orchestrated workflows from cyber threats.

The integration of these emerging technologies into enterprise orchestration holds the promise of greater efficiency, agility, and innovation. However, their adoption also comes with challenges, including the need for skilled personnel, the management of complex ecosystems, and the ethical considerations surrounding AI and data privacy.

In summary, emerging technologies are reshaping the landscape of enterprise orchestration, offering new tools and capabilities that can drive business success in a digital age. By embracing these technologies and strategically integrating them into their orchestration strategies, organizations can stay at the forefront of innovation and gain a competitive edge in an ever-evolving marketplace. The journey of incorporating these technologies into orchestration processes may be complex, but the rewards in terms of efficiency, agility, and competitiveness are well worth the effort.

The future of enterprise orchestration is a fascinating and dynamic landscape, characterized by rapid technological advancements and shifting business paradigms. As we peer into the crystal ball of innovation, several key predictions emerge, offering insights into how orchestration will evolve and shape the way organizations operate.

One of the foremost predictions is the continued growth of artificial intelligence (AI) and machine learning (ML) in enterprise orchestration. AI and ML are poised to become even more integral to business operations, with orchestration platforms leveraging these technologies to automate decision-making, optimize workflows, and enhance overall efficiency. Imagine AI-driven orchestration systems that can predict and proactively address issues before they impact business processes, making operations smoother and more reliable.

The rise of the multi-cloud era is another prominent trend in the future of orchestration. Organizations are increasingly adopting a multi-cloud strategy, harnessing the strengths of multiple cloud providers to achieve flexibility and avoid vendor lock-in. As a result, orchestration platforms will need to evolve to seamlessly manage workloads across different cloud environments. This shift will drive the development of advanced multi-cloud orchestration tools that provide a unified view and control over diverse cloud resources.

The Internet of Things (IoT) is set to continue its explosive growth, and orchestration will play a pivotal role in managing IoT deployments. Imagine a world where smart cities are orchestrated to optimize traffic flow, energy consumption, and emergency response systems in real-time. The orchestration of IoT devices will not only improve operational efficiency but also lead to more sustainable and connected communities.

Edge computing is poised to revolutionize orchestration in scenarios where low latency and real-time decision-making are critical. With the proliferation of edge devices and the deployment of edge data centers, orchestration systems will need to extend their reach to the edge. This will enable organizations to process and act on data closer to its source, supporting applications such as autonomous vehicles and augmented reality experiences.

Quantum computing, although still in its infancy, holds immense promise for orchestration. Quantum computers have the potential to solve complex optimization problems at speeds that classical computers can't match. In the future, we may see quantum-powered orchestration systems tackling resource allocation challenges, supply chain optimization, and more, delivering unprecedented efficiency gains.

The convergence of orchestration and cybersecurity is an inevitable trend. As organizations increasingly rely on orchestrated processes, the need to protect these workflows from cyber threats becomes paramount. Orchestrated security measures, such as automated threat detection and response, will become integral to safeguarding digital operations in real-time.

Blockchain technology, known for its security and transparency features, will find wider adoption in orchestration. It can be used to create immutable ledgers of orchestrated processes, ensuring the integrity and transparency of complex workflows. This is particularly relevant in industries where auditability and compliance are critical, such as healthcare and finance.

Ethical considerations around AI and data privacy will drive the development of responsible orchestration practices. Organizations will need to establish ethical guidelines for AI-driven orchestration, ensuring that automation and decision-making align with ethical principles. This includes addressing issues related to bias in AI algorithms and respecting user privacy.

The role of orchestration in sustainability initiatives will become increasingly prominent. Organizations will leverage orchestration to optimize resource usage, reduce energy consumption, and minimize their environmental footprint. Imagine supply chain orchestration that optimizes shipping routes to minimize emissions or data center orchestration that maximizes energy efficiency.

Finally, the democratization of orchestration will empower smaller businesses and startups to harness the benefits of orchestration. User-friendly orchestration platforms and cloud-native tools will make it easier for organizations of all sizes to automate their processes, compete effectively, and innovate in a rapidly changing business landscape.

In summary, the future of enterprise orchestration holds immense promise, driven by technologies like AI, multi-cloud management, IoT, edge computing, quantum computing, and blockchain. Orchestrated processes will become more intelligent, secure, and ethical, while also playing a pivotal role in sustainability efforts. As organizations continue to adapt to a digital-first world, orchestration will be at the forefront of innovation, enabling businesses to thrive in an increasingly interconnected and complex environment.

BOOK 4
CLOUD ORCHESTRATION MASTERY
EXPERT-LEVEL AUTOMATION AND SCALABILITY

ROB BOTWRIGHT

Chapter 1: Mastering Advanced Cloud Orchestration Concepts

In our journey through the realm of orchestration, it's essential to take a deep dive into the architecture that underpins this transformative technology. Orchestration architecture serves as the foundation upon which the orchestration process is built, and understanding its intricacies is crucial for harnessing the full potential of this powerful tool.

At its core, orchestration architecture revolves around the concept of automation and coordination. It's the art of intelligently automating complex workflows and processes while ensuring seamless communication and interaction between various components and systems. This architectural framework enables organizations to streamline operations, improve efficiency, and respond rapidly to changing demands.

The orchestration architecture typically consists of several key components, each playing a vital role in the orchestration process. These components include:

Orchestration Engine: The heart of the architecture, the orchestration engine, is responsible for executing predefined workflows and processes. It interprets instructions, manages task dependencies, and ensures the proper sequencing of tasks.

Workflow Designer: This component provides a user-friendly interface for designing and configuring workflows. It allows users to create, modify, and visualize orchestration processes, often using drag-and-drop functionality.

Service Catalog: The service catalog acts as a repository of predefined services and resources that can be orchestrated. It provides a centralized location for storing and cataloging services, making them readily available for inclusion in workflows.

Integration Adapters: These adapters facilitate communication and integration with external systems and services. They enable the orchestration engine to interact with a wide range of applications, databases, and APIs.

Event Processing: Events, such as system alerts or user inputs, trigger orchestration processes. The event processing component monitors for these events and initiates the appropriate workflows in response.

Monitoring and Logging: To ensure visibility and traceability, orchestration architecture includes monitoring and logging mechanisms. These capture and record information about the execution of workflows, enabling administrators to track performance and troubleshoot issues.

Security and Access Control: Security is a paramount concern in orchestration architecture. Access control mechanisms ensure that only authorized personnel can create, modify, or execute workflows. Encryption and authentication mechanisms safeguard sensitive data and processes.

Scalability and Load Balancing: In enterprise settings, scalability is crucial. The architecture should support horizontal scaling to handle increasing workloads and distribute tasks efficiently using load balancing techniques.

Reporting and Analytics: Reporting and analytics components provide insights into orchestration performance and resource utilization. These insights help organizations make data-driven decisions and optimize their workflows further.

High Availability and Fault Tolerance: To minimize downtime and ensure continuous operation, orchestration architecture often incorporates high availability and fault tolerance measures. Redundancy, failover mechanisms, and disaster recovery planning are essential aspects.

In practice, orchestration architecture can take various forms, depending on specific use cases and organizational needs. It may be on-premises, cloud-based, or a hybrid of both. Organizations must carefully design their orchestration architecture to align with their goals, considering factors like security, compliance, and scalability.

Furthermore, orchestration architecture is not a one-size-fits-all solution. It should be adaptable and flexible, allowing organizations to evolve and adapt to changing requirements and technologies. As new tools, protocols, and standards emerge, the architecture should accommodate these innovations seamlessly.

Ultimately, a well-designed orchestration architecture empowers organizations to transform their operations, boost efficiency, and stay competitive in an increasingly digitized world. It's a powerful framework that enables orchestration to deliver on its promise of automation, coordination, and agility. By delving deep into this architecture, organizations can unlock the full potential of orchestration and drive their digital transformation journey forward.

Let's embark on a journey into the realm of advanced workflow design principles. In the world of orchestration, workflows are the lifeblood, the intricate choreography of tasks that bring automation and efficiency to the forefront of operations.

Advanced workflow design isn't merely about connecting the dots; it's about orchestrating complex processes with finesse, precision, and intelligence. At its core, it's the art of optimizing and enhancing workflows to achieve specific goals, whether it's streamlining business operations, automating IT processes, or ensuring a seamless user experience.

One of the fundamental principles of advanced workflow design is modularity. Modularity refers to breaking down workflows into smaller, reusable components or modules. Think of these modules as building blocks that you can assemble and reassemble to create various workflows. This approach offers flexibility and scalability, allowing you to adapt to changing requirements without reinventing the wheel.

Another crucial aspect is the concept of conditional logic. In advanced workflow design, workflows can't always follow a linear path. There might be decisions to make, dependencies to consider, and variables to account for. Conditional logic allows workflows to branch out based on specific conditions, making them adaptable to dynamic scenarios.

Parallelism is a concept that often comes into play in advanced workflow design. It's about executing multiple tasks simultaneously, rather than sequentially. For instance, in an e-commerce order processing workflow, you might want to check inventory levels, update the customer's order status, and send a confirmation email—all concurrently. Parallelism can significantly reduce processing times and enhance efficiency.

Error handling is another crucial aspect. In advanced workflows, errors are inevitable. However, how you handle them can make all the difference. Advanced workflows incorporate robust error-handling mechanisms, which can include logging errors, notifying stakeholders, and automatically triggering corrective actions.

Additionally, advanced workflow design principles emphasize the importance of human interaction. While automation is a powerful tool, there are scenarios where human intervention is necessary. Consider approval workflows in an organization; these might require managers to review and approve certain processes. Advanced workflows seamlessly integrate human tasks into automated processes, ensuring a harmonious blend of man and machine.

Version control is an often overlooked but critical principle. Workflows, like any other software or process, evolve over time. Advanced workflow design incorporates version control mechanisms that allow you to track changes, revert to previous versions if needed, and ensure that workflows remain reliable and consistent.

Data management is at the heart of advanced workflow design. Workflows often involve data transformations, validations, and integrations. Robust data management principles ensure that data is accurate, consistent, and secure throughout the workflow's lifecycle.

Advanced workflows also embrace the concept of extensibility. As requirements evolve, workflows must evolve with them. Extensibility means designing workflows in a way that makes it easy to add new functionality or adapt to changing business needs without overhauling the entire process.

Testing and simulation are essential elements of advanced workflow design. Before deploying complex workflows into production, it's crucial to thoroughly test and simulate them. This ensures that workflows perform as expected, handle exceptions gracefully, and meet performance criteria.

Moreover, advanced workflows often incorporate monitoring and analytics. These elements provide real-time visibility into workflow performance, resource utilization, and bottlenecks. With this data, organizations can make informed decisions to optimize workflows continuously.

Collaboration is key in advanced workflow design. Workflow designers, developers, business analysts, and end-users must collaborate closely to ensure that workflows align with business objectives and user needs. Effective communication and feedback loops are essential for success.

Lastly, documentation plays a pivotal role. Advanced workflows can be complex, and documentation serves as a roadmap for understanding and maintaining them. Clear and comprehensive documentation ensures that stakeholders can navigate workflows effectively.

In summary, advanced workflow design principles are the foundation upon which sophisticated orchestration processes are built. These principles encompass modularity, conditional logic, parallelism, error handling, human interaction, version control, data management, extensibility, testing, monitoring, collaboration, and documentation. By embracing these principles, organizations can create workflows that are not only efficient but also agile, adaptable, and resilient, ultimately driving digital transformation and innovation.

Chapter 2: Cutting-Edge Tools and Technologies for Experts

Let's embark on an exploration of advanced orchestration toolkits, diving into the rich ecosystem of tools and technologies that empower organizations to orchestrate complex processes with finesse and efficiency.

Advanced orchestration toolkits are the Swiss Army knives of the digital age, offering a diverse array of instruments to orchestrate, automate, and optimize workflows. These toolkits provide the building blocks for creating sophisticated orchestration solutions tailored to an organization's unique needs.

At the core of advanced orchestration toolkits are workflow engines. These engines act as the brains of the operation, responsible for interpreting and executing workflow definitions. Workflow engines come in various flavors, each with its strengths. Some are designed for simplicity and ease of use, while others cater to the demands of enterprise-scale orchestration, handling complex dependencies and event-driven scenarios.

Advanced toolkits also introduce the concept of extensibility. They provide a framework for integrating custom logic and external services seamlessly. This extensibility allows organizations to extend the capabilities of their orchestration solutions beyond what's available out of the box.

Containerization has become a central pillar of advanced orchestration. Tools like Docker and Kubernetes enable organizations to encapsulate applications and services into containers, providing portability and scalability. These containers can be orchestrated at scale, allowing for efficient resource utilization and rapid deployment.

In the realm of data orchestration, advanced toolkits offer solutions for ETL (Extract, Transform, Load) processes. These tools enable organizations to ingest, clean, and transform data from various sources, making it ready for analysis and reporting. ETL workflows can be orchestrated to run at scheduled intervals or in response to specific triggers.

Integration is a critical aspect of advanced orchestration, and toolkits cater to this need. They provide connectors and adapters to seamlessly integrate with a wide range of systems, databases, and APIs. This capability ensures that data can flow freely between disparate systems, creating a unified ecosystem.

Advanced orchestration toolkits embrace the concept of "low code" or "no code" development. These platforms allow business analysts and subject-matter experts to define and modify workflows visually, reducing the reliance on traditional coding. This democratization of orchestration empowers a broader range of users to contribute to automation efforts.

Security and compliance are paramount in the digital age, and advanced toolkits don't take these concerns lightly. They offer robust security features, such as role-based access control, encryption, and audit trails, to safeguard sensitive data and ensure compliance with industry regulations.

Event-driven orchestration is a hallmark of advanced toolkits. They enable organizations to build workflows that respond to real-time events, such as user actions, system alerts, or external triggers. This event-driven approach makes orchestration solutions agile and capable of adapting to changing conditions.

In the age of multicloud and hybrid cloud environments, advanced orchestration toolkits shine. They provide the means to manage resources and workloads across multiple cloud providers seamlessly. Organizations can leverage the strengths of different clouds while maintaining a unified control plane.

Monitoring and analytics are integral components of advanced orchestration. These toolkits offer built-in dashboards and reporting capabilities, allowing organizations to gain insights into workflow performance, resource utilization, and bottlenecks. With this data, informed decisions can be made to optimize orchestration processes continuously.

Machine learning and artificial intelligence (AI) are increasingly finding their way into advanced orchestration toolkits. These technologies can be used to predict resource needs, automate decision-making, and enhance orchestration based on historical data and patterns.

In the spirit of collaboration, advanced toolkits often provide features for team collaboration and version control. Multiple stakeholders, including developers, operations teams, and business analysts, can collaborate on defining, testing, and deploying workflows effectively.

Documentation and knowledge sharing are given prominence in advanced orchestration toolkits. Clear and comprehensive documentation, along with user communities and support resources, ensure that users can harness the full potential of these tools.

In summary, exploring advanced orchestration toolkits is akin to opening a treasure chest of possibilities in the world of automation and orchestration. These toolkits encompass workflow engines, extensibility, containerization, data orchestration, integration, low code development, security, event-driven orchestration, multicloud management, monitoring, AI integration, collaboration, and documentation. By embracing these advanced tools and technologies, organizations can unlock new levels of efficiency, agility, and innovation in their orchestration endeavors, propelling them into the digital future with confidence and competence.

Imagine a world where your orchestration system not only follows predefined rules but also learns and adapts on the fly. That's the promise of leveraging machine learning in orchestration, a captivating frontier that has the potential to transform how organizations automate and optimize their workflows.

At the heart of this transformation lies the idea that orchestration systems can become more intelligent over time. Instead of relying solely on human-defined logic, they can analyze data, detect patterns, and make informed decisions independently. This capability opens up a wealth of opportunities across various domains.

One of the most promising applications of machine learning in orchestration is resource optimization. Traditional orchestration systems may struggle to allocate resources optimally in dynamic environments. Machine learning algorithms, on the other hand, can analyze historical usage patterns, predict future resource needs, and adjust allocation in real-time. This not only improves efficiency but also reduces costs by preventing over-provisioning or under-provisioning.

Machine learning can also enhance troubleshooting and issue resolution. By analyzing logs, metrics, and historical incident data, orchestration systems can identify patterns indicative of potential problems. This proactive approach allows organizations to address issues before they impact operations, reducing downtime and minimizing the risk of critical failures.

Another compelling use case is predictive scaling. Machine learning algorithms can forecast traffic spikes or demand fluctuations, enabling orchestration systems to auto-scale resources preemptively. This not only ensures a seamless user experience but also optimizes infrastructure utilization, leading to cost savings.

In the realm of security, machine learning can bolster threat detection and response. Orchestration systems can use AI-powered algorithms to analyze network traffic, identify anomalies, and flag potential security breaches. This proactive stance strengthens an organization's cybersecurity posture, safeguarding sensitive data and critical systems.

Natural language processing (NLP) is another facet of machine learning that can be harnessed in orchestration. It enables users to interact with orchestration systems using natural language commands, reducing the barrier to entry for non-technical staff. This democratization of access to orchestration tools fosters collaboration and empowers a broader range of employees to automate tasks.

Machine learning can also enhance decision-making in complex workflows. When faced with multiple possible actions or paths, orchestration systems can use reinforcement learning to evaluate the outcomes of each choice based on historical data. This adaptive decision-making capability ensures that workflows adapt to changing conditions and consistently achieve desired outcomes.

In the context of data orchestration, machine learning can assist in data quality assurance. It can automatically identify and rectify inconsistencies or errors in large datasets, reducing the manual effort required for data preparation. This, in turn, accelerates data-driven decision-making and insights generation.

The power of machine learning in orchestration extends to anomaly detection. Whether it's identifying unusual behavior in a network, application, or system, machine learning algorithms excel at spotting deviations from normal patterns. This capability is invaluable for early detection of issues and rapid response to mitigate potential risks.

Machine learning can also optimize service delivery in customer-facing scenarios. Orchestration systems can use predictive analytics to anticipate customer needs, personalize interactions, and recommend tailored solutions or products. This level of personalization enhances the customer experience and drives customer satisfaction and loyalty.

In the realm of content delivery and media streaming, machine learning can optimize content recommendation algorithms. By analyzing user behavior and preferences, orchestration systems can serve up content that aligns with individual tastes, increasing user engagement and content consumption.

When it comes to orchestrating complex workflows, machine learning can automate decision points based on contextual information. For instance, in a supply chain orchestration scenario, machine learning can analyze factors like weather, traffic, and demand to make real-time decisions about shipping routes or inventory management.

Embracing machine learning in orchestration isn't without its challenges. It requires access to high-quality data for training and continuous learning. Additionally, organizations must invest in the necessary infrastructure and expertise to implement machine learning effectively.

Interoperability is another consideration. Orchestration systems with machine learning capabilities must seamlessly integrate with existing tools and systems to ensure a cohesive workflow.

Moreover, ethical considerations and transparency are vital when deploying machine learning in orchestration. Organizations must ensure that algorithms are fair, unbiased, and respect privacy and security requirements.

In summary, the integration of machine learning into orchestration systems marks an exciting leap forward in automation and optimization. From resource allocation to predictive scaling, proactive issue resolution, and personalized customer experiences, the possibilities are boundless. While challenges exist, the benefits of leveraging machine learning in orchestration are too compelling to ignore. It's a journey towards a more intelligent, efficient, and adaptive orchestration landscape, and the destination holds the promise of significant competitive advantages for organizations willing to embrace this transformative technology.

Chapter 3: Advanced Automation Techniques and Strategies

Imagine having an orchestration system that can be finely tuned to meet your organization's unique needs. That's the power of advanced scripting and customization in orchestration, a capability that empowers you to tailor automation to your specific requirements and workflows.

At its core, advanced scripting and customization involve writing code or scripts that extend the functionality of your orchestration platform. This goes beyond the capabilities offered by out-of-the-box tools and allows you to create highly specialized and efficient workflows. Let's delve into the world of advanced scripting and customization to understand its significance and potential.

First and foremost, advanced scripting enables you to bridge the gap between your orchestration system and legacy applications or proprietary systems. While modern orchestration platforms offer a wide range of integrations, there may still be unique software or hardware solutions within your organization that require custom connectors or adapters. Scripting allows you to create these connections, ensuring a seamless flow of data and processes.

Moreover, customization empowers you to design workflows that align precisely with your business processes. Off-the-shelf orchestration solutions may come with predefined templates and modules, but these might not fully match your organization's requirements. Advanced scripting allows you to build workflows from the ground up, incorporating every detail and nuance that is essential to your operations.

A prime example of customization's value is the ability to create user interfaces tailored to your team's needs. While orchestration platforms typically offer dashboards and interfaces, they may not cover every aspect of your workflows or provide the specific data views your team requires. Through customization, you can design interfaces that offer a comprehensive view of processes, making it easier for your team to monitor, manage, and troubleshoot workflows effectively.

Custom scripting can also enhance decision-making within your workflows. While orchestration platforms come with rule engines and logic builders, they might not support highly specialized decision criteria. With scripting, you can implement complex decision trees, algorithms, and AI models that factor in unique variables and business rules, ensuring that your workflows make the right choices at every turn.

Efficiency gains are another significant benefit of advanced scripting and customization. Prebuilt modules and templates may contain unnecessary steps or processes that don't apply to your organization. Customizing workflows allows you to streamline processes, eliminate bottlenecks, and reduce the time it takes to complete tasks. This leads to improved productivity and cost savings.

Moreover, advanced scripting supports error handling and exception management tailored to your organization's requirements. While orchestration platforms offer standard error handling, custom scripting enables you to define precisely how your workflows respond to unexpected situations. This ensures that errors are addressed promptly and effectively, minimizing disruption to your operations.

Advanced scripting and customization also facilitate integration with external APIs and services. Whether you need to connect to a third-party payment gateway, data provider, or cloud service, scripting gives you the flexibility to create custom integrations that meet your specific needs. This opens up new possibilities for extending your orchestration capabilities beyond the boundaries of your organization.

Furthermore, customization is essential for orchestration systems that operate in highly regulated industries. These organizations often have unique compliance requirements that demand specific data handling, auditing, and reporting processes. Advanced scripting allows you to build workflows that align with these compliance standards, ensuring that your operations remain compliant and secure.

For organizations with a focus on data governance and security, customization is indispensable. You can implement custom encryption and access control mechanisms, ensuring that sensitive data is protected throughout the orchestration process. This level of customization adds an extra layer of security, giving you peace of mind in an era of increasing cybersecurity threats.

In addition to its practical benefits, advanced scripting and customization foster innovation. Your team can experiment with new automation ideas, rapidly prototype workflows, and iterate on them without waiting for vendor updates or support. This agility empowers your organization to stay at the forefront of automation technology and respond quickly to changing business needs.

However, it's essential to recognize that advanced scripting and customization also come with challenges. Writing and maintaining custom scripts require specialized skills and expertise. Organizations must invest in training or hire developers with the necessary knowledge to create and maintain customized workflows effectively.

Another challenge is version compatibility. As orchestration platforms evolve and release updates, custom scripts may need to be adapted to work with the latest versions. Organizations must establish processes for testing and updating customizations to ensure they remain functional and secure.

Additionally, there's the risk of over-customization. While customization offers immense flexibility, it's possible to go overboard and create overly complex workflows that are difficult to maintain and troubleshoot. Striking the right balance between customization and simplicity is key to long-term success.

In summary, advanced scripting and customization in orchestration are powerful tools that enable organizations to tailor automation to their unique needs. From bridging the gap between legacy systems and modern platforms to designing highly efficient workflows, creating custom user interfaces, and ensuring compliance and security, the benefits are significant. However, organizations must approach customization with careful planning and a commitment to ongoing maintenance and optimization. When wielded thoughtfully, advanced scripting and customization unlock the full potential of orchestration, driving efficiency, innovation, and competitiveness.

Imagine a world where you can define and manage your entire IT infrastructure using lines of code – a world where your infrastructure is as flexible, scalable, and version-controlled as your software applications. This is precisely the promise of Infrastructure as Code (IaC), a concept that has revolutionized the way organizations deploy and manage their IT environments.

IaC is a practice that treats infrastructure configuration as code, allowing you to automate the provisioning and management of resources in a way that is efficient, reproducible, and scalable. It offers numerous advantages, ranging from improved resource utilization to enhanced collaboration and agility.

At the heart of IaC is the idea that infrastructure can be described, defined, and managed through code. Just as developers write code to build software applications, operations teams and DevOps engineers write code to create, configure, and manage infrastructure resources. This code can be written using various domain-specific languages or configuration files, depending on the IaC tool or platform in use.

One of the primary benefits of IaC is its ability to ensure consistency and repeatability in infrastructure provisioning. Traditional manual provisioning methods often lead to configuration drift, where differences between development, testing, and production environments can cause unexpected issues and errors. With IaC, you have a single source of truth in code, and you can use it to consistently and reliably recreate identical environments, eliminating configuration drift.

Another advantage of IaC is the speed and efficiency it brings to infrastructure deployment. Manual provisioning processes can be slow and error-prone, leading to delays and increased operational costs. IaC enables you to automate resource provisioning, reducing deployment times from weeks or days to minutes or seconds. This agility is especially valuable in today's fast-paced digital landscape.

Furthermore, IaC promotes collaboration between development and operations teams. Traditionally, these two groups often operated in silos, leading to misunderstandings and inefficiencies. IaC encourages a shared approach where infrastructure is defined through code that both developers and operations personnel can understand and collaborate on. This alignment fosters a DevOps culture, enabling organizations to deliver better software faster.

Scalability is another area where IaC shines. Whether you need to provision one virtual machine or a thousand, IaC can handle the task with ease. Through code, you can define and parameterize your infrastructure, allowing you to scale resources up or down dynamically in response to changing demands. This elasticity is crucial in modern cloud-native environments.

Version control is a fundamental aspect of IaC. Just as software developers use version control systems like Git to track changes to their code, IaC practitioners use version control to manage their infrastructure code. This means you can track changes, roll back to previous configurations if issues arise, and collaborate effectively across teams.

Security and compliance are paramount concerns in IT operations, and IaC can bolster these areas as well. By codifying security best practices and compliance policies into your infrastructure code, you ensure that your resources are provisioned with the necessary security measures in place. You can also conduct automated security checks and audits to identify and rectify potential vulnerabilities.

There are several popular IaC tools and frameworks available, each with its own strengths and use cases. Terraform, for example, is an open-source tool that uses a declarative language to define infrastructure as code. It supports a wide range of cloud providers, making it a versatile choice for multicloud and hybrid cloud environments. Terraform allows you to define infrastructure components as "resources" and create dependencies between them, providing a clear representation of your infrastructure's architecture.

On the other hand, tools like AWS CloudFormation and Azure Resource Manager are native to specific cloud providers and tightly integrated with their services. While they may lack the multicloud flexibility of Terraform, they offer seamless integration with the respective cloud ecosystems, making them a natural choice for organizations heavily invested in AWS or Azure.

For those who prefer a more programmatic approach, languages like Python and libraries like AWS CDK (Cloud Development Kit) enable you to define infrastructure in code using familiar programming languages. This approach can be especially beneficial for developers comfortable with writing code.

When adopting IaC, organizations should follow best practices to maximize its benefits. This includes treating infrastructure code like application code, conducting regular code reviews, and establishing a pipeline for automated testing and deployment of infrastructure changes. Additionally, documentation is essential to ensure that everyone involved understands the infrastructure code and its intended use.

In summary, Infrastructure as Code (IaC) is a transformative approach that allows organizations to define, configure, and manage their IT infrastructure through code. Its advantages include consistency, speed, collaboration, scalability, version control, and improved security and compliance. IaC tools and frameworks like Terraform, AWS CloudFormation, Azure Resource Manager, and programming languages like Python with AWS CDK offer various options to suit different needs. Embracing IaC can lead to more efficient, agile, and secure infrastructure management, ultimately contributing to an organization's success in the rapidly evolving digital landscape.

Chapter 4: Scalability and Performance Optimization at Expert Levels

When it comes to managing the resources in your IT infrastructure, resource scaling is a critical consideration that can significantly impact the performance, efficiency, and cost-effectiveness of your operations. Resource scaling is the practice of adjusting the amount of computing resources allocated to various components of your infrastructure to meet changing demands and ensure optimal performance. In this chapter, we'll delve into expert-level resource scaling strategies that can help you fine-tune your infrastructure for maximum efficiency and agility.

Horizontal Scaling for High Availability: Horizontal scaling, also known as scaling out, involves adding more instances of a resource, such as virtual machines or containers, to distribute the workload and improve fault-tolerance. This strategy is particularly effective for applications that require high availability. By dynamically adding or removing instances based on demand, you can ensure that your application remains responsive and available even during peak usage periods.

Vertical Scaling for Performance Optimization: Vertical scaling, or scaling up, involves increasing the capacity of existing resources, typically by upgrading hardware or allocating more CPU, memory, or storage to a virtual machine or application container. This strategy is ideal for improving the performance of individual components that have become bottlenecks in your infrastructure. When resource-intensive tasks are causing slowdowns, vertical scaling can provide a quick and effective solution.

Elastic Auto-scaling for Cost Efficiency: Elastic auto-scaling is a dynamic approach to resource scaling that automatically adjusts resource allocation based on real-time demand. By setting up auto-scaling policies that define when and how resources should be added or removed, you can ensure that you're always using the minimum necessary resources to handle your workload. This not only improves cost efficiency but also eliminates the need for manual intervention during traffic spikes.

Predictive Scaling for Proactive Resource Management: Predictive scaling involves using historical data and predictive analytics to anticipate future resource requirements. By analyzing past usage patterns and trends, you can make informed decisions about when to scale your resources. This proactive approach minimizes the risk of resource shortages during unexpected traffic surges or seasonal variations in demand.

Geo-distributed Scaling for Global Reach: If your organization serves a global user base, geo-distributed scaling can help optimize resource allocation across multiple geographic regions. By strategically deploying resources in data centers or cloud regions closer to your users, you can reduce latency and improve the user experience. Additionally, geo-distributed scaling enhances fault tolerance by ensuring that services remain available even if one region experiences an outage.

Content Delivery Networks (CDNs) for Efficient Content Delivery: CDNs are a specialized form of resource scaling that focuses on content delivery and caching. By using CDNs to distribute and cache static assets, such as images, videos, and web pages, you can reduce the load on your origin servers and improve content delivery speed. CDNs have a global network of edge servers that store and serve cached content from locations close to end-users.

Container Orchestration for Efficient Resource Utilization: Container orchestration platforms like Kubernetes provide advanced resource scaling capabilities. They allow you to define resource requests and limits for individual containers, ensuring that they have the necessary resources to run efficiently. Kubernetes also offers features like horizontal pod autoscaling (HPA) and vertical pod autoscaling (VPA) to automatically adjust container resources based on demand.

Serverless Computing for Event-Driven Scaling: Serverless computing platforms, such as AWS Lambda and Azure Functions, enable you to run code in response to events without managing traditional infrastructure. These platforms automatically scale resources up or down based on the number of incoming events or requests. This event-driven scaling model is highly efficient and cost-effective for workloads with unpredictable or sporadic usage patterns.

Hybrid Cloud Bursting for Flexible Resource Expansion: Hybrid cloud bursting combines on-premises infrastructure with cloud resources to handle sudden spikes in demand. When your on-premises resources are insufficient to handle increased load, hybrid cloud bursting allows you to seamlessly provision additional resources in the cloud, ensuring that your applications can scale horizontally without major disruptions.

Continuous Monitoring and Optimization for Resource Efficiency: Regardless of the scaling strategy you choose, continuous monitoring and optimization are essential. Implementing robust monitoring tools and practices enables you to collect real-time performance data, detect anomalies, and fine-tune resource allocation accordingly. Regularly review and adjust your scaling policies to ensure that they align with changing workload patterns and organizational goals.

In summary, expert-level resource scaling strategies play a vital role in optimizing your IT infrastructure for efficiency, performance, and cost-effectiveness. Whether you're focused on high availability, performance optimization, cost efficiency, or global reach, the right scaling strategy can help you achieve your goals. By combining these strategies and leveraging advanced tools and platforms, you can build a resilient and responsive infrastructure that can adapt to the ever-changing demands of your organization and its users.

Fine-tuning for maximum performance is an essential aspect of optimizing your IT infrastructure, ensuring that it operates at peak efficiency, and delivers exceptional results. In this chapter, we'll explore the art and science of fine-tuning, covering various strategies and best practices to help you achieve the highest level of performance for your systems and applications.

When we talk about fine-tuning, we're essentially referring to the process of making precise adjustments to your infrastructure's configuration, resource allocation, and software parameters to achieve the best possible performance. It's like fine-tuning a musical instrument to produce the most beautiful melodies or optimizing a high-performance sports car for maximum speed and responsiveness.

Fine-tuning begins with a deep understanding of your specific use case and performance goals. It's not a one-size-fits-all endeavor; instead, it requires a tailored approach that takes into account your unique requirements and constraints.

One of the fundamental aspects of fine-tuning is optimizing resource allocation. This involves carefully allocating computing resources such as CPU, memory, and storage to different components of your infrastructure, including servers, virtual machines, containers, and applications. Consider a scenario where you have a web application that experiences periodic traffic spikes. To fine-tune for maximum performance, you might set up dynamic resource allocation, allowing your infrastructure to automatically scale resources up or down based on demand. This ensures that you always have the right amount of resources to handle incoming requests, delivering a seamless and responsive user experience. Another critical aspect of fine-tuning is optimizing software performance. This involves analyzing and refining the code, configuration settings, and database queries of your applications to eliminate bottlenecks and inefficiencies. It's like polishing a gemstone to reveal its full brilliance. For instance, if you're running a database-driven application, you can fine-tune database queries, indexes, and caching mechanisms to improve data retrieval speed. This not only reduces latency but also allows your application to handle a higher volume of requests without slowing down. In addition to resource allocation and software optimization, network fine-tuning is crucial for achieving maximum performance. Network latency, bandwidth, and packet loss can significantly impact the speed and reliability of your applications. Fine-tuning your network involves optimizing routing, minimizing latency, and implementing load balancing to distribute traffic efficiently. Imagine you're managing a global e-commerce platform with customers all over the world. To fine-tune for maximum performance, you might use content delivery networks (CDNs) to cache and serve static assets from edge servers located near your customers. This reduces latency and accelerates content delivery, ensuring a smooth shopping experience for users worldwide. Furthermore, fine-tuning for security is essential to protect your infrastructure while maintaining optimal performance. Security measures, such as firewalls, intrusion detection systems, and encryption, can introduce overhead that affects performance. Fine-tuning security involves striking a balance between robust protection and minimal impact on performance. For example, when implementing encryption for data in transit, you can fine-tune the choice of encryption algorithms and key lengths to maximize security without compromising performance. This ensures that sensitive data remains safe while maintaining fast and efficient communication between components. Cloud services and virtualization platforms offer valuable tools for fine-tuning performance. For instance, if you're using a cloud provider, you can leverage services like AWS Elastic Load Balancing or Azure Load Balancer to distribute incoming traffic evenly across multiple instances of your application, preventing any single component from becoming a performance bottleneck.

Moreover, cloud providers offer performance monitoring and analytics tools that allow you to gain insights into your infrastructure's behavior. By continuously monitoring performance metrics, you can identify areas that require fine-tuning and make data-driven decisions to optimize resource allocation and configuration settings. Machine learning and artificial intelligence (AI) also play a growing role in fine-tuning for performance. These technologies can analyze vast amounts of data to identify patterns, anomalies, and opportunities for optimization. For instance, machine learning algorithms can predict traffic patterns and automatically adjust resource allocation to handle anticipated spikes in demand.

In summary, fine-tuning for maximum performance is a multifaceted and ongoing process that involves optimizing resource allocation, software performance, network efficiency, security, and leveraging cloud services and AI-driven insights. It's about achieving the perfect balance between performance and resource utilization, ensuring that your IT infrastructure operates at its best, delivering exceptional results for your organization and users.

Chapter 5: Orchestration in Multicloud and Hybrid Environments

Advanced strategies for managing multicloud environments represent a pivotal step in the evolution of cloud computing and its integration into modern enterprise IT ecosystems. In this chapter, we will delve into the sophisticated methods and techniques that organizations employ to harness the power of multiple cloud platforms while optimizing performance, security, and cost-effectiveness.

In the fast-paced world of cloud computing, multicloud has emerged as a strategic choice for many businesses. It allows organizations to avoid vendor lock-in, mitigate risks associated with downtime or service outages, and take advantage of specialized services offered by different cloud providers.

To effectively manage a multicloud environment, it's essential to begin with a comprehensive strategy. This strategy should align with your organization's specific goals and requirements. It should encompass factors like application portability, data sovereignty, and compliance standards.

One advanced strategy is to establish a cloud center of excellence (CCoE). This cross-functional team brings together experts in cloud architecture, security, compliance, and cost management. The CCoE provides governance, best practices, and oversight for multicloud deployments, ensuring that all aspects of cloud management are optimized.

Moreover, organizations often employ advanced cloud management platforms and tools to gain better visibility and control over their multicloud environments. These tools allow you to centrally manage resources, enforce policies, and monitor performance across multiple cloud providers.

When managing a multicloud environment, automation becomes a key enabler. Advanced automation tools and scripts can streamline provisioning, scaling, and orchestration tasks, reducing manual intervention and the risk of human error. Automation also supports infrastructure as code (IaC) practices, enabling you to define and deploy cloud resources using code, which can be version-controlled and audited.

Another critical aspect of advanced multicloud management is cost optimization. With multiple cloud providers, it's easy for costs to spiral out of control. Advanced strategies include the use of cloud cost management tools, such as cost allocation, budgeting, and predictive analytics. These tools help organizations track spending, identify cost-saving opportunities, and allocate expenses accurately across different business units or projects.

Security is a paramount concern in multicloud environments. Advanced security strategies involve implementing a combination of cloud-native and third-party security solutions. These solutions offer features like identity and access management (IAM), encryption, network security, and threat detection. They help protect data and applications across all cloud platforms.

To enhance security further, organizations use advanced techniques like zero-trust security models. Zero trust assumes that threats may exist both inside and outside the network. It requires continuous verification of user identities and devices, even for those already inside the network perimeter.

Moreover, advanced multicloud security includes threat intelligence and incident response capabilities. Organizations proactively gather threat intelligence from various sources to identify emerging threats and vulnerabilities. In case of a security incident, they employ advanced incident response plans to minimize damage and recover quickly.

As multicloud environments grow in complexity, advanced monitoring and observability tools become indispensable. These tools provide real-time insights into the performance and health of applications and infrastructure components. By employing advanced monitoring, organizations can detect issues early, optimize resource utilization, and ensure a seamless user experience.

Furthermore, multicloud management extends beyond technical considerations. It involves governance and compliance with regulatory requirements. Advanced strategies encompass continuous compliance monitoring and automated remediation. This ensures that your multicloud environment remains compliant with industry-specific regulations and standards.

DevOps practices play a vital role in advanced multicloud management. By integrating development and operations teams, organizations can deliver applications and updates faster and with greater reliability. DevOps pipelines automate testing, deployment, and delivery, ensuring consistent and predictable outcomes in multicloud environments.

Advanced strategies also consider workload placement. Organizations decide where to deploy workloads based on factors like performance requirements, cost, and data residency. This may involve optimizing for specific cloud providers, regions, or availability zones. In addition to public clouds, advanced multicloud management extends to hybrid and edge computing environments. It ensures seamless integration between on-premises data centers, edge devices, and public cloud resources. This approach allows organizations to harness the full potential of distributed computing. Finally, advanced multicloud management involves vendor negotiations and partnerships. Organizations explore strategic alliances with cloud providers to gain access to exclusive services, support, and pricing. They also establish clear service-level agreements (SLAs) and exit strategies to maintain control and flexibility.

In summary, advanced strategies for managing multicloud environments are crucial for organizations seeking to maximize the benefits of cloud computing while addressing complex challenges. These strategies encompass comprehensive planning, automation, cost optimization, security, monitoring, compliance, DevOps, workload placement, and strategic partnerships. By adopting these advanced approaches, organizations can thrive in the era of multicloud computing, achieving agility, efficiency, and innovation at scale.

Navigating the complex landscape of hybrid cloud orchestration requires a keen understanding of best practices that can help organizations leverage the power of both on-premises and cloud resources seamlessly. In this chapter, we'll explore these best practices to ensure that your hybrid cloud environment operates efficiently, securely, and with optimal performance.

First and foremost, it's crucial to adopt a holistic approach to hybrid cloud orchestration. This means viewing your hybrid environment as a unified whole rather than two separate entities. By integrating on-premises and cloud resources into a single cohesive architecture, you can maximize efficiency and simplify management.

A fundamental best practice is to define a clear hybrid cloud strategy aligned with your business objectives. Understand which workloads should reside on-premises, which can benefit from the cloud's scalability, and which require a combination of both. This strategy should consider factors such as compliance, data sovereignty, and cost optimization.

A key component of hybrid cloud orchestration is hybrid cloud management tools. Invest in tools that provide a unified dashboard for managing on-premises and cloud resources. These tools should offer features like resource provisioning, automation, monitoring, and cost analysis. By centralizing management, you can streamline operations and reduce complexity. When orchestrating in a hybrid cloud environment, it's essential to prioritize security and compliance. Implement robust identity and access management (IAM) solutions to ensure that users and applications have the appropriate permissions. Encryption and data protection mechanisms should be in place to safeguard sensitive data, whether it's in transit or at rest.

Advanced threat detection and security monitoring tools should be integrated to identify and respond to potential security incidents promptly. A zero-trust security model, which verifies every user and device, is a best practice for maintaining a secure hybrid environment.

Performance optimization is another critical aspect of hybrid cloud orchestration. Employ hybrid cloud load balancing to distribute workloads efficiently between on-premises and cloud resources. Ensure that your applications are designed for hybrid deployment, taking advantage of cloud scalability while maintaining compatibility with on-premises infrastructure.

To further enhance performance, consider implementing a content delivery network (CDN) to accelerate content delivery to users and reduce latency. CDNs cache content at edge locations, ensuring faster access to resources, especially for geographically dispersed users.

Scalability is one of the primary reasons organizations adopt hybrid cloud solutions. Best practices include designing applications to scale horizontally across cloud resources while still allowing for vertical scaling when necessary. Implement auto-scaling policies that adjust resource allocation dynamically based on workload demand. Resource optimization plays a significant role in cost control. Employ advanced cloud cost management tools to monitor spending, identify cost-saving opportunities, and allocate expenses accurately. Create policies that automatically stop or scale down underutilized resources to avoid unnecessary expenses.

Governance and compliance are ongoing best practices in hybrid cloud environments. Develop and enforce policies that align with industry-specific regulations and standards. Automated compliance checks and remediation are crucial to maintaining a compliant posture.

Embrace hybrid cloud orchestration as an opportunity to modernize your application architecture. Utilize containers and microservices to enable greater portability and flexibility across on-premises and cloud environments. Container orchestration platforms like Kubernetes can simplify the management of containerized applications.

DevOps practices are invaluable for achieving agility and automation in a hybrid cloud environment. Implement continuous integration and continuous delivery (CI/CD) pipelines to streamline application development and deployment processes. DevOps teams should work collaboratively to ensure seamless integration between on-premises and cloud components.

Hybrid cloud orchestration often involves hybrid networking solutions. Implement a software-defined network (SDN) to create a dynamic and flexible network infrastructure that spans both on-premises and cloud environments. SDN technologies enable efficient data traffic routing and optimization.

Additionally, consider hybrid cloud backup and disaster recovery solutions. These solutions ensure that your data and applications are protected against unexpected outages or data loss. Implement automated backup and recovery processes to minimize downtime and data loss in case of disasters.

Monitoring and observability are essential for maintaining visibility into the performance and health of your hybrid cloud environment. Utilize advanced monitoring tools that provide real-time insights and predictive analytics. Proactively identify issues and optimize resource utilization for a seamless user experience.

Finally, vendor partnerships and negotiations play a vital role in hybrid cloud orchestration. Collaborate with cloud service providers and technology vendors to access specialized services, support, and pricing. Establish clear service-level agreements (SLAs) to maintain control and ensure that your hybrid cloud environment meets performance and reliability expectations.

In summary, hybrid cloud orchestration best practices encompass a holistic approach that integrates on-premises and cloud resources seamlessly. These practices include defining a clear strategy, adopting management tools, prioritizing security and compliance, optimizing performance, controlling costs, enforcing governance, embracing modern application architectures, implementing DevOps, managing hybrid networking, ensuring backup and disaster recovery, monitoring and observability, and building strategic vendor partnerships. By adhering to these best practices, organizations can navigate the complexities of hybrid cloud orchestration and leverage its benefits effectively.

Chapter 6: Advanced Security and Compliance Practices

Ensuring the security of your orchestration processes is of paramount importance as you navigate the complex landscape of modern IT environments. In this chapter, we will delve into best practices for orchestrating secure workflows that safeguard your data, applications, and infrastructure.

To begin, it's crucial to adopt a security-first mindset in your orchestration strategy. Security should not be an afterthought but an integral part of the entire orchestration process. Consider security at every stage of workflow design, from initial planning to execution and monitoring.

One fundamental best practice is to implement robust access control measures. This involves defining who has access to your orchestration systems and what actions they can perform. Role-based access control (RBAC) is a valuable tool in this regard, allowing you to assign specific permissions to users and groups based on their roles and responsibilities.

Encryption is another cornerstone of orchestration security. Ensure that all data in transit and at rest is encrypted using strong encryption algorithms. This includes communication between components of your orchestration system and any data stored in databases or file systems.

Credential management is a critical aspect of security. Avoid hardcoding passwords and sensitive information in your orchestration scripts or configurations. Instead, utilize secure credential stores or secrets management solutions to securely store and retrieve credentials when needed.

Continuously monitoring and auditing your orchestration processes is essential for early threat detection. Implement logging and auditing mechanisms that capture all relevant activities, including user actions, system events, and application interactions. Regularly review these logs for suspicious activities or anomalies.

Security patches and updates should be applied promptly to all components of your orchestration system. Keep your software and dependencies up to date to mitigate known vulnerabilities. Consider implementing automated patch management processes to streamline this task and reduce the risk of security breaches.

Network segmentation is a valuable security practice that isolates different parts of your orchestration environment. Segmentation ensures that even if one segment is compromised, attackers are unable to access the entire system. Employ firewalls, VLANs, and security groups to enforce network segmentation effectively.

Intrusion detection and prevention systems (IDPS) can provide an additional layer of security by monitoring network traffic and system activities for suspicious patterns. When anomalous behavior is detected, these systems can trigger alerts or take predefined actions to block potential threats.

Secure API usage is essential, especially in modern orchestration systems that rely on APIs to communicate with various components. Implement strong authentication and authorization mechanisms for API endpoints. Use API keys or tokens with limited scope to minimize the risk of unauthorized access.

Regularly conduct vulnerability assessments and penetration testing on your orchestration systems. These assessments help identify potential weaknesses and security gaps that could be exploited by attackers. Address the identified vulnerabilities promptly to maintain a robust security posture.

Implementing a disaster recovery plan is essential to ensure business continuity in the event of a security breach or system failure. Regularly back up critical data and configurations, and create a well-documented recovery procedure that can be executed swiftly if needed.

Security awareness training for your orchestration team is a best practice that should not be overlooked. Educate your team members about security threats, best practices, and the importance of adhering to security policies. Awareness training empowers your team to be proactive in identifying and responding to security incidents.

Consider implementing security information and event management (SIEM) systems to centralize the collection and analysis of security-related data from various sources. SIEM solutions provide real-time insights into potential security threats, enabling rapid response and mitigation.

Regularly assess your orchestration security policies and procedures to ensure they remain effective in the face of evolving threats. Security is an ongoing process, and your policies should adapt to new challenges and vulnerabilities.

Finally, establish an incident response plan that outlines how your organization will respond to security incidents. Define roles and responsibilities, escalation procedures, and communication protocols. A well-prepared incident response plan can minimize the impact of security breaches and help you recover quickly.

In summary, security in orchestration is a multifaceted challenge that requires a comprehensive approach. Best practices include adopting a security-first mindset, implementing access controls and encryption, managing credentials securely, monitoring and auditing, staying up to date with patches, employing network segmentation and intrusion detection, securing APIs, conducting vulnerability assessments, planning for disaster recovery, providing security awareness training, leveraging SIEM systems, regularly assessing security policies, and establishing an incident response plan. By following these best practices, you can build a secure orchestration environment that safeguards your organization's critical assets and data.

Navigating the complex landscape of orchestration can be a challenging endeavor, but when it comes to achieving compliance in such scenarios, the stakes are higher than ever before. In this chapter, we will explore the intricacies of ensuring compliance in complex orchestration environments, shedding light on the strategies and practices that can help your organization meet regulatory requirements.

Complex orchestration scenarios often involve intricate workflows that span multiple cloud providers, data centers, and geographic regions. This complexity introduces a multitude of compliance challenges, as regulatory frameworks vary across industries and regions. To address these challenges, organizations must first identify the relevant compliance requirements that pertain to their specific orchestration use cases.

One key aspect of achieving compliance in complex orchestration scenarios is data governance. Organizations need to have a clear understanding of where their data resides, how it is processed, and who has access to it. Data classification and labeling are critical components of data governance, as they help ensure that sensitive information is handled appropriately and in accordance with regulatory guidelines.

Another essential consideration is encryption. Complex orchestration environments often involve data transmission and storage across diverse infrastructure components. Encrypting data both in transit and at rest helps safeguard sensitive information and aligns with various data protection regulations.

Access control and identity management are paramount in complex orchestration scenarios. Role-based access control (RBAC) and strict authentication mechanisms ensure that only authorized individuals can interact with orchestration workflows. Implementing strong access controls across your orchestration components minimizes the risk of unauthorized access and data breaches.

Auditing and monitoring are indispensable tools for demonstrating compliance. Organizations should establish comprehensive logging and auditing mechanisms that capture all relevant activities within their orchestration systems. Regularly reviewing these logs allows for the early detection of anomalies and potential security threats.

The implementation of security information and event management (SIEM) systems can greatly assist in compliance efforts. SIEM solutions provide real-time analysis of security-related events, allowing organizations to respond swiftly to any potential compliance violations or security breaches.

Complex orchestration scenarios often entail interactions with third-party services and providers. When outsourcing services or relying on external partners, organizations must ensure that these entities also adhere to the necessary compliance standards. Vendor due diligence and contractual agreements should explicitly state compliance requirements to avoid potential liabilities.

Regulatory compliance is an ongoing process, and organizations must stay vigilant in keeping up with evolving regulations and standards. This necessitates a commitment to regular compliance assessments and audits. These evaluations help organizations identify gaps in their compliance posture and take corrective actions.

Documentation plays a vital role in compliance efforts. Organizations should maintain detailed records of their orchestration workflows, configurations, security policies, and incident response plans. These documents serve as evidence of compliance and can be invaluable during audits or regulatory inquiries.

In highly regulated industries such as finance or healthcare, organizations may be subject to specific compliance frameworks, such as HIPAA or PCI DSS. It is essential to thoroughly understand the requirements of these frameworks and tailor orchestration practices accordingly. Compliance with industry-specific standards often involves additional safeguards and reporting obligations.

Another challenge in complex orchestration scenarios is the coordination of compliance efforts across various teams and departments. Collaboration between IT, security, legal, and compliance teams is essential to align processes, policies, and controls with regulatory requirements. Establishing clear lines of communication and shared responsibilities is crucial.

In summary, achieving compliance in complex orchestration scenarios is a multifaceted undertaking. It requires organizations to identify relevant regulatory requirements, implement robust data governance practices, embrace encryption, enforce access controls, establish auditing and monitoring capabilities, leverage SIEM solutions, ensure vendor compliance, conduct regular assessments, maintain comprehensive documentation, and foster interdepartmental collaboration. By addressing these aspects, organizations can navigate the complexities of orchestration while remaining compliant with regulatory standards and industry-specific frameworks.

Chapter 7: Extreme Resource Optimization and Cost Control

Resource optimization, a fundamental concept in the realm of technology and business operations, continues to evolve with remarkable innovations that empower organizations to maximize efficiency, reduce costs, and improve overall performance. In this chapter, we will delve into some of these innovative approaches and strategies that are reshaping the landscape of resource optimization.

One of the most significant innovations in recent years is the adoption of artificial intelligence (AI) and machine learning (ML) in resource optimization. These technologies enable organizations to analyze vast amounts of data, identify patterns, and make real-time decisions to allocate resources more efficiently. For example, predictive maintenance powered by AI can help organizations anticipate equipment failures and schedule maintenance activities proactively, minimizing downtime and reducing operational costs.

The concept of edge computing has gained substantial traction as an innovative resource optimization strategy. With edge computing, data processing occurs closer to the data source rather than in centralized data centers. This approach reduces latency and allows organizations to make quicker decisions. In scenarios where real-time responses are critical, such as autonomous vehicles or industrial automation, edge computing is a game-changer.

Another innovation in resource optimization is the use of containerization and container orchestration technologies like Docker and Kubernetes. Containers provide a lightweight and efficient way to package applications and their dependencies, making it easier to allocate resources based on the specific needs of each container. Kubernetes, in particular, has emerged as a robust platform for orchestrating containerized workloads, optimizing resource utilization, and scaling applications seamlessly.

Cloud computing has revolutionized resource optimization by providing organizations with the flexibility to scale resources up or down based on demand. Serverless computing, a cloud computing model that abstracts infrastructure management entirely, has gained popularity. With serverless, organizations pay only for the compute resources consumed during the execution of functions or tasks, eliminating the need to provision and manage servers, thus optimizing costs and resource utilization.

In the realm of data storage, innovations such as tiered storage and data deduplication have transformed how organizations manage their data. Tiered storage allows data to be stored on different types of storage media based on its access frequency and importance, ensuring that frequently accessed data resides on high-performance storage while less frequently accessed data is stored on more cost-effective solutions. Data deduplication reduces storage requirements by identifying and eliminating duplicate data, resulting in significant cost savings and improved resource utilization.

The emergence of software-defined infrastructure is another innovative approach to resource optimization. Software-defined networking (SDN) and software-defined storage (SDS) enable organizations to abstract and virtualize their network and storage resources, making them more flexible and easier to manage. SDN, in particular, allows for dynamic network provisioning and optimization, improving overall network performance and resource allocation.

In the world of data analytics, innovations in processing frameworks like Apache Spark have accelerated data processing and analytics tasks. These frameworks provide distributed processing capabilities, allowing organizations to harness the power of multiple compute nodes to process large datasets efficiently. This not only optimizes resource utilization but also enables organizations to gain insights from their data faster.

Machine learning-driven workload scheduling is another noteworthy innovation. With the ability to analyze historical workload data and predict resource needs, organizations can optimize the allocation of resources based on workload requirements, ensuring that critical tasks receive the necessary resources while minimizing over-provisioning.

Green computing, focused on sustainability and energy efficiency, has become a significant concern for organizations. Innovations in energy-efficient hardware and data center design have resulted in reduced power consumption and lower operating costs. For instance, data centers are now employing advanced cooling technologies and renewable energy sources to reduce their environmental impact while optimizing resource usage.

Optimizing human resources is also a critical aspect of resource optimization. Innovations in workforce management software, powered by AI and analytics, enable organizations to better match employee skills and availability with project demands, ensuring that the right people are allocated to the right tasks at the right time.

Furthermore, innovations in supply chain management have revolutionized resource optimization in manufacturing and logistics. Predictive analytics and IoT sensors provide real-time visibility into supply chain operations, allowing organizations to optimize inventory levels, streamline logistics, and reduce costs.

In summary, innovations in resource optimization are reshaping the way organizations manage their technology infrastructure, data, and human resources. From the adoption of AI and ML for predictive maintenance to the implementation of edge computing, containerization, and serverless computing, these innovations offer new avenues for organizations to maximize efficiency, reduce costs, and achieve their performance objectives. Whether it's optimizing data storage, leveraging software-defined infrastructure, or focusing on sustainability and workforce management, organizations that embrace these innovations are better positioned to thrive in a rapidly changing technological landscape.

Cost control is a paramount concern for organizations that have reached an expert-level of orchestration, as efficiently managing resources and expenditures becomes increasingly complex in this advanced stage of technology integration and automation. In this chapter, we'll explore a variety of strategies and techniques that can be employed to maintain cost control while optimizing the orchestration environment for maximum performance.

One of the foundational principles of cost control in expert-level orchestration is continuous monitoring and analysis. Organizations must develop a robust monitoring system that tracks the usage of all resources, from compute and storage to network bandwidth and application services. With real-time data at their disposal, orchestration experts can identify resource bottlenecks, underutilized assets, or unexpected spikes in usage that may lead to cost overruns.

Capacity planning is another critical strategy in cost control. By forecasting future resource needs based on historical data and business projections, organizations can allocate resources more efficiently. This proactive approach allows them to avoid last-minute, costly resource provisioning or excessive underutilization, both of which can strain budgets.

In an expert-level orchestration environment, automation plays a pivotal role in cost control. Automation enables organizations to set up policies and triggers that automatically scale resources up or down based on demand. This dynamic scaling ensures that resources are allocated as needed, eliminating the need for manual intervention and the associated costs.

Organizations should also embrace the practice of rightsizing resources. This involves matching the type and size of resources to the specific requirements of each workload. For instance, using smaller, less expensive virtual machines for non-critical workloads and reserving larger instances for mission-critical applications can lead to substantial cost savings.

Furthermore, organizations should explore the possibilities of resource allocation policies that take advantage of spot instances or preemptible resources in cloud environments. These are typically available at a lower cost but come with the caveat that they may be reclaimed by the cloud provider with minimal notice. By strategically using such resources for non-time-sensitive workloads, organizations can achieve significant cost reductions.

Cost tagging and labeling is a best practice that helps organizations track spending by associating costs with specific projects, teams, or departments. This granular visibility into expenditures allows orchestration experts to identify areas of overspending, allocate costs accurately, and implement cost-sharing models where appropriate.

In addition to resource cost optimization, data transfer and storage costs are areas that require careful management. Leveraging data compression, deduplication, and data lifecycle policies can significantly reduce storage expenses. Moreover, optimizing data transfer by using content delivery networks (CDNs) or data caching can minimize bandwidth costs associated with data access and distribution.

Multi-cloud and hybrid cloud environments, while offering flexibility, can introduce complexity and cost challenges. To address this, organizations should implement cloud cost management tools that provide a centralized view of costs across various cloud providers and on-premises infrastructure. These tools can offer recommendations for optimizing resource allocation and identifying cost-saving opportunities.

For organizations dealing with high-availability requirements, load balancing strategies can be instrumental in cost control. Implementing intelligent load balancing algorithms ensures that resources are used efficiently and evenly distributed, reducing the risk of over-provisioning and the associated costs.

Another advanced technique for cost control is the use of serverless computing, which abstracts infrastructure management entirely. In a serverless environment, organizations pay only for the execution of code or functions, avoiding the overhead of provisioning and managing servers. This approach is particularly beneficial for event-driven workloads with sporadic resource needs.

Furthermore, organizations should keep a close eye on software licensing costs. By adopting open-source alternatives, exploring bring-your-own-license (BYOL) options, or optimizing software licensing agreements, orchestration experts can achieve substantial savings without compromising performance.

Finally, establishing a culture of cost-awareness and accountability across the organization is essential. Ensuring that teams responsible for resource provisioning and utilization understand the cost implications of their decisions can lead to more prudent resource management.

In summary, achieving cost control in expert-level orchestration requires a multifaceted approach that encompasses continuous monitoring, capacity planning, automation, rightsizing, cost tagging, and resource allocation policies. It also involves optimizing data transfer and storage, managing multi-cloud environments, implementing load balancing strategies, exploring serverless computing, and scrutinizing software licensing costs. By adopting these strategies, organizations can strike a balance between resource optimization and cost efficiency, ultimately maximizing the value of their orchestration investments.

Chapter 8: Orchestration for Big Data and AI Workloads

Managing big data workflows with orchestration is a complex and challenging endeavor, yet it's essential in today's data-driven world where organizations are inundated with vast amounts of data. In this chapter, we'll delve into the intricacies of orchestrating big data workflows and explore the key considerations, strategies, and best practices that can help organizations effectively harness the power of their data.

Big data workflows encompass a wide range of activities, from data ingestion and preprocessing to analysis and visualization. These workflows are characterized by their sheer volume, variety, and velocity, making them uniquely challenging to manage. To tackle this complexity, organizations turn to orchestration, which provides the automation and coordination needed to streamline big data processes.

One of the fundamental aspects of managing big data workflows is data ingestion. Orchestration tools enable organizations to automate the ingestion of data from diverse sources, such as databases, sensors, logs, and external APIs. This automation ensures that data is collected reliably and consistently, reducing the risk of data loss or errors.

Data preprocessing is a crucial step in the big data workflow. Orchestration allows organizations to automate data cleansing, transformation, and enrichment processes. By defining workflows that standardize data formats and handle missing or erroneous data, organizations can ensure that data is prepared for analysis effectively.

Scalability is a paramount concern when dealing with big data. Orchestration tools enable organizations to dynamically scale resources, such as compute clusters and storage, to handle data processing demands. This elasticity ensures that big data workflows can efficiently process large datasets without performance bottlenecks.

Data storage is another critical consideration in big data orchestration. Orchestration tools can manage data storage across various repositories, including data lakes, data warehouses, and distributed file systems. By automating data lifecycle management and data retention policies, organizations can optimize storage costs and data access.

Data orchestration also encompasses data movement, which involves transferring data between different storage locations or computing environments. Orchestration tools facilitate data replication, migration, and synchronization, ensuring that data is available where it's needed for analysis.

One of the key challenges in managing big data workflows is handling complex data processing tasks, such as machine learning model training, data aggregation, and ETL (Extract, Transform, Load) processes. Orchestration allows organizations to define workflows that automate these tasks, ensuring that they are executed in the correct order and with the appropriate dependencies.

Data security and compliance are paramount in big data orchestration. Organizations must implement access controls, encryption, and auditing mechanisms to protect sensitive data. Orchestration tools can enforce security policies and compliance requirements across the entire workflow.

Monitoring and observability are essential aspects of big data orchestration. Orchestration platforms provide real-time visibility into workflow execution, resource utilization, and data processing metrics. This monitoring allows organizations to detect and respond to issues promptly, ensuring the reliability and performance of big data workflows.

Error handling and fault tolerance are critical in big data orchestration, as large-scale data processing workflows are susceptible to failures. Orchestration tools enable organizations to define error handling and retry mechanisms, ensuring that workflows can recover gracefully from failures without data loss.

Collaboration and workflow versioning are essential considerations, especially in large organizations with multiple teams working on big data projects. Orchestration tools provide features for version control, collaboration, and workflow sharing, facilitating collaboration among data engineers, data scientists, and analysts.

In addition to managing the technical aspects of big data workflows, organizations must consider the cost implications. Orchestrating big data workflows efficiently involves optimizing resource utilization, minimizing data storage costs, and managing cloud service expenses. Organizations can use orchestration tools to implement cost monitoring and optimization strategies.

A crucial aspect of managing big data workflows is ensuring that the results of data processing are accessible to stakeholders. Orchestration tools can automate data delivery and reporting, making it easier for analysts and decision-makers to access insights derived from big data.

As organizations continue to embrace the potential of big data, orchestration will play an increasingly vital role in managing and optimizing big data workflows. The ability to automate and coordinate complex data processing tasks, ensure data security and compliance, monitor workflow performance, and control costs is essential for harnessing the value of big data.

In summary, orchestrating big data workflows is a multifaceted endeavor that involves managing data ingestion, preprocessing, scalability, storage, movement, complex processing tasks, security, compliance, monitoring, error handling, collaboration, and cost control. By adopting orchestration best practices and leveraging orchestration tools, organizations can effectively manage their big data workflows, extract valuable insights, and make data-driven decisions in today's data-rich landscape.

Orchestrating AI and machine learning (ML) pipelines is a critical component of modern data science and AI initiatives. In this chapter, we'll explore the intricate world of orchestrating AI and ML pipelines, delving into the complexities, strategies, and best practices that enable organizations to harness the power of artificial intelligence and machine learning effectively.

AI and ML pipelines involve a series of interconnected steps, from data collection and preprocessing to model training, evaluation, and deployment. The orchestration of these pipelines plays a pivotal role in streamlining the entire workflow, ensuring repeatability, reproducibility, and efficiency.

Data collection is often the first step in AI and ML pipelines. Orchestration tools allow organizations to automate data retrieval from various sources, including databases, APIs, sensor networks, and external data providers. This automation ensures a consistent and reliable data supply, which is crucial for model training.

Data preprocessing is a fundamental task in any AI or ML project. Orchestration enables organizations to create data preprocessing workflows that automate tasks such as data cleaning, feature engineering, and data augmentation. These workflows ensure that data is prepared in a standardized format for training and evaluation.

Model training is where the magic of machine learning happens. Orchestration tools can automate the training of ML models on large datasets, distributing the workload across multiple compute resources if needed. This scalability ensures that models can be trained efficiently, even on massive datasets.

Evaluation and validation of ML models are essential to ensure their accuracy and generalization. Orchestration allows organizations to define evaluation workflows that automate the testing of models against validation datasets and metrics. It also facilitates hyperparameter tuning to optimize model performance.

Once an AI or ML model is trained and validated, the next step is deployment. Orchestration tools assist in deploying models to various environments, whether it's in the cloud, on-premises, or at the edge. This deployment automation ensures that models are readily available for inference and decision-making.

Model monitoring and drift detection are crucial aspects of AI and ML pipeline orchestration. Organizations can set up monitoring workflows that track model performance in real-time and detect deviations from expected behavior. When drift is detected, these workflows can trigger alerts or retraining processes.

Scalability is a key consideration in orchestrating AI and ML pipelines. Orchestration platforms enable organizations to scale compute resources up or down based on workload demands. This elasticity ensures that pipelines can handle varying workloads efficiently.

Security and privacy are paramount in AI and ML pipeline orchestration. Orchestration tools provide features for access control, encryption, and audit logging to protect sensitive data and ensure compliance with regulations such as GDPR or HIPAA.

Reproducibility and version control are essential in data science and ML. Orchestration platforms allow organizations to version code, data, and model artifacts, making it possible to reproduce experiments and results accurately.

Error handling and automated retries are crucial in AI and ML pipeline orchestration, as processes can encounter issues such as data anomalies or infrastructure failures. Orchestration tools provide mechanisms for defining error handling strategies and retrying failed steps.

Collaboration is essential in AI and ML projects involving multiple data scientists, engineers, and domain experts. Orchestration platforms enable versioned workflows and collaboration features, facilitating teamwork on complex projects.

Cost management is a consideration in AI and ML pipeline orchestration, especially when dealing with cloud resources. Organizations can use orchestration tools to implement cost-monitoring strategies, such as auto-scaling and resource optimization, to control expenses.

Interoperability with other tools and frameworks is a key feature of AI and ML orchestration. Orchestration platforms can integrate with data storage systems, ML libraries, containerization tools, and deployment platforms, providing a seamless end-to-end workflow.

Orchestrating AI and ML pipelines is a dynamic and evolving field, driven by advancements in machine learning and data science. As organizations continue to adopt AI and ML to gain insights and make data-driven decisions, orchestration will play an increasingly vital role in ensuring the reliability, scalability, and efficiency of these pipelines.

In summary, orchestrating AI and ML pipelines involves automating and coordinating the various stages of data collection, preprocessing, model training, evaluation, deployment, monitoring, and scalability. By adopting orchestration best practices and leveraging orchestration tools, organizations can effectively harness the potential of artificial intelligence and machine learning, driving innovation and competitiveness in the digital age.

Chapter 9: Microservices and Serverless Orchestration

Microservices have become a dominant architectural style in modern software development, promising greater agility, scalability, and resilience. However, as organizations adopt microservices-based applications, they encounter the challenge of orchestrating these small, independent services into cohesive and functional workflows. In this chapter, we will delve into the fascinating world of microservices orchestration patterns, exploring the strategies and techniques that help organizations effectively manage their microservices ecosystems.

To understand microservices orchestration, let's start with the basics. Microservices are independently deployable units of software that perform specific functions within an application. These microservices communicate over the network, often using APIs, to collectively provide the overall functionality of an application. The key advantage of microservices is their modularity, allowing teams to develop, deploy, and scale individual components independently.

However, this modularity introduces challenges related to coordination and communication. Microservices need to work together seamlessly to deliver an integrated user experience. This is where orchestration patterns come into play. These patterns help in designing and managing the interactions between microservices to achieve specific business goals.

One of the fundamental orchestration patterns in the world of microservices is the "Choreography" pattern. In choreography, microservices communicate directly with each other to accomplish a task. Each microservice knows its responsibilities and the interactions required to complete a process. While choreography offers flexibility and decentralization, it can become complex to manage as the number of microservices grows. It's essential to establish clear communication protocols and standards.

On the other hand, the "Orchestration" pattern centralizes the coordination of microservices within an orchestrator service. This orchestrator service, often referred to as a workflow engine, defines the sequence of microservice invocations and handles error handling and compensation. Orchestration simplifies the coordination aspect but introduces a single point of failure and potential bottlenecks. Another prevalent orchestration pattern is the "Saga" pattern. Sagas are used to manage long-running and distributed transactions across multiple microservices. Each step of a saga represents an operation in a microservice, and the saga orchestrator ensures that the steps are executed in a predefined order. If an error occurs, the saga orchestrator can initiate compensating actions to revert changes made by previous steps.

"API Gateway" is an essential pattern in microservices orchestration. An API Gateway is a service that acts as a single entry point for client requests and manages requests routing to the appropriate microservices. It can also perform tasks like authentication, rate limiting, and response aggregation, simplifying the client's interaction with the microservices.

"Service Mesh" is another vital technology in microservices orchestration. A service mesh is a dedicated infrastructure layer that handles communication between microservices. It provides features like load balancing, service discovery, circuit breaking, and security, relieving developers from implementing these functionalities within their microservices.

Asynchronous messaging patterns play a significant role in microservices orchestration. "Event-Driven Architecture"

(EDA) allows microservices to communicate via events or messages. Events represent state changes or significant occurrences in the system, and microservices can subscribe to these events to react accordingly. EDA provides loose coupling between microservices and supports scalability.

The "Command Query Responsibility Segregation" (CQRS) pattern separates the read and write sides of a microservice application. The write side handles commands that modify data, while the read side deals with queries for retrieving data. CQRS enables optimizing each side independently, enhancing performance and scalability.

Scaling microservices horizontally to handle increased load is a common requirement. "Auto-scaling" patterns, both at the application level and infrastructure level, ensure that resources are allocated dynamically based on demand. Container orchestration platforms like Kubernetes have become popular for managing the deployment and scaling of microservices.

"Blue-Green Deployment" and "Canary Deployment" are deployment strategies used in microservices orchestration. Blue-Green Deployment involves running two environments, one with the current version (blue) and one with the new version (green). Canary Deployment gradually rolls out a new version to a subset of users, allowing early testing and minimizing the impact of potential issues.

While these microservices orchestration patterns provide powerful tools for building and managing microservices-based applications, it's important to choose the right patterns for specific use cases and architectures. Organizations should carefully consider factors like complexity, scalability, fault tolerance, and the unique requirements of their applications.

The world of microservices orchestration continues to evolve as new technologies and best practices emerge.

Organizations that successfully navigate the challenges of microservices orchestration can reap the rewards of agility, scalability, and resilience in their software systems.

In this dynamic landscape, it's essential for developers, architects, and organizations to stay informed about the latest trends and innovations in microservices orchestration. By doing so, they can harness the full potential of microservices while effectively managing the complexities that come with them.

To sum it up, microservices orchestration patterns are a crucial aspect of modern software development, enabling organizations to coordinate and manage their microservices-based applications effectively. These patterns offer solutions to challenges related to communication, coordination, and scalability in microservices architectures, allowing organizations to build robust and responsive systems that meet the demands of today's digital world.

In the ever-evolving landscape of modern technology, serverless computing has emerged as a transformative paradigm shift, redefining how we approach application development and orchestration. As we embark on this exploration of serverless computing and its synergy with event-driven orchestration, we will uncover the core concepts, benefits, and real-world applications that make this combination a compelling choice for organizations seeking agility and efficiency in their software systems.

To understand serverless computing, let's start with a fundamental question: What does "serverless" really mean? Contrary to its name, serverless computing doesn't mean there are no servers involved. Instead, it refers to a cloud computing model where cloud providers abstract away server management and infrastructure concerns from developers. In other words, developers can focus solely on writing code to run their applications without worrying about provisioning, scaling, or maintaining servers.

One of the key components of serverless computing is "Function as a Service" (FaaS). In a FaaS environment, developers write individual functions that perform specific tasks or handle discrete events. These functions are triggered by events such as HTTP requests, database changes, or scheduled tasks. When an event occurs, the associated function is executed, and the cloud provider takes care of resource allocation and scaling.

One of the most well-known serverless platforms is AWS Lambda, provided by Amazon Web Services. AWS Lambda allows developers to upload their functions and define the events that trigger them. This serverless model has gained immense popularity due to its cost-effectiveness and scalability. Other cloud providers, such as Microsoft Azure and Google Cloud, also offer serverless computing solutions.

Now, let's dive into the concept of event-driven orchestration. Event-driven systems are designed to respond to events in real-time. An event can be anything from a user clicking a button on a website to a sensor detecting a temperature change. Event-driven architecture (EDA) is particularly well-suited for serverless computing because it aligns with the serverless model's event-triggered execution.

Event-driven orchestration involves coordinating and automating a series of functions or microservices in response to events. Each function or microservice performs a specific task, and together they create a workflow or business process. Events initiate and guide the flow of execution, allowing for dynamic and efficient processing.

One of the primary benefits of event-driven orchestration in serverless computing is its inherent scalability. Functions are executed in response to events, and the cloud provider automatically scales resources based on the incoming event load. This means that applications can handle sudden spikes in traffic without manual intervention or overprovisioning.

Additionally, event-driven orchestration enhances fault tolerance. If a function fails to execute, it can be retried or handled gracefully, ensuring that the entire workflow continues without disruption. This fault tolerance is crucial for building reliable and resilient systems.

Event-driven systems are highly decoupled, meaning that individual functions or microservices do not need to be aware of each other's existence. This loose coupling simplifies development, as developers can focus on writing isolated, reusable functions without worrying about the intricacies of inter-service communication.

Event-driven orchestration is also well-suited for real-time data processing and analytics. Events can be sourced from various streams, such as IoT devices, application logs, or external services, and processed in real time to derive insights or trigger actions. This capability is invaluable in scenarios like fraud detection, monitoring, and personalized user experiences.

Let's explore a real-world example to illustrate the power of serverless computing and event-driven orchestration. Imagine an e-commerce platform that needs to process customer orders efficiently. When a customer places an order, an event is generated, triggering a serverless function. This function validates the order, updates inventory, calculates shipping costs, and sends order confirmation emails—all in response to a single event. As order volumes fluctuate, the platform automatically scales to handle the load, ensuring a seamless shopping experience for customers.

Serverless computing and event-driven orchestration also play a vital role in microservices architectures. Each microservice can be implemented as a serverless function, and events can facilitate communication and coordination between microservices. This approach simplifies the deployment and scaling of microservices-based applications. While serverless computing and event-driven orchestration offer numerous advantages, it's essential to consider some challenges. Cold starts, for example, can introduce latency when a function is invoked for the first time or after a period of inactivity. Developers need to optimize their functions and choose appropriate memory configurations to minimize cold start times.

Additionally, managing and monitoring a distributed system of serverless functions can be complex. Tools and services for observability, logging, and tracing are essential to gain insights into the behavior and performance of the system.

In summary, serverless computing and event-driven orchestration have revolutionized the way we build and operate software systems. This approach enables organizations to develop highly scalable, cost-effective, and responsive applications. By harnessing the power of serverless and embracing event-driven orchestration, businesses can stay competitive in the fast-paced world of technology, delivering innovative solutions to meet evolving customer needs.

Chapter 10: Pushing the Boundaries: Expert-Level Cloud Orchestration Challenges and Innovations

In the world of modern technology, where complexity often begets innovation, solving complex orchestration challenges has become a critical endeavor. These challenges arise from the growing complexity of applications, distributed systems, and the need for seamless coordination and automation across various components. As we delve into the realm of addressing these complex orchestration challenges, we will uncover the strategies, techniques, and best practices that guide us toward efficient solutions.

At the heart of complex orchestration challenges lies the need to manage intricate workflows and dependencies. When organizations build and operate large-scale systems, orchestrating various components and tasks becomes a daunting task. This complexity can manifest in several ways, including coordinating microservices, managing data pipelines, and ensuring resource optimization. Let's explore some of these challenges and how organizations are tackling them.

Microservices orchestration is a prime example of a complex orchestration challenge. In a microservices architecture, applications are decomposed into small, independently deployable services. While this approach offers flexibility and scalability, it also introduces the need to coordinate these services efficiently. Service A may rely on Service B, which in turn depends on Service C. Managing the flow of data and control among these services requires robust orchestration solutions.

Container orchestration platforms like Kubernetes have become indispensable tools for managing microservices.

Kubernetes provides features like service discovery, load balancing, and automated scaling, which simplify the orchestration of containers running microservices. Organizations can define complex deployment patterns and specify how services interact, ensuring that microservices work together seamlessly.

Another intricate challenge arises in managing data pipelines, particularly in the context of big data and analytics. Organizations are constantly dealing with vast amounts of data that need to be ingested, processed, and analyzed in real-time or batch mode. This requires orchestrating a series of data processing tasks, including data ingestion, transformation, and storage.

Apache Airflow is a popular choice for orchestrating data pipelines. It allows organizations to define complex workflows as code, specifying dependencies between tasks and handling retries and error handling. Data engineers can design intricate data processing pipelines that automatically scale to meet demand and ensure data quality and reliability.

Resource optimization is another complex challenge that organizations face when orchestrating workloads. Ensuring that computing resources are used efficiently while meeting performance requirements is a delicate balancing act. Cloud providers offer a range of tools and services to help organizations optimize resource allocation.

Auto-scaling, a capability provided by many cloud platforms, allows organizations to dynamically adjust resource allocation based on workload demand. This ensures that applications can handle increased traffic during peak times and scale down during periods of lower demand. Additionally, organizations can use machine learning-based tools to predict resource usage patterns and optimize resource allocation accordingly.

Security and compliance pose significant complexities in orchestration. Organizations must ensure that sensitive data is protected and that their systems adhere to industry-specific regulations and security best practices. Achieving this requires the orchestration of security measures throughout the application lifecycle.

DevSecOps, an extension of DevOps, integrates security practices into the development and operations processes. Automation plays a crucial role in DevSecOps, with tools for vulnerability scanning, identity and access management, and security policy enforcement. Organizations use these tools to automate security checks, detect vulnerabilities, and respond to security incidents promptly.

Hybrid and multicloud environments introduce yet another layer of complexity in orchestration. Organizations often rely on a mix of on-premises data centers and cloud providers to meet their computing needs. Coordinating workloads across these environments while maintaining data consistency and security is a significant challenge.

Multicloud management platforms and tools help organizations manage resources and applications across multiple cloud providers. These tools provide a unified view of resources, automate workload placement decisions, and ensure data synchronization between different cloud environments.

As organizations address these complex orchestration challenges, they are increasingly turning to infrastructure as code (IaC) and automation. IaC allows organizations to define infrastructure configurations as code, making it possible to version, test, and automate infrastructure provisioning. This approach brings the benefits of code development practices to infrastructure management, enabling organizations to treat infrastructure as a programmable resource.

Automation extends beyond infrastructure provisioning to encompass entire application workflows. Continuous integration and continuous delivery (CI/CD) pipelines automate the building, testing, and deployment of applications. By automating these processes, organizations reduce manual intervention, decrease the risk of errors, and accelerate the delivery of new features and updates.

To successfully navigate these complex orchestration challenges, organizations need to adopt a comprehensive and strategic approach. This involves:

Assessment and Planning: Understanding the specific challenges and requirements of the organization, including identifying critical dependencies and performance bottlenecks.

Selection of Tools and Technologies: Choosing the right orchestration tools and platforms based on the organization's needs, such as Kubernetes for microservices or Apache Airflow for data pipelines.

Automation and IaC Adoption: Embracing automation and infrastructure as code to streamline provisioning, configuration management, and application deployment.

Security Integration: Implementing security practices as part of the orchestration process, including vulnerability scanning, access controls, and encryption.

Monitoring and Optimization: Continuously monitoring the performance and resource utilization of orchestrated workloads and making adjustments to optimize resource allocation and cost-efficiency.

Compliance and Governance: Enforcing compliance with industry regulations and internal policies and maintaining governance over orchestrated workflows.

Scalability and Resilience: Designing orchestration solutions that can scale to handle increasing workloads and ensuring resilience in the face of failures.

In summary, solving complex orchestration challenges is a multifaceted endeavor that requires a combination of technology, automation, and strategic planning. Organizations that embrace modern orchestration practices, leverage the right tools, and prioritize security and compliance will be well-positioned to thrive in today's dynamic and ever-evolving technology landscape. By addressing these complexities head-on, organizations can achieve greater efficiency, agility, and innovation in their operations and service delivery.

In the ever-evolving landscape of cloud computing, innovations in expert-level cloud orchestration have been at the forefront of reshaping how organizations harness the power of the cloud. These innovations are driven by the growing demands for agility, scalability, and efficiency in managing complex workloads across diverse cloud environments. As we delve into the world of these innovations, we'll explore the exciting developments that are shaping the future of cloud orchestration.

One of the most transformative innovations in expert-level cloud orchestration is the rise of serverless computing and event-driven architectures. Serverless computing enables organizations to build and run applications without the need to manage traditional infrastructure. In this paradigm, functions or "serverless" components are executed in response to specific events or triggers. This approach offers unparalleled scalability and cost-effectiveness.

Providers like AWS Lambda, Azure Functions, and Google Cloud Functions have paved the way for serverless computing. Organizations can now develop applications that automatically scale to meet demand, paying only for the actual compute time consumed. This innovation has revolutionized how organizations handle tasks like data processing, image resizing, and real-time event handling.

Container orchestration has also witnessed remarkable innovation, with Kubernetes emerging as the de facto standard for container management. Kubernetes provides a unified platform for automating the deployment, scaling, and management of containerized applications. It offers features like service discovery, load balancing, and self-healing, which simplify the orchestration of container workloads.

Kubernetes has become a cornerstone of cloud-native application development. Its robust ecosystem of tools and extensions, combined with its portability across cloud providers, makes it a compelling choice for organizations seeking to achieve true multi-cloud and hybrid cloud strategies. Kubernetes innovations continue to drive the evolution of container orchestration, with improvements in resource management, security, and observability.

Another notable innovation is the increasing adoption of infrastructure as code (IaC) principles. IaC involves defining and managing infrastructure configurations using code. Organizations can use tools like Terraform, AWS CloudFormation, and Azure Resource Manager to declare their infrastructure requirements in a readable and version-controlled manner.

IaC brings numerous advantages, including reproducibility, consistency, and automation. It allows organizations to provision and configure cloud resources programmatically, reducing manual errors and accelerating the deployment process. Innovations in IaC tooling have made it easier to manage complex infrastructure setups, optimize resource allocation, and adopt infrastructure best practices as code.

Automation and orchestration have also seen significant advancements in managing big data workloads. Organizations dealing with vast datasets and complex analytics pipelines rely on orchestrating data processing tasks efficiently. Innovations in tools like Apache Airflow have transformed how organizations design, schedule, and monitor data workflows.

Apache Airflow provides a flexible and extensible platform for defining, scheduling, and executing data workflows as code. With its growing ecosystem of operators and sensors, organizations can automate data ingestion, transformation, and pipeline orchestration. This innovation is particularly valuable in the context of data lakes, data warehouses, and real-time analytics, where the efficient orchestration of data processing is paramount.

In the realm of security and compliance, innovations have been driven by the need to secure cloud environments and protect sensitive data. Cloud-native security solutions, such as cloud access security brokers (CASBs), offer real-time monitoring and control over cloud services. These tools help organizations enforce security policies, detect threats, and ensure compliance with regulatory requirements.

Furthermore, innovations in identity and access management (IAM) have strengthened cloud security. Organizations now have the ability to define fine-grained access controls, implement multi-factor authentication, and manage identities at scale. Cloud providers offer IAM services that integrate seamlessly with existing on-premises directories and provide robust identity federation capabilities.

Machine learning and artificial intelligence (AI) have made their mark on cloud orchestration by enabling intelligent automation and predictive analytics. Organizations are leveraging machine learning models to optimize resource allocation, predict workload demand, and automate routine tasks. AI-driven solutions are transforming how cloud resources are managed, leading to cost savings and improved operational efficiency.

Additionally, innovations in monitoring and observability have become essential for maintaining the health and performance of cloud workloads. Cloud-native monitoring solutions offer deep insights into application and infrastructure metrics. They employ AI and machine learning algorithms to detect anomalies, troubleshoot issues, and provide predictive analytics.

Innovations in expert-level cloud orchestration are not confined to technology alone. Cloud service providers continue to evolve their offerings, introducing new services and features that empower organizations to achieve more with the cloud. These innovations span a wide range of areas, from machine learning and artificial intelligence to serverless computing and hybrid cloud management.

Furthermore, the adoption of best practices such as DevOps and DevSecOps has become a driving force behind cloud orchestration innovations. These practices emphasize collaboration, automation, and continuous improvement, fostering a culture of innovation and agility within organizations.

In summary, the world of expert-level cloud orchestration is undergoing a continuous transformation driven by innovation. Organizations are reaping the benefits of serverless computing, container orchestration, infrastructure as code, and advanced automation. These innovations are enabling them to achieve greater efficiency, scalability, security, and compliance in their cloud operations. As technology continues to advance, we can expect even more exciting developments in the field of cloud orchestration, shaping the future of how organizations harness the power of the cloud.

Conclusion

In "Cloud Orchestration Unleashed: Comprehensive Journey from Novice to Guru," we embarked on an enlightening voyage through the multifaceted world of cloud orchestration. This four-book bundle, comprising "Cloud Orchestration Demystified: A Beginner's Guide," "Mastering Cloud Orchestration: Intermediate Techniques and Best Practices," "Cloud Orchestration for Enterprise: Advanced Strategies and Case Studies," and "Cloud Orchestration Mastery: Expert-Level Automation and Scalability," has provided readers with a comprehensive and holistic understanding of cloud orchestration.

In Book 1, we started our journey as novices, unraveling the fundamental concepts and principles of cloud orchestration. We demystified complex terminologies, explored foundational technologies, and laid the groundwork for the exciting chapters that followed. Readers gained the confidence to navigate the intricate landscape of cloud orchestration, setting a strong foundation for their learning.

Book 2 elevated our understanding as we delved into intermediate techniques and best practices. We explored the orchestration of containerized workloads, harnessed the power of automation, and optimized resource management. Through practical examples and real-world scenarios, readers honed their skills and became adept at orchestrating cloud environments effectively.

In Book 3, we took a deep dive into the world of enterprise orchestration. Advanced strategies and real-life case studies illuminated the path to orchestrating complex workflows, ensuring compliance, and achieving optimal performance in enterprise settings. Readers were equipped with the knowledge and insights needed to tackle intricate orchestration challenges within their organizations.

Finally, in Book 4, we reached the pinnacle of expertise in cloud orchestration. Expert-level automation and scalability techniques were unveiled, empowering readers to manage large-scale deployments with finesse. Innovations in orchestration architecture, resource scaling, and performance optimization were explored, making readers true masters of cloud orchestration.

As we conclude this comprehensive journey, readers have transformed from novices into orchestration gurus. They are now equipped with the knowledge, skills, and confidence to navigate the ever-evolving world of cloud orchestration. Whether orchestrating workloads for personal projects, leading orchestration initiatives within their organizations, or architecting complex multicloud environments, readers of "Cloud Orchestration Unleashed" are well-prepared for the challenges and opportunities that lie ahead.

The journey doesn't end here; it's merely a stepping stone. Cloud orchestration continues to evolve, and as technology advances, so too will the techniques and best practices. As readers embark on their own unique orchestration journeys, they are encouraged to remain curious, adaptable, and committed to continuous learning.

With "Cloud Orchestration Unleashed," we've unlocked the doors to a world of possibilities in the cloud. It's a world where automation, scalability, efficiency, and innovation converge to shape the future of IT. Whether you're a novice, an intermediate practitioner, or an expert, this bundle has been designed to empower you to orchestrate the cloud with confidence and mastery.

So, dear reader, as you embark on your own orchestration adventures, may your clouds be ever clear, your workflows seamlessly orchestrated, and your journey through the cloud orchestration realm filled with success and fulfillment.

About Rob Botwright

Rob Botwright is a seasoned IT professional with a passion for technology and a career spanning over two decades. His journey into the world of information technology began with an insatiable curiosity about computers and a desire to unravel their inner workings. With a relentless drive for knowledge, he has honed his skills and expertise, becoming a respected figure in the IT industry.

Rob's fascination with technology started at a young age when he disassembled his first computer to understand how it operated. This early curiosity led him to pursue a formal education in computer science, where he delved deep into the intricacies of software development, network architecture, and cybersecurity. Throughout his academic journey, Rob consistently demonstrated an exceptional aptitude for problem-solving and innovation.

After completing his formal education, Rob embarked on a professional career that would see him working with some of the most renowned tech companies in the world. He has held various roles in IT, from software engineer to network administrator, and has been instrumental in implementing cutting-edge solutions that have streamlined operations and enhanced security for businesses of all sizes.

Rob's contributions to the IT community extend beyond his work in the corporate sector. He is a prolific writer and has authored numerous articles, blogs, and whitepapers on emerging technologies, cybersecurity best practices, and the ever-evolving landscape of information technology. His ability to distill complex technical concepts into easily understandable insights has earned him a dedicated following of readers eager to stay at the forefront of IT trends.

In addition to his writing, Rob is a sought-after speaker at industry conferences and seminars, where he shares his expertise and experiences with fellow IT professionals. He is known for his engaging and informative presentations, which inspire others to embrace innovation and adapt to the rapidly changing IT landscape.

Beyond the world of technology, Rob is a dedicated mentor who is passionate about nurturing the next generation of IT talent. He believes in the power of education and actively participates in initiatives aimed at bridging the digital divide, ensuring that young minds have access to the tools and knowledge needed to thrive in the digital age.

When he's not immersed in the realm of IT, Rob enjoys exploring the great outdoors, where he finds inspiration and balance. Whether he's hiking through rugged terrain or embarking on a new adventure, he approaches life with the same inquisitiveness and determination that have driven his success in the world of technology.

Rob Botwright's journey through the ever-evolving landscape of information technology is a testament to his unwavering commitment to innovation, education, and the pursuit of excellence. His passion for technology and dedication to sharing his knowledge have made him a respected authority in the field and a source of inspiration for IT professionals around the world.

www.ingramcontent.com/pod-product-compliance
Lightning Source LLC
Chambersburg PA
CBHW071234050326
40690CB00011B/2105